PEOPLE WHO SAY GOODBYE

INDEPENDENT VOICES

PEOPLE WHO SAY GOODBYE

Memories of Childhood

P. Y. BETTS

A CONDOR BOOK

SOUVENIR PRESS

1

There were sudden voices, and a scurry of people across the hall from right to left and through a door which was slammed. The voices, still agitated, faded.

On the polished floor was left a small puddle of yellow froth, like beaten egg. (So this was what 'foaming at the mouth' must be.)

Mrs Barlow and Miss Dowdy, who had been craning their necks from the armchairs where they were sitting, settled back, though Mrs Barlow still looked hoity toity and affronted. She often did.

'She really shouldn't be allowed to use our lavatory. We might catch fits.'

'If fits are catching.'

'You never know.'

Mrs Barlow and Miss Dowdy were residents. Whenever we came on holiday to Brattle Place they were always there. Florrie Milton, the daughter of the house who helped to run the boarding establishment, was known to have fits occasionally, though this was the first and only time I witnessed an episode, over the several visits, up to the age of eleven, when I stayed there with my parents or my maternal grandparents.

Florrie did not reappear amongst us that day.

There was nothing odd about Florrie. She was just a grown-up who saw to things around the house. She was pleasant enough, rather preoccupied, pale with frizzy but subjugated hair, and had obviously been grown up rather longer than her sister Jessie who, not exactly remembered but by no means forgotten, had been a mother's help in our family at the beginning of my life. Jessie, who did not have fits, had left to better herself, as was the way of maids employed by my mother. Come to think of it, I never heard that any of the maids we

1

had had left anywhere else to better themselves with us.

Florrie was assisted by Marie (to rhyme with starry) who was not young and not old, small, very quick and bright, rosy with blue eyes and a pointed nose. Privately, because of her name, I thought of her as French—after all, Brattle Place was on the way to Dover and she might have slipped over into Kent before my time, to better herself. France, it was understood, was not all that far away, for we could hear, on certain still days, the dull sound of the guns in France. 'Listen to the guns in France,' grown-ups would say. I knew about the war, I knew that the sound of the guns was the sound of soldiers being killed, killed at that very moment. Blood in the mud. France was not so far away. Marie had done well to better herself at Brattle Place, if she could put up with living with Mrs Milton.

Mrs Milton was really frightful. Old enough to be the mother of grown-up daughters, she had fuzzy iron-grey hair and a plum-coloured face laced with broken veins. Her usual stance was embattled, with arms akimbo as if ready to fight off complaints as they arose. Her eyes were murky, the colour of muddy blue clay, and her expression one of settled bad temper. She frowned. What was her most ghastly and atrocious feature was an undershot jaw ensuring that her incomplete set of lower teeth were ever on display. The general effect was of a tusked boar—she could have rootled for truffles.

By hindsight it would be easy to write off Mrs Milton as a bad-tempered Irish bruiser with a taste for the bottle, but the fact that she was a protegée of my evangelically teetotal grandfather would seem to rule that out. There was a family tradition, origins lost in that vague hinterland before my time, that Grandpa had somehow or other set Mrs Milton up in her boarding-house. There was no firm hint of impropriety about this, for Grandpa was a Victorian poor man's great man who was known to do charitable deeds, not always by stealth. No facts were ever available about the link between my grandfather and Mrs Milton but it was plain that she doted upon him and thought him wonderful —only for him did she ever achieve that unforgettable glimpse of pure frightfulness, her smile. So taken up was I

2

with staring horror-struck at Mrs Milton when her smile happened, that I never thought to look at Grandpa to see how he was taking it. He was a handsome and arrogant man with a known intolerance of ugly or stupid people and his connection with Mrs Milton remains inexplicable. I am inclined to think that it must indeed have been some act of pure generosity on his part and that her atrocious smile may have been one of pure gratitude. With her equipment, after all, how could she have smiled prettily?

My mother and Mrs Milton detested one another. For one thing, my mother plainly was very good-looking and knew it. Their acquaintance must have dated back a long way, as I deduced, in my Sherlock Holmes phase, from the fact that Mrs Milton had a pony called Kitty and two Jersey cows, Clover and Daisy respectively, no doubt named after the pony my mother had driven called Kitty and the Jerseys Clover and Daisy kept as house cows long ago when my mother was eighteen and her family had had a house and a few acres, long since pulled down and built on, at Sunbury-on-Thames. Perhaps it was then that she had taken against Mrs Milton and her mysterious association with my grandfather—we shall never know.

Because of this connection, whatever it was, between my mother's family and Mrs Milton, Brattle Place had come to be a convenient holiday place for us and for our friends. In those days it seemed to be in deep country yet was reasonably accessible from London. My own family got there by train, being met at the station by the grumpy Brattle Place groom with the pony and trap. When I travelled with my grandparents it was in grandeur in the Leon Bollet, driven at 25 m.p.h. by the chauffeur who wore a cockade in his cap because Grandpa was a JP. This meant that we were saluted by all the policemen on point-duty as well as by the AA and the RAC scouts, and I saluted back. I was a snob about this. There was not much else I could be a snob about, given my mother's wayward and regardless attitude to all that was good form and the done thing.

Red squirrels were common in the south of England in those days. One had been caught and kept in an outside cage at Brattle Place. My mother and I, mooching around, had come upon this tatty and hapless animal. Not a word was spoken, but as we looked at one another revolutionary signals flashed between us. Which of us unlatched the cage I do not remember, it was an act of dual control. The squirrel hesitated, did a double take and suddenly was springing away into the trees, free again. Afterwards, though nothing was said as far as I know, there was some background unpleasantness and I think it likely that suspicion fell upon us as early animal liberationists.

Visits to Brattle Place seem telescoped and blurred, in a way one long visit, beginning with a Christmas when I was three and ending with my mother and Mrs Milton confronting one another, embattled, across the bed in which I lay with a pain in my tummy tentatively diagnosed as appendicitis but attributed by my mother to food-poisoning somehow brought on by Mrs Milton's cooking. The clash of antagonisms across my bed was awful—that was the final visit. But in between, in the everlasting summer of childhood, friends and relations came and went, new visitors were introduced and even a few strange people, complete outsiders, ventured to board at the place from time to time. These tended to be looked down upon, somehow pitied, by the regulars.

Mrs Barlow and Miss Dowdy were always there. They seemed never to change. Mrs Barlow was fairly tall and stately with a peevish classy face and a diadem of small grey curls above her forehead. Miss Dowdy was shorter and dumpier with grizzled gingery hair and a sandy, freckly face. She wore glasses. She was not, like Mrs Barlow, always grumbling and there was a look about her that she might be fun if one ever got her alone. But Mrs Barlow was always there. Miss Dowdy occasionally had a niece to stay, another Miss Dowdy, a young woman not unlike her aunt, interestingly distinguished by several pale warty blobs on her face. No other connections of either Miss Dowdy or Mrs Barlow were known to exist. Now, one wonders about those two. What were their lives? They were not outstandingly old, early sixties at most. Presumably their means were modest or they would not have settled at Brattle Place, a made-over farmhouse a mile or two from the village, miles from Maidstone. What did they do all day? What about the winters? They were not tweedy sporting types who

tramped about the chalky lanes. They were displaced suburban persons with nothing to do but knit and embroider,
for this was years before the wireless, let alone television,
and they were a little too grand to pig it in the kitchen with
the Miltons and Marie, giving a hand with the marmalade-
making or the Christmas puddings. Books? I never saw
them read a book. There must have been newspapers,
which were of great importance in those days, eagerly
awaited, snatched jealously, read up or handed over,
sometimes page by page.

The casualty lists were in the papers. They were the first
item readers turned to: obituary notices of the young. I did
not read the casualty lists. I was able to read but did not read
the casualty lists. The casualty lists were dull, just long lists
of names. But the grown-ups turned to them first.

A lot of men were in uniform. One of these was Fred
Dimbleby. Some generations of Dimblebys had been
friends of my mother's family and I had often been taken by
my grandmother to tea with old Mrs Dimbleby at Richmond. She was nice, with brown eyes, not much neck, on
the fat side and, like so many old ladies of her day,
apparently permanently seated, everlastingly pouring tea.
I thought she was rather like Mrs Hippo in the Tiger Tim
strips. Fred was one of the sons. He was like a hippo too. He
turned up at Brattle Place in a tight, crumpled uniform, a
major's. His cap had a softened, battered top. It was said
that very young officers kicked their caps around to give
them that chic used look, but I had no doubt that Fred
Dimbleby's cap was genuine—it went with the crumpled
uniform. He had a pretty wife called Gwen. From somewhere he produced a big green apple and gave it to me. I bit
into it and at once the toothmarks turned brown, a bad sign
in an apple. While I was looking at it, wondering whether to
take another bite or take it away in the hope of getting some
sugar to put on it, a beautiful fair boy, a bit younger than
me, ran up to his mother and father, asked a question,
and ran away again: a boy like an angel come and gone,
Dick. He grew up to be Richard Dimbleby, the famous
broadcaster, father of the current Dimblebys.

My mother said that Fred had been sweet on her once but
had expressed the opinion that she would be too much of a

5

handful, whatever that meant. I was glad that, whatever the reason, she had settled for my father rather than Fred. Fred Dimbleby looked like a hippo but my father looked like a cad which, in a father, was a big advance on a hippo.

My father was not in uniform. He said he was gun-shy. Being gun-shy, he explained, would not have been enough to keep him out of the army if he had not also had some useful varicose veins. These were spectacular in appearance and effectively disqualified him from military service. Being a strong and healthy man, proud of his good physique, he was at once piqued in his vanity at being turned down as unfit yet gratified that he would not have to be shot at by guns. He said he had seen what a gun could do to a rabbit and frankly he was afraid of guns. A man could not stand up against a gun, so bully for varicose veins.

His varicose veins, incidentally, never gave him a moment's discomfort to his life's end.

That my father was gun-shy never gave me any feelings of embarrassment. I knew he was brave and strong. He had caught burglars, struggling hand to hand with desperate men. The occasion had been only a week or two before I was born, indeed it was because of the imminence of my birth that my mother had stayed at home while he had gone out to join some neighbours at cards. It would have been whist in those days. This was before the war, the Edwardian heyday. The card party was just up the road at the house of a middle-aged couple with a young son, Bertie, who was in the Navy and then on leave. Next door, a corner house, was occupied by two of their nieces, of not much more than twenty: Frances and Florence Marwood, who had come over from Trinidad to live in London. It was a neat arrangement, giving them independence free from the taint of Edwardian raffishness that might have touched them, lively girls in their own establishment, but for the presence next door of Uncle Marwood who was respectable enough to get his living close to the editorial heart of *The Morning Post*.

They were all in the uncle's house at cards when faint odd sounds were heard from the house next door, the girls' house, which they had left empty. My father, followed by young Bertie, went to investigate. Quietly unlocking the front door they listened, then stole up the stairs. The place was in darkness but it was easy to find the way because the house was a replica of our own. There were sounds from a back bedroom. They rushed in, grabbed what they could find. Bertie's burglar broke free, jumped out of the window and landed on a rockery, breaking a leg. My father tackled the second man; all in darkness, no electric light, they tumbled together and rolled down the stairs, over and over, gripping each other's throats and grunting. My father said afterwards the man's throat was like gripping solid rubber, it was so muscular he felt he was making no impression on it, but luckily he came out on top at the bottom of the stairs and held the man until the bobby on the beat (never far off then) arrested him. 'Get him orf me! Get him orf me!' the chap is reported to have cried to the policeman. 'The bugger's bloody strangling me!'

This was a legend of my childhood. I was safe. My father was stronger than other men. He could subdue them with his bare hands. It was of no consequence that he was gun-shy when he could strangle people.

This episode, before my birth, was a very clear event in my mind, part of the continuum of childhood of which the Marwood girls were flesh and blood. Still young even to my youthful eyes, they stayed on in their burgled house for another five or six years, Florence gay and pretty, Frances rather elegant, very well-dressed and considered clever. Later they moved to a flat on the other side of the Common. Who knows whether their adventurous uprooting from their family in Trinidad, to set up house in London, came near to their expectations? So many of the young men of that generation were blasted away by war. Perhaps for them that became a happy time for them to look back on, a time full of hope, playing cards and fooling with their cousin Bertie and my caddish and flirtatious father, the night of the burglary.

Neither ever married.

* * *

Brattle Place was not, of course, the only place that I had been to for holidays. By the time I was six I had been to a number of different places and, by a coincidence that struck me as marvellous, they all began with B: Broadstairs, Bournemouth, Brattle Place, Barton, Bognor and Bexhill. For ages I had known the alphabet with its twenty-six letters, and as the tally of holiday places mounted, all beginning with B, the same as our surname, my sense of wonder increased. There were plenty of other places where people went for holidays, no farther away—Eastbourne, Ramsgate, Hastings, Torquay—yet all the places we went to began with B. The improbability of the thing hinted at the intellectual beauty of mathematics and engrossed me with a sense of the marvellous.

Something else that lent itself to prolonged contemplation was the black against white, opposite image, chessboard effect of my mother's and father's families.

His father was fairly short and (had been) dark haired, her father was taller and (had been) fair.

His mother was tall and fair, her mother was short and dark-haired.

His people were poor, hers were (comparatively) rich.

He had one sister and two brothers. She had two sisters and one brother.

His people lived in the country, hers lived in London.

He was the eldest of his family, she was the youngest of hers.

He was dark. She was fair.

He was a man. She was a woman.

And from this coming together of opposites, this clash of matter and anti-matter, I had come.

It took a lot of thinking about. It was a marvel.

Such coincidences and correspondences gave me a grave and balanced pleasure. It could not be shared with the boys I played with. It was only in my own head. Strange perceptions and marvels were not for sharing.

There was an old discarded oak draining-board lying about at the bottom of our garden in London. It was a perfectly quiet, sunny afternoon, almost hot, but of its essence not like a summer afternoon. It was different. Why? It was different because it was not summer, it was October. This was important. It was unusual, in my

8

experience, for October to be as warm as this. The event must be recorded.

I went into the house and came back with the brass-bound magnifying-glass with the mother-of-pearl handle. I settled down for the afternoon with the draining-board and the burning-glass, focusing the hot spot of sunlight on the wood.

Years and years later the old draining-board was still lying about with the legend burnt into it:

October 6th 1915.

It was a time for marvels. I was six.

*   *   *

Our house backed onto a field of eleven acres bounded by the gardens of houses built four sides of a square. It was a real meadow with hedges and ditches and many big trees. In the summer hay was cut there and after the hay sheep were turned in to graze. Usually there was nobody there, at most two or three children from the neighbouring houses, playing. One summer evening, when I was six, I went with my father strolling in the field and near their garden gate met for the first time a young man and woman who had just moved into the house the Marwood girls had recently left. A sturdy young tabby cat was with them. I occupied myself with the cat which they said was on the wild side and might scratch me, but didn't, while the grown-ups above my head got to know one another. The new couple's name was Hirst, soon to be known as Frank and May. He was fair and rather colourless, a very polite young man with regular features, a lawyer. His wife was fairly big and somehow soft, with dark hair and dark blue, very shy eyes. She blushed a lot. They had been married only a few weeks and this was their first home.

There was a special atmosphere about this meeting, not a word of which remains with me except to mind the cat. The summer evening, a quiet evening smelling of flowers and grass, seemed to stand still for hours. It was transfixed in some way that was not tedious as grown-up encounters often were but as if suspended in a time of its own. I have realised since that what I was enjoying were the faint

9

vibrations of the controlled sexual tension of those others, the grown-ups. The honeymoon electricals held that summer evening entranced in their field of force.

From then on the Hirsts joined those of our friends who turned up from time to time at Brattle Place. They soon had a car, partly to get about in, partly for Frank to tinker with. He was an able man who qualified as a professional organist before studying law and he could make anything work. When wireless came in he had receivers all over the house, on the stairs and hanging from every ceiling, all on at once, *fortissimo*, in an attempt to get the stereo effect from orchestral concerts long before true stereo was available. The huge noise, and the clutter, nearly drove his wife mad; but that was in the future when the honeymoon electricals were things of the past. In years to come Frank went on to become Public Trustee and was given a knighthood. He asked my father what he should be known as.

'As your second name is Wyndham, certainly Sir Wyndham,' my father advised. 'Nobody is going to remember Sir Frank, but Sir Wyndham is *Sir Wyndham*.'

So Sir Wyndham he became. Nobody in his life had ever called him Wyndham but Sir Wyndham he suddenly became. Unlike some other yuppies of that time who lived on our housing estate but moved on when they got their knighthood or sterling equivalent, the Hirsts stayed in their modest house till old age moved them on. Four bedrooms were more than enough for a childless couple, after all.

May Hirst had a pretty young sister, Bea, yellow-haired with big blue eyes and a ringing laugh. She was like a high-class barmaid. Flashier than her shy sister, she was an outrageous flirt. As my mother's name was also Bea, short for Beatrice, my father judiciously nicknamed this Bea Mark II, Fifi, a nonsense name which permitted a degree of nonsense behaviour. My mother was perfectly tolerant of this rather stagey little flirtation which, by bringing it right out into the light of day, she turned into a situation comedy. No doubt she was aware that nothing disinfects the germ of romance as effectively as laughter. The thing became a family joke in which the two participants were happy to play their farcical parts.

There was a wood near Brattle Place known as Little

Switzerland—not that there was anything particularly Swiss about it, as I remember. What was special about it was its reputation, as imparted to me by my maternal grandmother. She said she had seen snakes hanging from the trees there. I cannot believe that Grandma was an outright liar, but perhaps she was a little fanciful or her eyesight was unreliable and she had put this unnerving interpretation upon heavy growths of ivy climbing the trees, or something. Whatever got into Grandma, the idea scared the daylights out of me. I was frightened of snakes. Not long before, running on a narrow path ahead of the usual gaggle of grown-ups 'going for a walk', a feature of holidays then, I had almost stepped on a frog-coloured one that slithered out of the wood on my left, across my path and down into the quarry on my right. I screamed. I screamed. My screams echoed dramatically across and across the quarry and all the grown-ups came running. They tried to comfort me with reasonable assurances that the snake was probably only a harmless grass snake, that it would have been more frightened of me than I was of it and that, anyway, it had gone. And why was I always running ahead of everybody else anyway, when we went for walks? Running ahead alone was asking for trouble. I was eight.

I did not care to explain that I had recently been reading Conan Doyle's *The Speckled Band*, a most disquieting story in which a venomous snake had been trained to climb through a grating between one bedroom and another, down a bell-rope, on to the pillow of the sleeping victim. The sleeper was then to be fatally bitten and the deadly snake, mission accomplished, climb at a whistle up the bell rope again through the grating and back into its box where goodies awaited it, placed there in readiness by its exultant master/murderer. In my bedroom at home there was a cord hanging down the wall behind my bed with a bell-push on the end of it. I had come to an uneasy truce with this bell-cord, reasoning that it was an electric flex, not a great woolly bell-rope, and incapable of accommodating any poisonous snake, however skinny, that my mother in her bedroom on the other side of the wall might be thinking of slipping through to me. My father, who could not fail to be

11

awakened by all the rustlings and fidgeting that this manoeuvre must entail, like undressing under a nightie, would not allow such a thing to happen because he loved me best. Against this, my mother loved my brother best . . . Admittedly the whole thing was improbable, physically impossible—even I knew that, I was not a fool . . . nevertheless it was a mental minefield, an unexploded shell, a snake-pit . . . Snakes scared me and I never went into Little Switzerland for fear of meeting a few hanging from trees, low enough to brush against people.

All the same, I was quite happy to go into Little Switzerland if somebody else was going too. The hanging snakes would only be interested in one person at a time. I liked woods. There was a special feeling about them—the green light and the mystery, the feeling of suspense, something wonderful about to happen.

One day my father and Fifi went for a walk in the wood and I went with them.

We walked on through the wood. They were talking. I was not interested in what they were talking about until my father asked Fifi if she would like some chocolate. They stopped and my father took a packet of Cadbury's Mexican Chocolate out of his pocket. This was a plain chocolate in shiny blue paper. My father couldn't stand milk chocolate, he said it smelt of sick babies. So there was only plain chocolate to offer Fifi, even if she preferred milk chocolate as I did myself at that time. My father unwrapped the chocolate. It was in a slab, hard-looking, dark brown. He took out his penknife, a small silver knife with two sharp blades. I was watching, facing him, Fifi close behind me, no doubt watching too. He held the thick slab of chocolate flat on his palm, his other hand poised above it with the blade of the knife pointing down.

This was no way to break up a slab of chocolate. I knew my father was ham-handed, no use at all at putting up shelves or fixing things like Frank Hirst, but this beat everything. It was idiotic. He was not even looking at the knife and the chocolate, he was looking at Fifi over my head, with that half mocking, half caressing look that was special to my father but out of place when dismembering chocolate. But I was not much concerned because the

12

green feeling in the wood was becoming very strong, the lovely feeling that something wonderful was about to happen.

What happened was that my father, mind not properly on the job, jabbed down at the chocolate with the pointed knife, clean through the chocolate and into his hand. Blood poured out of it, heavy drops onto the leafmould.

I have no recollection of Fifi moving in with instant first-aid skills. I managed to salvage some sizeable bits of chocolate from the blood. I doubt if those two got any. We went back to Brattle Place where my mother saw to the bandaging.

'How did the fool manage to do a thing like that? Couldn't he break off a bit of chocolate like anybody else?' she said to me. 'I suppose he was flirting with Fifi and wasn't watching what he was doing?'

'I suppose so,' I said.

'A fool,' decided my mother.

My phobia about snakes, though not extreme, continued to bother me for several years. The bell-cord syndrome wore off pretty quickly, but I still had an unspoken fear of walking among bracken on sandy heaths. When I was twelve a few girls with an interest in natural history were taken on a visit to the zoo. One of the mistresses at my school was related to the curator of reptiles there, so we were taken behind the scenes, as it were, to the backdoor of the reptile cages. Nothing of the talk we were given stays in my mind; all I remember is the moment when a fairly large grey snake, about six feet long, was withdrawn from its cage and displayed before us. It was non-venomous, we were assured. It lay in a loose, lazy coil on a bench, its grey back smartly patterned with black markings like natty suiting.

'Anybody care to touch it?' invited the curator. 'It's quite harmless.'

Nobody volunteered. It was quite a big snake. We looked at it. Suddenly something uncontainable boiled up inside me, like milk boiling over on a hob; the diverse workings of cowardice and of pride. If this was to be my Laocöon, so be it.

'I will touch it,' I said.

13

I had expected it to be slimy but it was dry and firm, neither warm nor cold, like a very muscular arm. There was nothing revolting about it at all. It was all right.

The other girls reached out experimental hands. The critical moment was over. I had overcome. From then on, though I knew snakes could be poisonous and should be avoided, they ceased to be things of horror for me. They were no more horrifying than bulls, who were best avoided too. That a thing were better avoided did not automatically turn it into a Medusa's head, I decided.

But this apocalyptic event was yet in the future. For me there was still a long time to go before the snakes in Little Switzerland came down from the trees and silently stole away.

* * *

Room Number One was the best room at Brattle Place. When my grandparents were there No 1 was the room they occupied, naturally. The house was long and low, possibly several cottages knocked into one, and No 1 was a gable end with windows on two sides. It was my parents' room on this occasion. I have no recollection of what the room was like because it was in darkness except for a candle. There were a number of people in the room, my mother and father and presumably my brother, Fifi of course and very likely the Hirsts. There was the dull boom of anti-aircraft fire not very far off but nobody seemed to be listening much to this, they were all squashed together on the bed, laughing at their own jokes. I asked what the guns were firing at—there were searchlights raking the sky outside the little gable window.

'The anti-aircraft gunners are practising,' Fifi explained. I knew this to be nonsense, but humoured her. This was the real thing.

Someone said we had better put up the black-out curtain but my father said just to blow out the candle would be enough. Fifi laughed her ringing laugh, her teeth shining for a moment before the light went out. I was aware she was in favour of darkness.

'Why blow out the candle?' I asked.

14

'It might get in the gunners' eyes and dazzle them,' my father improvised.

The disgust I felt at grown-ups with their silly ways and subterfuges was so strong that it has acid-burned the rest of that night clean out of memory.

We went back to London by train. It was after dark. The train was packed and I had to sit on my mother's knee. I dozed. Later I woke up, eyes still kept closed, to hear my mother talking to the other people in the carriage. She was garrulous in trains, unlike my father who wished she would shut up sometimes.

'We tell her it's a practice. She doesn't know it's a raid. Please God she never knows,' my mother added with a touch of drama.

I kept my eyes shut. I knew my mother knew I knew. I knew she was showing off to the strangers in the train, Outside her own home she sometimes went stagey; I was not keen on her then.

It was better to keep my eyes shut if she was in her stagey mood.

* * *

My next holiday at Brattle Place must have been after the war was over because Grandpa had got his car back on the road—it had been laid up for a spell in the middle of the war. I was taken down with them in pomp to Brattle Place, acknowledging with gracious impartiality the salutes of the police, the AA and the RAC men.

There were outsiders at Brattle Place this time. Usually the guests—there were never many of them, perhaps a dozen—ate at a long table all together, rather like school dinner. It was an arrangement I found congenial. But when we were accompanying Grandpa, that great Victorian, things were different. My grandparents, two aunts and myself were creatures set apart at a table on our own and were waited upon personally by Mrs Milton and dreadfully smiled upon by her tusks. Possibly the lesser breeds at the common table looked upon us with envy; equally they may have found us absurd and stuck-up.

On this visit there was a little monkey-faced girl about my

15

age who was with her grandmother, a lady in black with a sad and worried look. The times being what they were, it is likely that the child's father had been killed in the war. I have an idea she told me she was fatherless but I had little to do with her and seem never to have known her name. My cousin Dudley, also my age, came over one day from Maidstone and we hid in the hay in the barn when it was time for him to go home, to delay things; perhaps Monkeyface was with us but I do not remember playing with her. All I remember about her is that on the last day of her short stay she came into my bedroom to say goodbye. She handed me a very small package.

'This is a keepsake,' she said, 'so that you will remember me for ever.'

Interested, I tore open the offering. Inside was a pack of miniature playing cards with pink backs. They were not glossy and slippery like the cards I had been used to playing with. These seemed to be made of thin cardboard like postcards and bore traces of the minute splinters of wood pulp that bedevilled all notebooks and school exercise books because of the paper shortage during the war. I was a stationery fetishist and looked doubtfully upon the little cards and their pink backs which I thought were soppy. But I knew my manners and thanked Monkeyface somehow.

'I want you to remember me all your life,' the little girl insisted. Though she was my age she was much smaller than me, bony and anxious. I was tall and strong for my age. Her monkey face looked up at me intently. 'Will you remember me all your life?' she insisted.

I considered this question. I thought it over. Then I said:

'I shouldn't think so. I'm ten now and I expect it will be years and years before I die. There will be lots of things to remember between now and then so I shouldn't think I'll remember you.'

But I have remembered her. Seventy years have gone by with much to remember in between and most forgotten, but her I have remembered. Nameless, gone whither? She has been remembered all my life with her small bony body and plain monkey face. Did she remember me? I see now that she was a lonely little girl who wanted to be with me to partake of those supposed blessings which I took so much

16

for granted and which she lacked—stuck-up relations who sat at a separate table and had a posh car with a chauffeur, mother and father and big brother at home and even a rumbustious boy cousin who hid in the hay because we were enjoying ourselves so much he didn't want to go home. Possibly she envied me but there was no malice in it, only a kind of longing to partake, if only in not being forgotten.

And the keepsake? The little pink patience cards? I never played with them, their quality was too rough and poor. But I never threw them away either. From time to time they turned up in a box or at the back of a drawer. I could never throw them away. They must be about still, somewhere or other.

I have remembered her all my life.

2

Because my mother had a low opinion of education, as a process which tended to unfit children for life, I was not sent to school till I was seven and a half. Even in those days children were required to attend school from the age of five and this rule was supposed to be enforced by a school inspectorate. No school inspector ever approached my mother, as far as I know. Either she was never shopped by the neighbours, whose own young regularly attended kindergarten, or perhaps an inspector had called one day and had afterwards gone missing, died of wounds. Way back she had taught me to read and spell and in due course to write, add up, subtract, multiply and divide. More than that no one needed to know. If the young had any sense they could pick up the rest as they went along; if they hadn't any sense it was all up with them anyway. She herself had been to the best school in her neighbourhood till the age of eighteen. It was the former Greek Embassy near Clapham Common and had beautiful ceilings painted with cupids and angels and dolphins. However, all she had learnt there, she said, had been a lot of Bach cantatas and the single fact that the capital of Portugal was Lisbon on the Tagus. That was not much to show for all those years of going to school, she remarked, was it?

For this reason I had a longer exposure to what may be called 'home influence' than most children. The summers, apart from holidays away, were mostly spent playing with the local small boys in the field where my father and I met the Hirsts and their cat. A great part of the winter, after the first fog gripped my throat as I bowled my hoop in November, was spent indoors coughing and wheezing and often alarmingly struggling to breathe. Nowadays I suppose it would be said that I was allergic to the sooty fogs of those winters and the cure would have been to send me

18

away out of London to school. Nothing of the sort ever crossed anybody's mind. I stuck it out, wheezing my way through the winters, in the care of our family doctor, Dr Biggs.

I am sorry to have to speak ill of the dead, but Dr Biggs was a fool. I knew this early on. So did my brother. My father also had strong suspicions. But my mother said he was a very clever doctor. This would have been surprising in view of her wholesale dismissal of fools in general except that I had come to know, by the osmosis of family life, that men who flattered her were never perceived by her to be fools. Dr Biggs was old, really old, too old to flirt; all the same he had a way of buttering my mother up as she stood on the other side of the bed while he dabbed the cold stethoscope on my chest.

His first words, when he entered the bedroom were:

'And how are the bowels?' He pronounced 'bowels' in two distinct syllables, as if hyphenated, and all his aitches were heavily aspirated. My father called him 'Old Whhhen-and-Whhhhatski' and my mother would retort that he was a very clever doctor. He was scrupulously clean, a dandy. While he was uttering his heavily breathed-on inquiry about the bow-els, he would often be standing at the washstand, washing his hands in the hot water provided, drying them on the towel my mother, his handmaiden, offered him, before turning to the patient on the bed.

In his dress, which was immaculate, he was a relic of a former generation. I knew nobody else who dressed like Dr Biggs. He was snuff-coloured all over. He wore a frock coat, a long wrapped-over affair, with trousers of the same colour, and spats. He carried gloves and a snuff-coloured trilby hat bound round the edge with snuff-coloured ribbon —these items left downstairs, of course, in the hall. His waistcoat had pearl buttons. He always wore wing collars with a horrible fold of old wattled neck at the gap. His wide tie was dove grey, more like a stock, and his tie pin was an opal, for bad luck.

I suppose his hair, such as it was, must have been a kind of grey-snuff colour too, but all I am sure of is that he was not bald, and that whatever grew on his head lay flat. His skin was parchment-coloured with big pores, but there

19

were no black dots in the pores as with some old men. His nose was rather big and fleshy, with deep, heavy lines going down to the corners of his mouth, which I always thought of as nose-strings, like the drawstrings on shoe-bags. His eyes were a weak brown with a bluish *arcus senilis* round the pupils. It could have been the face of some enormous unclassified bird of prey. There was no mercy in it, but there was no cruelty in it either. He seemed about to swoop but all he did was dab with a stethoscope.

Dr Biggs would have qualified around 1875, and as he smelt faintly of disinfectant forty years later, it may be assumed that he had heard of Joseph Lister. He must also have been instructed in the use of the stethoscope, if not in the interpretation of its messages, which his keen listening ears—seen from where I lay to be as big as an elephant's —took always to be a requirement to prescribe a brown sedimented medicine called cough mixture, to be followed after a few weeks by a clear red potion with a faint whiff of meth., known as tonic. Treatment by Dr Biggs consisted of nothing else—1) dab dab with a cold stethoscope on warm chest, now turn over to dab dab with slightly warmed stethoscope on back; 2) brown cough mixture to be shaken and taken three times a day after meals, and 3) red tonic ditto. At no time during my childhood did he take a peek into my ears which often ached hellishly and received only *ad hoc* medication from my mother in the form of what felt like boiling oil poured into them. Years later an ENT consultant told me that both my ear drums had been perforated and were badly thickened. By rights I should be fairly deaf, why wasn't I? (No good asking me. Ask Dr Biggs.)

Outside the house, during his visits, waited Dr Biggs's brougham with his coachman. Other doctors already did their rounds by motor car but Dr Biggs was a carriage and horse man to the last. That was the nicest thing about him. One supposes that his horse, when it was out of sorts, was doctored with the same brown physic and red physic that were all his patients ever got, but in somewhat larger doses.

* * *

20

The War of 1914–18, which occupied the timeless years of my childhood, was to end on Armistice Day 1918 with a triumphant bang, but it had begun with a whimper. We were at Bognor on holiday and for some time there had been talk of some friends of my parents who had been in Mexico where there was a war. Fleeing from the slaughter these people (for ever unknown to me) had managed to get away 'on the last boat'. Not having any idea of an ocean-going liner, I had a vivid mental picture of this couple splashing down the wet sand and pushing off a small rowing boat, jumping in and rowing away like mad from the war. This lower case war became merged in my mind with the upper case War we had to get to know so much nearer home.

At Bognor our family occupied apartments, a civilised arrangement which made it possible for pestilential small children to be kept out of grown-ups' hotels while sparing their mothers the bother of keeping house in a rented cottage. They were furnished rooms, from choice on the sea front, where a whole family could be accommodated without annoying other people. The landlady would shop for whatever meals were ordered, cook them and serve them up in the family's own dining room. It was thus in Bognor in the year the War began. There was another family, name of Dry, in their own apartments in the same seaside house. They had a little girl called Effie, marked down to be my friend for the holidays, but I had been used to playing with boys and did not care much for Effie. We all went, both sets of parents, my brother, Effie and I, one shining late afternoon westward for a walk along the wet sands, dazzling under the tide going out. I hated a crowded walk with a lot of people and, as on that future day when the snake crossed my path, I ran on ahead and, as on the day of the snake, came to no good.

I ran on ahead towards the sun across the shining, shining sands and fell plop into a pool. For a moment I was totally immersed but felt no shock or fear because the water was warmed through by the sun and rescue was immediate. A young man, known as such by a pair of grey flannelled legs, plucked me out of the water as soon as I fell in. The young man, no doubt soon to die in the War like all

21

the other young men, fades from the scene as the other six walkers of the party draw near. There I am standing, five years old, soaked cotton dress clinging to my tummy, hip-long hated hair dripping with sea water heavily tinctured with the famed Bognor effluent—surely an object of pity and of love? Not a bit of it. My mother comes up laughing, completely unconcerned.

'Ha!' she says. 'Effie Dry and Phyllis Wet, I see.' This humiliating pun was the end of the afternoon for me and the beginning of the War. I wished I could have pushed off in the last boat, across the sea, far far away from all the people and from Effie Dry, to Mexico.

On that same holiday we went to a circus. We had some little-known distant relations who lived nearby and we went with them. Children were supposed to like circuses but I disliked the strained yellow light coming through the canvas of the big tent, the worn-out grass under foot, the smell and the mangy-looking lions that I felt sorry for. Clowns gave me the creeps. There were many empty seats. At one stage, perhaps at an interval in the show, I was on my own with nobody I knew around me, just strange distant grown-up cousins talking among themselves in the big smelly tent, when a very small boy ran up to me. He was about six. He had on a prep school cap ringed in yellow and brown and a brown blazer striped with yellow. He seemed small inside his clothes. He had big brown eyes. He held out to me a penny bar of chocolate in its red paper, the kind that came out of machines. He looked straight at me. I took the chocolate. No word was spoken. We looked straight at one another for a moment and then he ran away again, back to his grown-ups. I felt better. It was not just the chocolate. I never knew who he was. I never forgot him.

Later that year, back in London, my parents had a letter from these Bognor distant cousins to say that one of the children who had been at the circus that afternoon with us had been ill and had died. It was a little boy.

I was sure it was that little boy, the one who had looked straight at me. He had been so small inside his brown and yellow blazer and his big brown eyes had been so big.

To this day I feel a faint desperation that I know nothing

22

about that child who for one everlasting moment was known to me so well, known by heart.

* * *

In the early months of the First World War, large numbers of Belgian refugees, fleeing before the German invaders, came pouring into London. Everybody seemed to know of a family of Belgian refugees but only those few who spoke French, let alone Flemish, understood what they were talking about. They came babbling to tea. My mother whose education, it will be remembered, began and ended with the knowledge that the capital of Portugal was Lisbon (on the Tagus) did her best at making do with sign language, which she was not bad at. What she wanted to tell her Belgian guests was that her husband, who had been educated partly in France, spoke excellent French but he unfortunately was working late at the office because the auditors were there, so he would not be home until (tapping vigorously at her wristwatch) nearly eight o'clock. Whenever Mother tapped her wristwatch the Belgian ladies would become restive, making French twittering noises and half rising to their feet, when my mother would push them down again and offer them whatever was going, which might well be bread and dripping as she was not one to stand on ceremony with anyone, let alone foreigners.

The Belgian ladies had no husbands but they had children. These came to tea too. One of these was an exasperating child of my own age. It was not long before Christmas and my brother and I were making paper chains. We sat at the dining room table with the coloured strips of paper, gummed at the ends, in front of us. The thing was to pick a strip at random, moisten the ends with a damp sponge and link it through the previous ring, which must not be of the same colour. Red, blue, green, white, yellow, purple, pink—it was lovely work as the finished links piled rustling up. Our guest, not exactly loved but tolerated because we had a common enemy, sat beside us at the table and was free to take part in this blissful occupation. One would have thought that just seeing the thing done would have been enough for anyone, even deaf and dumb, to get the hang of it, but no, petite Mignon did not seem to cotton on at all. Again and again she kept picking up a strip of one colour and linking it on to a link of the *same* colour—red, red, red, etc., or green, green green . . . In vain we laid strips of differing colour alongside each other, nodding savagely and crying, 'OUI! OUI!' then putting the same colour together, the same the same the same, and screaming, 'NON!' In vain. It made me mad. Paper chains were precious and she was wasting them. I thumped the table. 'NON!' My brother was a clever, thoughtful boy, five years older than I and advanced for his years, but not even his careful demonstration of how paper chains should be made, and his tentative '*Comme ca?*' had the slightest effect on our guest. Was she exceptionally stupid or plain obstinate? Were Belgian paper chains all made of the same colour and did she think our variegated ones crude and garish, vulgar tasteless British kitsch?

We were never to know. She did not come to tea again. Later that winter, aghast grown-up talk going on over my head revealed that she had fallen in the fire and was dead.

When my brother came in from school I told him the news. We agreed it was a good job she was dead. People who couldn't make paper chains properly had no future anyway. The fire was the best place for them.

* * *

Our suburb was a favoured one on account of its wide roads and many open spaces. Not only was there the Common, there was a nursery garden full of flowers, threaded with footpaths, there were enchanting glimpses through wrought-iron gates of the secret gardens of the big houses in the road between two commons where my grandparents lived. No wonder our estate, with its comfortable modern housing, pulled in youngish couples who were, they expected, going to get on in the world. There were so many trees. There was such abundance of fresh air. It was incidental that much of the fresh air blew in from the domains of madness, crime, wounds and death, each of which required a large acreage of living space, if living is the word.

Madness was accommodated in the large lunatic asylum

with its own farm, not far from the Common. In the days of my youth there were no euphemisms for mental disturbance. If you were mentally ill you were mad and if you were mad you went to a lunatic asylum and no messing. If you were very, very mad they put you in a padded cell.

My mother of course had something to say about lunatic asylums because as a girl she had visited one. Her father had taken her when he went there on business. He was a Commissioner in Lunacy, whatever that may have been —something to do with committing patients, I suppose, as he was a Justice of the Peace. While he went off to attend to what may have been gruesome business she remained behind, engaged in conversation with a pleasant gentleman to whom she had been introduced. They were on an upper floor with a view of the hall below, and when in due course her father came in sight, talking to an official, my mother's companion walked with her to the head of the stairs, where he bowed and took his leave, explaining regretfully that he was unable to accompany her down the stairs as his legs were made of glass and might break.

(His glass legs were vivid in my mind. They were like the very solid chunky kind of cut glass tumblers that stood ranged on shelves in my grandparents' butler's pantry.) But my mother had a more disturbing story than this. It was about a woman in a padded cell. I doubt whether she had been invited to see for herself, more likely her father had told her about it, but its impact on my mind was powerful and lasting. The madwoman was raving, flinging herself at the walls of her padded cell and screaming that she was burning to death, burning to death . . . This horrified me. It seemed to me that being deluded that you were burning to death was far worse than really being burnt to death, because being burnt to death would end, in death, but being burnt to death *in the head* would go on and on. It was merciless. It was an eternity of torment. It was hell itself.

Glass legs, comparatively, were a bagatelle. You could lead quite a happy life on one floor, preferably the ground floor.

But that was in the past. In my own day no especial horror stories came out of the asylum. There were high walls round the grounds. Sometimes a happy band of more

25

or less presentable inmates would issue forth in the care of their keepers, busily chattering. I liked to look at them though I was not supposed to. Their enjoyment was intense. They were mostly, if not all, female, with bright excited eyes and frizzy grey hair, darting jubilantly in and out of the parade of shops facing the Common, clutching small purchases.

'They always buy sardines,' my mother said, and it was true: fourpenny tins of sardines gleamed in their hands as they emerged, discarding paper bags, afternoon light blazing back from their shining eyes. My mother would point out that mad people usually had either lank hair hanging in dank hanks or fuzzy stuff frizzing up all over their heads, and the frizzy sort was more often seen.

The hair style of the happy lunatics came naturally. Their hair stood on end of its own accord. In my own generation, for people near the age of the century in its last decades, the chosen hair style of nearly all old women is a similar frizzy mop, more or less veiling the pink skin beneath. The only difference is that now their faces are not bright with joy as were those of the happy loonies of my early childhood, nor are they joyfully clutching tins of sardines.

* * *

The domain of crime was the prison which, with its ancillary buildings, was as big as a village, whole streets of warders' houses and big houses with gardens for the Governor, chaplain, doctor. There was a *cordon sanitaire* of open ground around it, leased off to bowls and tennis clubs. Opposite our house was a rough field with a footpath leading away into the prison hinterland, whence sallied forth at times a hooligan family of red-haired boys, warders' children, to terrorise clean little prep school boys in their grey flannels. Neighbours tut-tutted about these boys, who seemed ripe for imprisonment themselves. Occasionally an active prep school father would catch and beat one of the redheads, as could be lightly undertaken in those days without fear of a suit for assault. Bad boys were not easy to catch, but once caught, they could be beaten —that was the way of it then.

The façade of the prison was sombrely impressive, a fortress. It had a huge main gate like the gate of a mediaeval castle, with a small door let into it. Onto the main gate was posted the notice of execution when a murderer was hanged. When she was young, my mother said, they would run up a black flag which could be seen at a distance when a hanging had been done, but now there was only the notice, posted up by a warder. I was told that when the notice was posted a great sigh, a communal collective exhalation, would go up from the crowd that had assembled in front of the prison at the time of execution. I thought of this enormous sigh as the last breath of the hanged murderer, all the breath that had ever been in his lungs going out into the world without him.

On winter mornings before it was light on the day of an execution there would be a clippety-shuffle noise on the pavements outside our house. It was the sound of the leather-shod or hobnailed booted people from the bottom of the hill coming up to watch outside the prison in time for the execution at eight o'clock. They walked without a word. They would stand in silence waiting for the deed to be done on the hour, and from them would go up the great sigh. Whether that sigh was of pity or of grief, satisfaction at justice done or fear of the wrath of God, it went up into the raw air as a single sigh such as a man might heave before taking up again his burden.

At home, no impairment of appetite was felt at breakfast on execution mornings. That was how things were. You took a life, they took your life. It was a simple trade-off. We had been warned.

* * *

Our house in London was at about the middle of a long, very wide road lined with (then) young plane trees. The top of the road near the Common was the 'better' end, going down past our house and other houses like it and then more steeply downhill to a stretch not built on, a vague area of slightly messed-up open spaces, a Board school with its shrieking playground, and the cemetery. The Board school was for pupils, drawn from the nether regions at the bottom of the hill, who were too poor to pay fees, though some of the more ambitious parents, according to my mother, scraped together fourpence a week to pay for violin lessons. She was full of a sort of exasperated pity for these needy little aspirants scraping away on their tinny fiddles till their fourteenth birthday pitched them empty-handed into the nearest factory, which was a smelly one. I never knew what was made there. Something to do with glue, I think, or gas.

At the bottom of the road was a short terrace of run-down Victorian houses, not far from the railway, where the road met at right angles a main road of tramlines, cheap shops and shabby people. Charwomen came from somewhere round here. There was also a most interesting sewage farm.

Down this road on winter afternoons came the military funerals. No doubt they came on summer mornings too, like the ordinary funerals—they came all the time, several a day—but it is the winter afternoons that I remember. These were the funerals of the soldiers who had died of wounds in the military hospital up the road and round the corner. Going down the hill where I stood on a chair by the window watching, they went at a measured pace, the hooves of the horses—ordinary brown horses not black funeral ones—clopping soberly by. Behind the pairs of horses came the gun carriage with its coffin draped with the Union Jack. There were mounted soldiers, khaki-clad, useful-looking riders without ceremonial trappings. Following the gun-carriage were usually some ordinary mourners, people as distinct from soldiers, in carriages drawn by undertakers' black horses. The number of following carriages and the amount of flowers varied. Some flag-draped coffins had no mourners following. Why?

The procession would go by, down the hill into the wintry afternoon with its faint foggy smell that gripped your throat if you were out in it. It was the smell of coal fires and winter. The sky, when the cortège had gone out of sight, would be smoky grey with red streaks over the low-lying ground beyond the cemetery. Those afternoons were very quiet. The road seemed scarcely used. I would wait. Then faintly the bugle would sound, final and sad, the lamenting never-coming-back notes of the Last Post. It seemed to me a dark, smoky, red slash of sound against

28

the quiet grey of the London winter evening coming down.

Not long afterwards the soldiers and the horses were to be heard coming back at a smart trot, the coffin and the flag gone from the gun-garriage. The soldiers were hurrying home to their barracks for tea with plum-and-apple jam.

My mother would come in with a loaf of bread and a stone jar of dripping. We would toast the bread at the fire, by the light of the fire. With luck the dripping would be used up to near the bottom of the jar, where delicious beef-jelly could be reached. This would improve the toast enormously.

'What happens to all those dead people who are put into graves?' I asked my mother.

'They rot,' she replied, spreading dripping.

* * *

Because of the funerals passing the house so regularly on the way to the cemetery, the idea of death had always been familiar to me. I liked the way my father raised his hat when a funeral passed by on the road. Older ladies bowed and I liked that, too. However, I did not feel equal to bowing as they did; at six years old my waist was somehow too near the ground. One day, when I was missing, my mother asked a passer-by if she had seen a little girl in a blue woolly hat. 'Yes,' the stranger replied, 'she's standing at the corner up the road, raising the hat to funerals.' No doubt I had found it wiser to pay my respects to the dead out of sight o my mother. I would not have wanted to bring on another Effie Dry situation.

On the other side of the road from us there were only two houses, built close together. They were bigger and older than the modern houses on our side. One was the under-taker's, the one next door was a small private school. The undertaker's family lived over the shop, which had a big front showroom with a display of coffins and artificial flowers under glass domes. Behind this there was the joiner's shop where the coffins were made. There must have been a mortuary too, because in later years, when refrigeration became common, my mother had the bright idea of getting round the undertaker to store her furs in the cold room there during the summer—it was so much handier than the Army and Navy Stores. Cheaper too, no doubt—just one or two of my mother's dazzling smiles would do the trick with the undertaker, whose customers were so much less lively than my mother.

The private school was run by Mrs Stroud, who had white hair and a quite young face. Her husband was an optician who went off every morning to work elsewhere, like all the other fathers. They had a little girl whose name was Molly. I knew Molly, though not well. It might have been expected that we would play together, two small girls in a neighbourhood of small boys only, but by hindsight I can see that as I went to no school, let alone Mrs Stroud's as might have been expected, a certain strangeness may have attached itself to me. Mrs Stroud's school was a sort of happy bedlam, not at all up-market. It catered for children of all ages and both sexes, boys of kindergarten age and girls from tiny children to what appeared to be ripe woman-hood. What made it down-market was that its pupils were drawn almost entirely from *down the road*. Shopkeepers' daughters went there, well-nourished girls whose fathers wielded cleavers behind butcher's blocks, or kept pubs. These were far from needy, though considered, of course, common. But some of the girls who went to Mrs Stroud's school came from families who were only a pay packet away from the Board school, families who must have had a struggle to pay the fees, low as they were, at a down-market private school. From my window where, wheezing, I watched the military funerals go by, I would see the children across the road coming out of school and trooping down the hill to tea in parlours behind shops.

It was in the Christmas holidays, a quiet time, that we heard that Molly Stroud had caught measles. I had already had measles, very badly but quite unremembered as I was only eighteen months old at the time. Somehow I had survived Dr Bigg's two medicines, but from that time began the boiling oil treatment down the ears that was such a feature of my childhood. Measles, they said, did bad things to ears and sometimes to eyes, too. Complications, these bad things were called.

Molly Stroud began to have complications. Her kind of measles was special. It was called black measles. When I asked what black measles was I was told that it was a sort of measles that did not come out properly but went inward and did deadly damage. To this day I am no wiser about what black measles may be and have never heard of anyone else having it. But Molly Stroud died of it.

Children's funerals were not uncommon when I was a child. Less riveting than the military funerals, they were somehow more interesting than the funerals of grown-ups. They were identifiable at a glance because of the small size of the coffin and its different disposal in the hearse—crosswise behind the coachman instead of fore and aft. These small coffins were always heaped with flowers. Their occupants would have died usually from infectious diseases against which there was no protection. Immunisation, except for smallpox, did not exist. Except for a child's natural resistance, there was no defence against tuberculosis, whooping cough, tetanus, measles, polio and diphtheria. Many children caught these illnesses and some died of them. Tubercular meningitis was a certain killer; there was no hope for its victims. However skilled the nursing they received, these children were doomed to scream for a few days and then to die.

Molly Stroud's funeral was to take place on this winter afternoon. Her house was in full view of ours. Surprisingly, there was no hearse, no top-hatted coachmen with their black horses. Instead their front door opened and out came Mr Stroud and the undertaker, bare-headed, each bearing on a shoulder the weight of the small coffin. Mr Stroud was bald with a pink scalp and the remains of some reddish hair. They turned downhill, carrying the coffin, and that was all. Away they went, two men and a small coffin borne carefully down to the cemetery. It was the quietest funeral I had ever seen, and the most sobering. I went to my tea that day in a serious mood. That a father should carry his child to the grave was a solemn thing.

My mother naturally was matter-of-fact about this. Full of sympathy as she was for the Strouds, going as far as to wipe away a tear on their behalf, she was quick to point out that for people living so close to the cemetery and with a coffin

31

so small and so light, the expense of the full panoply of hearse and horses would have been unjustifiable. Nor was the present arrangement, or something even more informal, unprecedented. There had been Mr Batsford up the road. When his wife had had a dead baby—born at home, as most babies were then—Mr Batsford had put the baby in a shoebox, parcelled it in paper and string and had taken it, after dark, down the hill to the cemetery.

'Did he dig a grave for it himself, then?' I asked.

'No, of course not. He gave it to the gatekeeper to put into a grave that had been newly dug, with some earth over it, under the next coffin to be lowered down.'

'That would be cheaper than a proper funeral?'

'Much cheaper. I expect he gave the gatekeeper five bob at most. People often do that with their dead pets, you know, cats and dogs. Instead of burying them in the garden they take them down to the cemetery after dark and tip the gatekeeper half a crown to pop them into an open grave.'

'But a dead baby would cost more than half a crown, say five bob?'

'Probably, yes.'

'But supposing Mr Batsford had wanted the gatekeeper to bury Biff,' (Biff was a Great Dane weighing hundredweights actually belonging to the Batsfords), 'wouldn't it have cost more than burying a baby?'

'No.'

'Why?'

'Because Biff is still alive and the baby was dead,' replied my mother with unanswerable firmness.

Future archaeo-anthropologists, meticulously uncovering skeletons, will note that it was sometimes the custom, in suburban England c. AD 1915, to bury domestic animals with their owners. Theses will be written on the subject and doctorates handed out.

* * *

The school kept by Mrs Stroud was not the only one in the neighbourhood. There were also a sort of kindergarten, where I attended when first sent to school, a larger private school for girls where I spent a year when about nine years old, and a preparatory school for boys. This last was a good, small school where the pupils were properly grounded in the required subjects. (The same could not be said of any of the local schools that I attended.) Boys from this school were usually of a standard to go on to a public school. My brother, a brainy boy, was a pupil there up to the age of thirteen.

The headmaster, Canon Stowe, was a tall, lean, likeable middle-aged man, known as a Trinity man. Though he was a clergyman, apart from the giveaway big Adam's apple and ecclesiastical voice projected from somewhere behind nose and tonsils, you would not have known it. There was no side to him, he did not give off an uncomfortably high moral tone, and he rode about on an old bicycle painted black. From this perch he would call out a cheerful high-pitched greeting to me as he pedalled by. Every Boat Race day he arranged a school trip to Mortlake. A bus was hired for the occasion, an open-top bus of course. For some reason I was always included in the trip, the only girl among a bus-load of prepubescent boys. Who arranged this I never bothered to think. Being a girl I was naturally ostracised but suffered no pain from this, knowing that boys had to behave as other boys expected them to behave and that no personal slight was intended. Individual small boys could fraternise with a small girl but when in a pack they must ignore her. At Mortlake we piled on to a barge, wore favours and yelled as the crews shot past. I forget now who was for Oxford and who was for Cambridge, though I remember at one stage I transferred my allegiance from one university to the other, in an effort to balance up the support which was heavily weighted in favour of Oxford (or was it Cambridge?). I did not really care who won and I expect most of the boys didn't either—it was an outing, rarer then than now.

Canon Stowe had a somewhat faded but still pretty and elegant wife. She wore a grey squirrel coat and a bunch of Parma violets. What made her interesting was that she was said to be a great invalid who had survived, but only just, that operation which was spoken of as 'having all her insides out'. As a consequence of this heroic surgery her digestion was delicate (and no wonder, with no insides left)

33

to the point that her diet consisted only of oysters and champagne. I had no idea what champagne was but somehow it had acquired a romantic aura, probably from the uncensored trash I read in *Woman's World*. This was a twopenny weekly, delivered on Monday mornings, mostly made up of instalments of three or four serials dealing with mill girls and gaffers, shop girls and commercial travellers, or the kitchen maid and the young master. It was a weekly aimed at the lower end of the market, to be read mostly by servants—certainly none of the yuppie mothers of the small boys I played with would be seen reading it. My mother, however, enjoyed it greatly and so did I. I do not doubt that my acquaintance with champagne was made through the medium of this excellent publication, probably at the wedding reception of the young master and the kitchen maid.

Mrs Stowe was not the only lady to have all her insides out. She had a grown up son, but there was also a childless class of lady who would have loved children but had parted with her insides, as if there were a connection between no insides and a passionate love of children. I had observed that those couples who loved children very much never had any of their own. This was perfectly understandable. My own mother, who had retained her insides, did not love her children all the time.

Not only were there several ladies walking about who had had all their insides out, but my mother had known one who had actually burst. Her name had been Rose Layton, one of a family my mother had known as a girl, and she had burst.

'How, burst?' I asked.

'Her stomach swelled up and she burst.'

'What had she eaten to make her burst?'

'How do I know what she had eaten?'

'Well, you were there, weren't you?'

'No.'

'Didn't you ask her what she'd eaten to make her burst?'

'How could I, you little idiot? She was dead.'

Another case of all the insides gone.

My mother was obviously not in a child-loving mood, or I

would have asked her whether Rose Layton would have loved to have children.

* * *

Ladies' insides were not the only personal fittings to be summarily whipped out. Teeth could go the same way. Chicken-pox at the age of five brought on an eruption of second teeth in my mouth, unfortunately before the first ones showed any sign of loosening, so I soon had the beginning of a grotesque double row.

The situation required a number of visits to Mr Crocker the dentist on the other side of the Common. It was a walk of more than a mile each way. During this walk on the first occasion, my mother told me that having a tooth pulled out hurt terribly, it was really a very bad pain but one that lasted so short a time that by the time it was felt it was over. I had better expect the pain but it would be over at once. Afterwards we would go home and she would give me sixpence and a slice of cake hot from the oven. Clara had just popped it into the oven so that it would be ready for me the moment we got home.

We went into the dentist's and Mr Crocker settled me in a big chair. I opened my mouth and he wielded his forceps and gripped. There was a sudden awful pain and a crunch inside my head.

'There!' said Mr Crocker, wielding a white tooth with bloody roots. I was yelling hard but soon stopped as the pain stopped. Mr Crocker explained that it had been unusually firmly rooted with fangs like a grown-up tooth —milk teeth normally had a shallow root with a kind of suction grip and gave up easily. All my teeth that were later pulled had these strong grown-up roots and must have hurt as much as grown-up teeth would have hurt, but not knowing that other children had it easier I had no complaints. An anaesthetic was never suggested—milk teeth were supposed to be loose. Mine were not.

After the extraction I was led away to the kitchen to bleed for a few minutes in the company of Mr Crocker's nice fat housekeeper and her enormous tabby cat, who became a friend of mine. My mother stayed chatting with Mr

35

Crocker, an old chum, for there never seemed to be any other patients.

If it was winter, before we left the house my mother would wrap a scarf round my mouth to keep the cold out and we would set out to cross the Common again, while my tongue probed the seemingly bottomless bloody cavern that was a new feature of my mouth. Sure enough, when we got home there was the hot cake and the sixpence. My mother had her faults but she kept her word. If she said it would hurt badly, hurt badly it did, but not for long, as she had promised. She could be counted on.

By the next morning the cavern had lost its pulpiness and by dinner-time was forgotten.

This procedure was followed a good many times, until my second teeth had all emerged unimpeded. It hurt badly every time but because I had been warned I never dreaded it. I knew that some mothers lied to their children about wounds and death but I should have been ashamed to have had a soft-centre mother like that. My mother was rather unlike other children's mothers in her ways, but though she could be embarrassing I was quite proud of her, and of my father too, because they were bold and good-looking. I should not have liked the funny-looking parents who fussed about everything that some children had.

3

I never met Clara because she had always been there. She had always been there though she was not there always.

There can be no first impressions unless there have been remembered first meetings, so it seems to me that I never met Clara.

She was there before I was born. More accurately, before I was born she had come and gone. By the time I remember her, therefore, she was always there but not there always.

Clara had been my newly-married parents' first little maidservant, a fourteen-year-old up from Somerset. That was in a house I never lived in, the other side of the Common. My brother was born there. Later my parents moved to the modern house where I was born, but by that time Clara had left to better herself in the ritual fashion of all my mother's maids.

When I was about three she was employed by people called Day, a better family than the Bettses presumably, who lived at Streatham. On her afternoons off Clara often came to see us because by now, thanks to my mother's unorthodox and egalitarian ways, she had become 'as family', a familiar friend who lent a hand.

There was one afternoon of great happiness when she took me out on her day off. We went on a bus to a common, not the common Common I knew but a common that was quite uncommon, touched with the light that falls just so on a lifetime only once. It was afternoon, autumn, with fallen leaves. We walked through rustling leaves to a kiosk where Clara bought me a thick slice of yellow cake studded with currants and sultanas. Then we sat on a bench while I ate the cake in the misty autumnal tea-time light. The cake was intensely enjoyable, packed with a taste and texture so satisfying in the mouth that to remember it nourishes me still.

One day when I was four, towards the end of a gas-lit afternoon at about the hour when Clara usually left to go back to the Days at the end of her visit to our degraded family, she was standing in the kitchen tying behind her back the strings of a big white apron. Usually now she would be putting on her coat. She stood tying the apron, looking down at me.

'Aren't you going now, Clara?' I asked.

'No,' she said, 'I'm not going away any more. I'm staying here now.'

A surge of joy swept through me. I hugged her round the waist, which I could reach. *'No I'm not going away any more. I'm staying here now.'*

Those are the only words of hers that I have remembered. But they were potent words and all, really, that I needed to know.

(Clara was not the only one of my mother's maids who, having bettered herself by moving on to a classier family, worsened herself again by coming back to live with us.)

Clara was a quiet person. Her face was gentle. She was pale, with blue eyes and straight, dark hair. She was very faintly buck-toothed so that she seemed to smile easily, but she never said much. Perhaps that is why I remember nothing she said over all those years except her announcement that she was staying, though, when I come to think of it, what people say is not usually what one remembers about them. All those hours of talk are soon forgotten. I remember people only as beings, much as I remember companionable animals long dead. Even the clever ones, the witty ones, their words are soon gone. Only what they were remains in the memory.

Once someone with not long to live said to me:

'Now after I am dead you must be sure to remember that . . . you must never forget that . . .' but what it was I was supposed to remember, must never forget, never even reached me, let alone could be recalled, as a pattern of words. None of the words got through, only the look, the sense of another being, the message.

When Clara was cutting bread and butter for tea I would stand beside her and ask for 'a tasty bit'. This was a crusty knob torn off, not cut off, a Coburg loaf, crowned with a dab of butter. With all that butter about, this must have been before the War. Another treat was to get Clara to come and talk to me for a few minutes after I was in bed, for what I called 'a friendly chat'. For some reason friendly chats were not frequent; Clara seemed to find it difficult to fit them in. By hindsight, I think it likely my mother put the boot in. I had become conscious, when I was four, that my mother was no longer my favourite person, Clara was. My change of heart had, no doubt, been observed and not enjoyed. Her egalitarianism did not encompass the affections.

Clara stayed with us for three years, till she left to get married. She married George. George did not quite fit into things. She had met him at one of the places where she had gone to better herself, a standard family with a slightly bigger house than ours, with a father in a bowler and a thick dark blue overcoat, who went to an office, and two children destined for public day schools. George, surprisingly, was an uncle, a brother of the father. Far from being glossy and prosperous like his brother, Clara's employer, George had something shabby and kicked-in about him. He was not tall and his nose was rather long and sad. He looked quite old, about forty. He was in the Army but he was only a private. He was a mechanic and never went to the front. He had a motor-bike and sidecar. I stood at an upstairs window, feeling irritable, and saw Clara get into the sidecar and stutter away on her day off. I felt strongly that George was not good enough for Clara.

After the War he worked in a garage. They lived in the upper part of a small house not far away. When I was bigger I would sometimes walk there to visit Clara. George was never there, he was always working at the garage. They seemed quite poor, unlike George's brother in his thick navy overcoat. What Clara and I talked about on these visits is unremembered.

My mother said Clara had never been strong and that she worried too much about the future. It was my mother's opinion that a future too much worried about might never come. Clara had worried herself into an ulcer. She was often not at all well and looked paler than ever.

Clara was ill and was taken into St Mary's Hospital, Paddington. I went with my mother to see her there. She was in a long ward with many beds. Her face was bony and peculiarly pale but she looked pleased to see us. Her lips did not slide properly over her teeth. When we were leaving she smiled at me but because her mouth was dry her lips seemed stuck and her smile went on too long, somehow fixed, as if it might go on for ever with her teeth showing.

Half a lifetime later there was a story in the paper about a young French mountaineer who became trapped on an icy ledge in the Alps with the *bise* blowing and no hope of rescue. He would have been hopelessly frostbitten but was still living. He could be seen up there, far off, and the paper published a picture of him taken with a long-distance lens and blown up to seem quite near. Dying of cold, he stood there, transfixed, with his teeth bared in a sort of shuddering grin. I knew that his lips must have been too stiff, and his teeth too dry, for that smile ever to leave his face.

Some time later my mother remarked that George had put up a headstone for Clara and on it he had described her as 'my noble wife'. For all her imperviousness to education my mother had an ear for words and the description struck her as ridiculous. It amused her. Certainly it was inappropriate, I could see that, but somehow it did not amuse me.

I never again saw George nor did I ever go to see for myself that silly adjective on Clara's headstone.

* * *

When Clara left us to get married it was in the middle of the War. Soon afterwards I was sent to school for the first time. Far from being the traumatic experience so often suffered by people who write books about it, school was at once painless and meaningless. I was never set upon by bullies. It was a small private school run by a lady with kindergarten qualifications and a goitre. To assist the pupils with their reading, the books we were issued with were printed with hy-phens in between the syll-ables. As I had been reading the daily papers for a long time this struck me as laughable (in fact my bro-ther and I start-ed at home a cult man-ner-ism of talk-ing to one an-other in hy-phen-ated syll-ables). We sat at little desks of varnished deal—or pine as it is now called. One day, bored, I took the corner edge of my ruler and, pressing down hard with it, inscribed my name in intaglio on the varnished surface of the desk.

The next morning when I arrived at school there was my goitred headmistress already stagily installed, fitting tightly into the small desk, yellow duster at the ready, facial expression ratcheted into more-sorrow-than-anger, rubbing away at my indented signature. She lifted her head as if in surprise at my entrance and started in on a pained reproof. That finished her for me. A woman who thought strong dents could be rubbed off with a duster was not fit to teach me, I could teach her.

The gym uniform at this school was a pleated tunic in navy blue serge worn over a reseda green blouse of tussore silk. In this garb we walked in crocodile across the Common to a gym where sometimes we did gym things like jumping or climbing ropes or, ludicrously, galumphed about pretending to be fairies or toads. I could not see any sense at all in these antics. They had nothing to do with real life nor were they in any way satisfying to the imagination. Soon the winter with its annual gift of fog, asthma and bronchitis put an end to the farce of school for many weeks. I remember nothing of my last term there. The following autumn I went to another school.

Meanwhile at home, minus Clara, we were 'without'. 'Without' meant being without domestic help and was accepted verbal currency among ladies who customarily employed. Even my grandparents who kept several servants were partially without—Minnie the parlourmaid had gone for a soldier, a female soldier in the WAACs. My mother revelled in this deprivation. She had long striven to sink socially and now here was her chance. We ate in the kitchen. A kitchen in those days was usually a room with a cooking range, a lot of cupboards and a deal table. Unlike the kitchens of our day, where families eat and have their being, there was no sink in the kitchen of the past. The sink was in the scullery, along with the gas cooker and possibly a copper for boiling sheets, with a firebox underneath. Nobody would think of eating a meal in a room containing a sink, with its connotations of drains and sludge. A maid

41

would not be expected to eat in a scullery, because of the sink.

My father, exiled from the comforts of dining room meals, reminisced with an added touch of bitter prophecy. He reminded my mother that when they were first married they had a breakfast room, with main meals in the dining room. This was before my mother had shaken off the habits of her affluent upbringing. When the breakfast room had become the nursery they still had the dining room to eat in but now that, too, had been taken from him.

'Next move, the scullery,' he prophesied, 'and after that, meals eaten off the croquet box.' The croquet box, like an upended coffin, stood in the backyard opposite the coal shed and was usually covered with crumbs and scraps that my mother had put out for the birds. We had no cat then.

My father had always kept a dog or dogs. At the time of the outbreak of war we had a deerhound called Rona. Being so big, she was housed at night in a luxurious kennel, with two apartments, later to become a playhouse for me, at the end of the garden. Because she ate so much my father wisely decided to part with her to a grocer we knew who would have access to plenty of bacon bones and broken biscuits if rationing became tight.

At this period, when we ate in the kitchen with the door to the scullery open and the back door open to the yard and garden beyond, birds began to come into the house. They were mostly sparrows. They came right in, pecking crumbs round our feet, perfectly bold. They would come in while my mother was rolling pastry, mixing up cakes and puddings. Animals loved my mother. With them she was a natural. She could terrorise human beings but mice and spiders were safe with her. The bird invasion continued till she brought home a kitten. Some old friends of hers, two impoverished spinsters (sisters of that Rose Layton who had burst so interestingly) lived deprived lives in Richmond in a house where, for fourteen shillings a week and free accommodation, they kept open, under the auspices of an animal welfare society, a shelter for stray cats; hence Toodles.

Toodles was a half-Persian tabby with white socks and a neck almost free of hair. He had lice and he had worms. He

42

messed anywhere. He seemed untrainable. There was talk that he might have to go. Hearing this, I wept. Toodles jumped on to my knee, dabbed my face, seemed to wish to dry my tears. Softened by this performance, my parents granted Toodles a reprieve, after which he immediately reformed. He learnt clean ways, his neck fur grew in, he fattened, he grew beautiful and magnificent. But the birds, of course, had gone by then.

At the time of the Russian Revolution in 1917 my father rechristened Toodles Toodlumski, soon shortened to Umski, and so he was known till his death.

Umski was the only cat we ever came by honestly. From then on we were never without a cat but they were never ours by right. Cats moved in on us. Sometimes they were cherished cats belonging to neighbours who came and carried them home, begging us not to feed them and to shoo them away. We shooed them away for a bit, but they still came back. We always had our cats free, after Umski. But a cat had to be fed.

Cats were fed differently in those days. Tins of cat or dog food were unheard-of. Instead, there was the cats' meat man. He would come hawking along the road with a small cart drawn by an old horse (soon to end up as stock-in-trade of the cart itself). He peddled partly-cooked, smelly little slices of horse-meat sold by the stick on which they were impaled, kebabs for cats. Some cats liked this stuff very much and would mob his cart, but my mother had noticed that cats, unlike dogs, did not really enjoy meat that was going bad, so she resorted to the cats' meat man only when the cat food of choice ran scarce. When possible, she fed Umski on lights or cod's head. Both these delicacies, if obtainable, would be given away free to regular customers of the butcher or fishmonger, or sold for a few pence. Fish heads were penitential fare for those that did not eat them. Boiling, they stank the house out. Then they had to be boned. My mother would stand in the scullery, hands sunk in a bowl of steaming cod's head, feeling out the bones. The eyes, boiled, were peculiarly horrid—solid white, the size of a small damson, rattling about on Umski's tin dinner plate as he nosed the boiled eye around at the end of his meal, trying to bite it, a feline version of bobbing for apples.

Boiling lights stank too, not of going bad like the cat's meat kebabs but the steamy reek of insides boiling. The nastiest thing about lights was the newspaper they were wrapped in. They came in a big wobbly parcel as heavy as a baby. The newspaper was bloody and had to be torn off in strips where it had stuck. Boiled newspaper was not considered good for Umski, who was greatly cherished.

Food was chancy during the First World War. Rations were not as evenly distributed as in the Second War; there were many scarcities. Pondering the problem of Umski's food, my mother reasoned that there might be less of a run on lights in the City than in the suburbs, so she badgered my father into pestering the butchers in the neighbourhood of his office, which was on Ludgate Hill. My father was a handsome, well-groomed man, glossy with health, even his shapely eyebrows enhanced with a trace of Pears solid brilliantine. In summer he wore grey flannel suits and a flower in his buttonhole. All this manly elegance, so much esteemed by my mother as caddishness in happier circumstances, counted for nothing when it came to obtaining lights for Umski. My father was compelled to ingratiate himself with the few City butchers and bear home with him on his suburban train the bloody parcels, sagging with lengths of dreadful piping. Umski was not very fond of lights pipe but the visiting cats in the garden found them really welcoming. The house continued to be filled with offensive steams.

My mother had the siege mentality. She took naturally to hard times and was a notable food-gatherer. She laid in tins of cabin biscuits, the last resort of shipwrecked sailors on liferafts. These biscuits were absolutely hard and completely tasteless; one had to be very hungry indeed to tackle them. Towards the end of the war, when they were only beginning to be weevily, my mother was inspired to offer up cabin biscuits fried. Even then they were not well received. Tins of the things were still about at the beginning of the Second World War, when I was better placed to avoid eating them.

Contrary to present dietary thinking, my mother was convinced that growing children would not grow up healthy if they were not given ample supplies of *animal fat*.

She was insistent that *children must have animal fat*. To this end I was liberally fed with bread and dripping, bread and lard, bread and bone-marrow—scraped raw out of shin bones later rendered down for stock and for more fat. Other foods shovelled into me were herring roes on toast, sheep's brains, porridge made of coarse oatmeal cooked overnight, suet puddings of all kinds, mounds of turnip tops and hateful parsnips roasted round the joint, if any. Most of this food was perfectly acceptable to me and went down a treat. My brother was fussier. Bits of spat-out gristle edged his plate but I chewed mine up till it could be swallowed because I was always hungry. Any hungry gap at the end of the day would be filled with bread and cheese and onions, all the green of the onions to be eaten up and the cheese rind (of mummified cheesecloth) not to be cut off but scraped, in the interests of economy.

Economy of materials became second nature. My youthful doodlings were not on the lavish sheets of paper squandered by later generations of children but fitted in round the edges of print in old magazines. There were a few colouring books around but mostly I made do with the Army and Navy catalogues, of encyclopaedic size, lying around from before the War. Matches were rare and precious, as well as more needed then than today, with open fires and gas lighting still usual. I would be set to folding spills out of letters and any odd paper that was about. At an early age I had perfected the art of thrusting a spill into a fire downstairs then pelting upstairs in darkness but for the flaring spill, along a short corridor and into the lavatory at the end. This little room, like the scullery, had only a gas jet to light it, a miniature version of the bigger flares on market stalls before the black-out snuffed those cheerful lights. I had to clamber on to the seat to light the lavatory gas-jet. All the other rooms in the house, except the scullery, had gas fittings with mantles, deemed too fragile to be poked at with a lighted spill by a technical infant. My mother had no inhibitions about children handling fire. It was something they had to learn and the sooner the better. They must learn to be careful unless they wanted to be burned. We learned.

Knives were another example of my mother's learn-as-you-burn methods. Table knives were not then of stainless steel but of bone or horn handles with blades of soft steel that could take a keen edge. Because they tarnished readily, these knives had to be cleaned after every meal. Most people thrust them into a knife-machine, a round object like a big cheese with slots round the edge for the knives. When a handle was turned, something went on inside the cheese that cleaned the knives. My mother had no use for knife-machines. She said there was nothing like a knifeboard. This was a strip of wood about two feet long and six inches wide, covered with hard leather about as thick as the soles of dancing pumps. This would be sprinkled with a yellow abrasive powder and the knives rubbed vigorously back and forth, both sides, till they came bright. My mother was a virtuoso at the knifeboard, sweeping the knive outwards with a ringing sound, first one side, then the other, as if conducting a band. This technique had the effect of not only cleaning the knife, but finishing it off sharp as a razor front and back. Our knives would slice a tomato as easily with their backs as with their conventional cutting edge. Despising machine-cleaned knives as non-functional, my mother would import her own yellow-handled, worn-down, double-bladed little killer to meals in the restaurants of five-star hotels, wiping it off between courses. It was with knives like these that I learnt to cut up my food and whatever else I thought needed cutting up. My mother, when queried about this seemingly dangerous practice, would reply that sharp knives were much safer for children —they cut where they were supposed to cut and did not skid off surfaces and cut unsuitable objects such as fingers or knees.

In the event, my fingers were no bloodier than other children's.

During the War I had a bath only once a week. I expect the others did too but my bath was the first, immediately before my bedtime. The fire under the copper was lighted for this ritual for, though there was a hot water system heated by the kitchen range, this was considered too extravagant of fuel. The copper, once started, would be kept going on rubbish, the kind of soft muck like lights paper that most people put in their dustbins (not my mother: only

46

inorganic ashes, tins, and broken crocks went into her dustbin; she was an early ecologist and besides, she had sympathy for the dustmen, shouldering bins of smelly garbage). Pails of near-boiling water would be baled out of the copper and carried upstairs by my father and brother to be tipped with great issue of steam into the bath. Except on bath night I washed in cold water. I thought nothing of this. Nor did I think to compare my circumstances with the different conditions in my grandparents' house, where hot water gushed from taps in spite of all that the Germans could do.

Working on the principle that a fat person loses weight more slowly than a thin person because of the differing ratios of skin surface to body weight, my mother decreed that a useful economy would be to use bar soap in the bathroom. The preferred brand was Primrose soap, like Sunlight in appearance but considered milder. It came in double bars and the usual form was to screw these apart, converting it into two stout blocks. This was considered wasteful by my mother. The two Siamese bars should be left twinned, resulting in the least possible exposure to the wasting effects of water. A double bar of this yellow soap was placed in the bathroom for the use of all. In due course it would develop a sort of waist from being held, finally dwindling to the point of separation of the two diminished halves. That was the economical usage of soap that my mother envisaged but she had reckoned without my father's reaction. He would not put up with washing with laundry soap, let alone a double bar of the stuff. He complained. My mother was adamant: there was a war on. How would he like to be up to his neck in mud in the trenches? He would be glad of a bar of Primrose then, wouldn't he?

No he would not. He would never be glad of it. He stormed back to the bathroom. But there the only soap was a double bar of Primrose. Suddenly there was a roar and the sound of impact outside the kitchen window, which was under the bathroom. My father had chucked the soap out of the window. It had landed on the quarry-tiled area below —what a better class of family might have called the patio but which we called by-the-lilac. Clara, then still with us,

47

was bidden go and pick it up. It was brought, sadly pitted with London grit, into the kitchen for inspection. The Primrose was not what it had been. One wondered what its effect might be on skin.

'Take it upstairs again, Clara, and give it back to him.'

Upstairs went Clara, to return visibly resisting laughter. She had knocked on the bathroom door, which had been opened a few inches by my father.

'Your soap, sir,' Clara had explained. A bare arm had emerged and received the soap.

'Thank you, Clara,' my father, always polite, had said. As she was telling us this there was another roar from upstairs and down came the soap again with a thump on the by-the-lilac.

'Fetch it in, Clara.'

This time the bar of soap was showing serious signs of wear and tear, indeed it appeared gravely damaged, with one corner flattened out and much abrasive grit imbedded in it. But my mother was unrelenting. Clara was told to take it up again. The performance was repeated—door opening, bare arm extended, soap accepted, polite thanks tendered and then CLUNK! on to the quarry tiles outside.

As it was time for me to go to school I am not sure how this conflict of wills ended, but it must have been by compromise. Primrose soap continued to appear in the bathroom but in single bars, on a more human scale, better suited to family life as it was lived.

* * *

Notwithstanding my mother's insistence on household economies and her zest for hunting and gathering, she was the very opposite of mean. Food, once hunted for and gathered, was provided in abundance. Helpings were generous and plates could be sent back for more. Once properly filled up at meal-times, however, we were forbidden to eat between meals. The little boys I played and fought with had kind mothers who gave them biscuits or cakes with a glass of milk in the middle of the morning, but I was expected to last out till dinner. The mid-day meal was dinner. ('Lunch' for children meant elevenses. Luncheon was for people like my grandparents who kept servants and were waited on at table. We did not use the word, we had dinner.) On this regime, washed down, as they say, with cold water only—we both disliked tea and milk—my brother and I grew like mushrooms.

A word, but only a word, about my brother. He was my senior by five years and will be rarely mentioned. The reason for this is that he is still living, in his middle eighties with all his wits about him, capable, and perhaps quite willing, to sue me for libel should a loophole for a libel action present itself. Anyone who has had a brother will understand that it is difficult to write about him without incurring the risk of a libel action. *If you can't say something kind, don't say anything at all.* We have all heard that. So I am not saying anything at all about my brother, or at least not much.

It will not be libellous to note that on my mother's diet, to which he did not always take as readily as I did, my brother, at thirteen, was a grown man, just under six feet, with voice broken, shaving every day and pursuing girls industriously at any moment that could be snatched from his studies. Such precocious development is not common even today and in 1917 was highly unusual. My manly thirteen-year-old brother, trawling the summer evenings on his bicycle for girls, would be accosted by women, though not in the way he might have fantasised. They called after him: 'Why aren't you in the Army?' It would be neat to write that they offered him white feathers but I cannot bring myself to believe that women went about provided with a clip of white feathers ready to offer one to the next thirteen-year-old with over-active hormones who might happen along, riding the summer dusk on his gleaming Swift, darting predatory glances from behind his studious spectacles.

It may be of interest to parents with sons of nineteen who have not yet started to shave and still sing treble in the bathroom that my brother's chosen and invariable teatime diet was butterless brown bread and golden syrup taken with cold water.

My brother was a brainy boy, a scholar of St Paul's. His interests were simple: mathematics and girls. His mathematics helped him to keep count of the girls.

My only companions up to the age of nine were small boys. There were several of these living in the houses which, like ours, backed on the Field, where we played the war games natural at the time. It just happened that the parents living near us seemed to produce only boys and often only one boy at that. Being only boys they were pampered by their mothers, readily wrestled to the ground and their heads sat on. Once, when I was about eight, some bigger boys of twelve or thirteen set up a boxing match between me and the boy next door, Percy, who was two years older than I was. Percy had been a lifelong buddy of mine, always ready to oblige with an interesting parabola of pee. He had bad teeth and a pleasant, weak, personality. I bore him no ill-will but when the fight was set up and a ring of big boys formed, there was no choice but to fight him.

Having spent many hours of my bed-fast asthmatic winters reading and re-reading my brother's huge red annuals of *Chums* and *Boys' Own Paper*, I considered myself well-versed in the mystique of boxing matches—seconds out of the ring, the clinch, the quick jab to the ribs, straight left, straight right, the stagger against the ropes, the bell . . . on and on and on for fifteen rounds or so, pounded, bloody, until knocked or knocking out.

It sounded fearfully painful. The boys in the school stories took it bravely enough on the chin, but when you came down to it they were only story boys. This, the loose ring of bigger boys, the hazel coppice behind them, Percy my opponent opposite me, smiling a nervous smile of bad teeth—this was real life. It was going to go on a long time till one of us was out for the count, so I had better begin. A whistle sounded (no bell available) and I raced into the ring, meeting Percy with a solid punch on the nose before he was well out of his corner. He tottered back as blood poured from his nose. Immediately a shout of applause went up from the cruel boys who had staged the match, the ring broke up and Percy was offered a second hanky. The fight was over!

It was nice to find out that sometimes, just sometimes, life on earth went more smoothly than life in books.

It was in this little glade, sheltered by hazel bushes, that I had my statutory early experience of sex—better still, child

50

abuse. There was a big boy of eighteen, a young man really, ten years older than me, who lived in one of the houses on the other side of the Field. He had younger brothers and sisters, all older than me, whom I knew only slightly. His name was Tom. He was an art student but for how long I do not know. He was there in the glade and then later on he was not there any more, so very likely he went to the War and was killed. We would lie down in the bushes and he would cuddle me. He would look at me a long time and then ask if he could kiss me. I was not keen on being kissed so he took a Wolff's Lightning Eraser out of his pocket and said he would give it to me if I would kiss him. Being a stationery fetishist I found the india rubber irresistible and let him kiss me. The kiss did not affect me emotionally, all my desires were focused on the rubber. We met in the hazel coppice several times. Each time he would cuddle me and ask to kiss me. I began to hold out for brand new Wolff's Lightning Erasers, spotless white ones with geometrically sharp corners. He never did anything but cuddle me, look at me, kiss me gently and hand out quantities of new india rubbers, wonderful for swopping at school or keeping and gloating over. It all ended without my noticing. Perhaps the art school got suspicious about the run on erasers, or perhaps Tom was called up and got killed. I did not notice when it ended. I had enough rubbers to be going on with. Their smell was so alluring, so satisfying.

4

My mother had a horror of laundries. She was disgusted at the thought of a whole neighbourhood's dirty linen tossed in together. This revulsion was reinforced by Mrs Allen, then our charwoman, who had once worked in a laundry, and described vividly the vats in which the soiled sheets of strangers heaved and jostled in a vile soup of suds, bleach and body fluids.

There were no launderettes then, so all the family washing except dress shirts was done at home, and with zest. My mother was an enthusiastic washerwoman. Her aim, if the weather was fine, was to get the washing done, wrung through the mangle, hung out, dried, brought in, ironed, folded and hanging in rows on the kitchen airers, all in one day. This tight schedule demanded an early start, which it got. On washing days, when I was a child, my mother rose at four in the morning.

No one, except my mother, loved these early mornings much. My father grumbled at the commotion of his wife getting up and dressing at four in the morning and at some time must have put his foot down, or the boot in, because there was a period when I used to wake up to my mother getting out of my bed, where she must have been sleeping, and dressing in my room. In her youth she had been a frequent and active sleepwalker, wandering about the dark house disturbing her parents and siblings, warning of burglars, and in the confusion sometimes being mistaken for one—two hands on doorknobs either side of the door, turning opposite ways in the dark. Her family must have been glad to be rid of her when she married. She had calmed down a bit by my time but still carried on occasionally, and more than once woke me during the brief nights before washing day mornings by sitting up in bed, clutching my arm and hissing to me to listen! there was somebody in the wardrobe. This warning did not alarm me at all. For one thing, I knew there was no room in the wardrobe for a burglar, however stunted. It was crammed with clothing old and new and stacked with hoards of non-perishable foodstuffs. Also, I registered at once that my mother, usually so dependable, was at the moment 'not herself'. I would growl at her that there was nothing there and to shut up and lie down, and lie down again she would, perfectly docile for once. So it must have been with the children who, we were told, would be sent to the pub to call out their drunken fathers and lead them safely home. Grown-ups, for one reason or another were sometimes 'not themselves' and then a little child could lead them.

Sleeping in my bed before washing days did not go on for long. Either she kipped down somewhere else or slipped very quietly out of the marital bed and dressed in the bathroom. However she managed, she was up at four and before long the plumbing would be honking. It was called an airlock but it sounded like a carthorse plodding through an iron echo chamber. The house shook with it. My father would be heard cursing and groaning and, beneath the clamour, the hurrying feet of my mother hastening to turn on, or off, the tap that healed. By the time the house had settled again, bar the intermittent thundering of the airlock returning, an alarm clock would be heard shrilling. This meant that it was six o'clock and time for the maid of the moment to rise and join her mistress in the scullery's steaming hell. My mother reckoned herself to be a pretty indulgent employer who would let her maid hog it in bed till six when she herself had been up for two hours getting the steam up. But the truth was that my mother enjoyed washing days, the heat and burden of it, the gamble with nature and the weather, the harvest home.

On bright March mornings as I got up, I would see my mother down there in the windy weather in the garden, pegging out a sheet, reaching up, both hands busy and her strong teeth too, clamped on a hem of linen as it billowed and flapped, beating out a rhythm like a dog being sick. Oblivious of everything but the job in hand, her eyes shone triumphant.

Breakfast was in the kitchen. My brother and I ate ours

first as we had to be off to school: our parents somewhat later. There was always porridge, coarse oatmeal steeped overnight and brought to the boil in the morning. On Monday mornings, washing day, we had sardines and bread and butter. The sardines came in a giant tin as big as a thick paperback, never seen these days. I liked sardines. Another bonus on Monday mornings was the arrival, with the daily papers, of *Woman's World*. While the plumbing thumped and honked and jets of soapy steam forced their way under the door from the scullery, I would be reading *Woman's World* as quickly as possible, keeping up with the serials, which were all at different stages of completeness so that there was never a time when a bottom line could be drawn and the order for *Woman's World* cancelled. My brother, neat in his black jacket and waistcoat and striped trousers, would groan softly, 'Oh for a little peace, a little comfort!' as the steam surged under the door and round the edges. He read *Woman's World* too, when he could lay hands on it, but affected to treat it as a joke, as I soon came to do. One great event was when Our Editress, who conducted a discreet 'agony aunt' column and was depicted week after week in a line drawing as a grave but sweet Edwardian lady, was suddenly brought up to date as a breezy 1918 type, everybody's game little chum. There were household hints, too, with particular regard to the proper treatment of piano keys and woollens. Woollens that came up bobbled from wear or washing should be trimmed off close with scissors, a job that must have required the expertise of a brain surgeon.

By now I was at my second school, a petty private enterprise grandiloquently named Queen's College. It was a school for girls only, which took some getting used to because up to then my only companions had been boys. Entirely different social skills had to be learnt. Girls were not for hitting, they were for being bitched at. Having been used to being treated to a line in searing contempt by my brother, I was well placed to adapt this technique to my new classmates, fortified by the knowledge that if it came to it I could pound the little prigs into the ground.

People talk a lot nowadays about peer pressures but I am bound to say I never felt them. Anyone who has been sent to a school still wearing a gym tunic in the colours of a previous school because it has not yet been grown out of, will have either succumbed to peer pressures without trace or become indifferent, and for life, to passing fads. My mother naturally had no patience with each silly little school insisting on its own colours. There was nothing wrong with gym tunics and blouses being sometimes in different colours and my next outfit could certainly be brown and Cambridge blue or whatever it was, but not before the hem of my navy blue and reseda green job had been let down and grown out of. In the end I got my brown tunic and Cambridge blue blouse, but by that time I was only one term away from my next school, where they wore navy blue and scarlet for gym.

Of lessons at that school I remember nothing except learning pages of French verbs by heart—preterite, pluperfect, indicative, subjunctive moods: all quite meaningless to me because never explained, yet learnt by heart and somehow muddled through. I also learnt, note-perfect but by chance, *Nymphs and Shepherds* and *Sleepers Awake*, sung again and again by a chorus of big girls in another part of the house. Such was the scope of my education at the age of eight or nine. I could not be said to be well grounded academically.

There were quite a number of big girls at that school, some of them up to ten years older than me. My mother had made me a fur hat, a kind of Cossack job, the idea being to keep my head warm. Nothing could have been more sensible, yet as soon as my mother tried it on my head my heart sank, instantly recognising another station of the cross. However, it had to be faced, like getting a tooth pulled, so off I went to school with my new hat on. Sure enough, it was greeted with gusts of laughter.

'Wearing your grandmother's hat today?'

'Did the dog die?'

'Picked up something at the Zoo?' and so on.

Some of the bigger girls, those of about fifteen, laughing more kindly but still laughing, urged me to go up an iron staircase, leading to a balcony at the back of the school—it was only a big private house—because one or two of them with Brownie cameras wanted to take a snap of me.

I did not demur. I did not have to be pushed up the stairs like the Speaker being pulled into the House of Commons. I went willingly. Impassivity was all. If I went of my own free will the power of the others would begin to leak out of them and the laughter would die. The thing was not to care—not to pretend not to care but really not to care.

The cameras clicked once or twice. To this day in inherited albums, somewhere, there may be a faded snap of a round-faced eight-year-old in a big fur hat looking stolidly out from an iron balcony, like an infant version of a dignitary of the *Politburo* reviewing a rumble-past of tanks.

The giggling died down as the big girls paused to wind the film round in their cameras. They began to drift away and I came down from the balcony. I continued to wear the fur hat to school. There were a few more, ever fainter, references to 'Grannie's hat', but they soon died down. If my hat and I were immovable, if we did not yield, we became part of the landscape of the accepted things that were no longer laughable.

Years later I happened to mention this incident to my mother. She was rueful.

'Why didn't you tell me at the time? I always thought that hat suited you well, you looked rather nice in it.'

'What could you have done about it, anyway?'

'Well . . .' she hesitated, '. . . you needn't have gone on wearing it, or . . .'

Or . . . I knew all right. Or . . . or a militant march to the headmistress, untold damage to my good name, for giving up wearing the hat would never have been tolerated. A good warm hat should be worn until worn out. I had been wise not to mention a word about the hat incident at home. Home and school would have been a fatal encounter. How much better to brave it out and live it down and learn not to care.

This was a time of sadness and weariness among the grown-ups. After four years of a heartbreaking war there was scarcely a family not touched by loss. Three younger cousins of my father's, brothers, had all been killed. In neighbours' houses there were so many photographs of dead young soldiers looking out from silver frames. I used to look and look at the eyes of these soldiers, wondering

56

what they had seen. Their eyes were bright or resolute or sombre and they were all dead. Closed. Or shot out.

As for those at home, life had gone grey for them. Everybody was tired and few were well nourished. When the great influenza epidemic struck, its victims offered little resistance. Those who died were often in the prime of life. Those who survived suffered from terrible depression. My father was one of these. From being an easy-going if quick-tempered man he became, for a few months, a household misery, snapping at everyone and complaining about everything. On Sunday afternoons he napped in an armchair in the dining room, and if I crept in for a book left behind he would groan and curse at me for waking him up and fling one of his felt bootees at my head, though missing it. As for my mother, she became defensive and cross. Food was at its worst and life was not as enjoyable as it had been.

This was at about the time of the fur hat. I lay in bed one early morning and considered my situation. All around were gloomy grown-ups, always grumbling about something. They seemed abstracted and anxious if not actively disagreeable. School was uncongenial in a negative sort of way. All those French verbs were extremely tedious and there was the matter of the hat, though I was weathering that. Was there nothing at all that was agreeable about daily life?

I found I was humming under my breath. The humming came up louder. It was *Sleepers Awake*, splendid and heartening. I hummed louder—I had no idea of the words —only the invigorating notes sang out, full of hope and courage.

From his bedroom my father shouted at me to for God's sake shut up. I shut up, but only slightly. I still sang under my breath and felt suddenly wonderfully cheerful. Things were not so bad, really. Out snowballing not long before I had stuffed a lot of snow down the neck of a girl who soon after had been among those who had laughed loudest at my hat, and this last week she had been off school with pneumonia. The two events had not connected in my mind before but now they did, and I was not sorry to think that I had given her pneumonia, on account as it were. *Tit for hat*.

57

Life was not so bad if one did not take it too seriously. One could hand it out as well as take it.

Sleepers Awake!

I had become friendly with a girl who lived in the next road to mine. We walked home from school the same way. She was two years older than I but not so tall. Her name was Marion Morris. She was a very pretty little girl with regular features and fair curly hair tied back with a ribbon. Her experience was limited, in that she seemed never to have done anything naughty, never fought with anybody or even climbed trees. They had a typewriter at home, she said, the kind that had the letters set in a circle. She had once had a Bulldog printing set but most of that had been lost when it got knocked off the table and her mother had swept it up and burnt it. This had been a great loss. My mother would never have done a thing like that, I said, because she would often lay a meal at one end of the table in order not to disturb a game I had set up at the other. Marion said nothing. She was a quiet child.

She had two older sisters, Midge who was fifteen and also at Queen's College, the other really old, twenty-two and engaged to be married, Cathie. The elder one kept house at home. Their father had a much more interesting job than mine, who was merely the secretary of a building society. Their father was manager of Price's factory at Battersea and he often brought home reject candles. She would give me some small coloured barley-sugar Christmas ones if I liked. Our friendship strengthened.

I had never had a companion of my own sex before. It was nice for a change to have someone who would talk instead of always playing war games. I was able to interest her in codes, secret messages and invisible ink, necessary matters she had never even heard of. Private detection was another of my sidelines. One day, walking across the Common, I spotted a scrap of paper with a handwritten address scribbled on it. It was number, say 193, in Acre Lane, Brixton.

'This is a clue,' I exclaimed. 'We must follow it up!'

We had between us enough pocket money for the bus fare there and back, so we walked to the nearest 37 bus stop and bought tickets to Acre Lane. We gazed rapt at number

58

(say) 193, a blank commercial house-front. The thrill of achievement was deeply felt by both of us—we had successfully followed up a clue. Then we boarded a returning 37 bus and went back home. Marion was not in the habit, as I was, of spending much of her pocket money travelling the bus routes. This was not our only excursion. I doubt whether anybody in her subdued, carefully-run household got to know of them. My mother would not have cared. A knowledge of London bus routes was a better preparation for life, she would have agreed, than years at a desk being talked at by school teachers.

Marion came much more often to my house than I went to hers. It was easier at my house. Not that her big sister Cathie was unwelcoming—she always smiled at me in a favourable way as if she liked me—but I usually only called there to pick up Marion. Mrs Morris was not always to be seen and when seen was rather weird. She was a good deal older than my mother, with grey curly hair and a face very wide at the temples and from there diminishing in width, with no pause for cheekbones, to end in a pointed chin. Her eyes were sad and wild, angry yet questing, as if ransacking each arriving minute for its expected load of misery. She was hungry for bad news. I did not take to her at all, though liking all the other members of the family. She was a fanatical housewife, dusting and polishing all the time. But not always to be seen.

One day, when the house was quiet, I suggested to Marion a spell of messing about with the candles at her kitchen table. We had two candles lighted, one each, and with their flames melted other coloured candles into a kind of swirling coloured pool in an old dish. Some of the pool overflowed here and there in blobs of blue or red candle grease onto the deal table—nothing to worry about, a negligible occupational hazard, something my mother would have made nothing of. But not Mrs Morris. She entered unexpectedly. Her sudden rage was awful. She screamed at us. *Dirt! Mess! Filth!* She burst into tears, shooed me out of the back door, pursued Marion raving into the depths of the house. I fled, only too anxious to escape from this madwoman.

'I think Mrs Morris has gone mad,' I told my mother. 'She

59

had a kind of fit because we spilled a few blobs of candle grease on the kitchen table. The *kitchen* table . . .' and then I remembered and told my mother . . . 'and do you know, the other day I was in their dining room when Cathie came in to lay the table, and when she took off the tablecloth—I mean the thick green tablecloth with the tasselled edges —when she took that off to put on the white cloth for the meal, what do you think? Guess?'

'I have no idea,' said my mother absently. 'That poor child. Mrs Morris is sometimes *not herself*, you know, she has melancholia.'

'Something else she has too, you couldn't possibly guess . . . you know what, underneath that green cloth their dining room table is just plain deal like a kitchen table, but because it has dining table legs nobody knows, when the cloth is on. What do you think of that, a dining table with a kitchen table top?'

My mother thought nothing much about it at all. Perhaps it had once been a kitchen table, an exceptional kitchen table with polished legs. The Morrises came from the north somewhere, didn't they? Midge, that pretty girl, still spoke with that kind of fat voice they had in Lancashire, probably it was some Lancashire thing to have tables like that. What of it? How people lived was their own business. What was serious was poor little Marion being brought up like that, never being able to lead a natural child's life because of a mother who ought to be in a lunatic asylum . . . 'but don't on any account mention any of this to anybody else,' she added. 'It wouldn't be fair on Marion and her sisters.'

I agreed it would not be fair to talk about Marion's having a mad mother. So my mother took me more into her confidence and told me what Cathie, whom she sometimes met out shopping, had told her. It seemed that Mrs Morris, always subject to moods of gloom and irritability, had been more or less permanently out of bounds for many years now, in fact since Marion had been born. She was not considered quite bad enough, on average, to be committed to a lunatic asylum, but she was certainly quite bad enough to make life for her family unhappy most of the time. Cathie had taken on the housekeeping at an early age because Mrs Morris, though obsessive about cleaning the house, had quite given up on things like shopping or cooking or making laundry lists. No servant would stay with them.

My mother hoped to goodness that Cathie's young man would come back safely from the war and marry her. Ten years of minding a mad mother and running a home were more than enough.

'Who would look after Mr Morris and the house then, if Cathie married and went away?'

'Well, then it would be time for Midge to take her turn,' my mother said.

But what I had seen of Midge led me to think that easy outcome was unlikely. Midge—she of the fat voice—was extremely pretty, all blue eyes and golden curls and rosy plumpness, much livelier in manner than either of her sisters. I happened to know that my brother, younger than her by a couple of years though a head taller, was slightly in love, at a distance, with Midge. There was quite a list of the bigger girls at Queen's College that my brother, though at a distance, was slightly in love with. He suggested that I should enlarge my private detection activities to take in some casual surveillance of the comings and goings of the better-looking big girls and report back to him.

'I know you like taking notes and writing reports and things, don't you?' he said. 'You would enjoy it.'

'I can't do it unless I have proper paper for writing on. It must have lines, otherwise I can't keep straight.'

'I'll give you some foolscap paper.' And he did. It was unbelievable. I never found out where he got it from unless he had filched some from our grandfather's writing table. Foolscap was like gold.

The police court proceedings in the local paper were written in a style I found admirable, so I adopted it for my reports. Written in ink, with a few blots and splutters from the nib when it picked up a wisp of Umski's fur from the inkwell, it wavered, more or less on the lines, over the sacred page of foolscap, which I delivered each evening to my brother. How he received them I was not to know. He never reacted. He was inscrutable.

Tuesday Feb. 13—Acting on information received, emerging from school the observer observed the party in question (Midge Morris) accompanied by another party (Eileen Baverstock) proceeding in a northerly direction along Prison Road in the direction of the Post Office where the observer opines they bought sweets at least one of them did because coming out of the Post Office they had a sherbet dab between them Party Number One that is Midge probably being the one who paid for it as she was holding it. They came back. On the way back the observer observed them approaching Nan and Betty Scott with their mother Mrs Scott hereinafter known as Party Number Two and Party Number Three not counting Mrs Scott who doesnt count going the other way. Midge and Eileen said good afternoon or something like it I couldn't hear but the observer depones that Mrs Scott sort of bowed so they must have said something. Nan and Betty and Mrs Scott walked on they never speak much. They proceeded in a northerly direction they were wearing grey until lost to sight.

(Signed) Detective Betts

The beautiful and mysterious Scott family were the subject of much speculation. Arriving in the neighbourhood out of nowhere, the two girls were enrolled for a short time, perhaps a couple of terms, at Queen's College. There, being so old (eighteen and nineteen), they went immediately into the top form, beyond my ken. But they never seemed to make friends with anybody. They were either together or, out of school, with their mother. The three of them might be seen from time to time, passing by, walking in beauty.

Everybody, parents as well, agreed they were strikingly good-looking. All three were very tall, slender, with long legs like the models in fashion drawings. Their mother walked in the middle, a daughter on either side, never looking at what was near to them, always seemingly looking into the distance, heads held high, gazehounds, with great dark eyes. Their skin was neither pink nor pale, their cheekbones delicately moulded, their noses straight and at exactly the right angle. They had perfect mouths. Their hair was very dark, the mother's lightly touched with grey. And they always wore grey, impeccably tailored coats and skirts. They never carried bags of shopping.

Nobody seemed to know anything about them. My own opinion was that their father, no doubt a colonel in the Black Watch and laird of countless heathery acres, had been killed in the War heroically. The estate (I guessed) had passed to some distant cousin and the three lovely Scott women, mother and daughters, bereaved and dispossessed, had travelled south with their grief, but it walked always with them as they paced the roads and Common, heads held high, looking at nothing that was near: tragic thoroughbreds.

I was aware that my brother lusted after them but he never came nearer to them than reading the reports of Detective Betts. Nor did anybody else. After a few months they went as silently as they had come, out of our world. Perhaps they proceeded in a northerly direction again, wearing grey, until forever lost to sight. They were too beautiful to stay with us for long.

* * *

The tedious course of school and the happy companionship of Marion were both interrupted by a severe sore throat. I was put to bed and Dr Biggs called in. After inquiring about the state of the bow-els, dabbing front and back as usual with his stethoscope and prescribing the well-known brown medicine, Dr Biggs went away again. But my sore throat grew no better and Dr Biggs returned. This time, after the stethoscope routine, he looked down my throat and told me to say 'Ah'.

'Ah,' I said. And again, 'Ah.'

'Ah,' said Dr Biggs. 'I think we have here a case of diphtheria.' He would return in due course, he said, with a dose of antitoxin and a throat swab. Meanwhile to continue with the cough mixture and to keep the bowels open.

Dr Biggs returned. First he choked me with a wodge of cotton wool on a stick that he poked down my throat and joggled about like a dolly-washer, making me retch. Then he produced a giant syringe with a spike on it the size of a carpet needle, which he stuck up to its hilt into the muscle of my buttock. The pain was tremendous and I shrieked. The pain did not go away but matured into an agonising stiffness that made it impossible to put weight on that side of my rear end, soon to be compounded by a swollen itchy rash from waist to knee. I suffered.

Meanwhile a dark thrill had gone through the neighbourhood at the news that there was diphtheria in our house. My brother was throat-swabbed too and kept home from school. Queen's College went more or less on hold, those parents who wished keeping their daughters at home without the slur of absenteeism. Diphtheria was a killer. Mothers and fathers shrank at the sound of the word.

Dr Biggs returned. The result of the swab had come through. It was negative. I did not have diphtheria. I had tonsilitis. A course of red tonic was prescribed. That evening the first bottle, made up in the good doctor's own dispensary, was delivered by messenger to the house, meticulously wrapped in white paper sealed with red wax. The seal was to ensure that no unauthorised lips took a swig of the healing fluid before it reached my bedside—only his patients must benefit from Dr Biggs's unique skills.

My father looked in on me that evening. He gave me a kiss.

'So glad to hear you're all right, sweetheart,' he said. 'You had us a bit worried.' And he added, to my mother, 'That silly old bugger should be put out to grass. Doesn't know his job.'

'Dr Biggs is a very clever doctor,' said my mother defensively. 'It's much better to err on the safe side.'

'The old fool errs on the top side and the backside too, if you ask me—so wrapped up in the state of the bow-els by now he doesn't know the difference between a throat and an arsehole.'

'Will!' exclaimed my mother severely. 'In front of the child! Really!' but her eyes were laughing. My father slapped her lightly on the bottom as he went out of the room, saying something in French that nobody else understood. I could see he was in a good mood because I was not going to die yet.

My brother came in to see me for the first time since quarantine had been imposed. He grumbled about

64

being kept home from school. Unlike me, at school he shone.

'I hear our worthy doctor has committed another act of Biggery,' he said, in a prepared speech. Little did he know that worse was to come, roll on a few more years.

No doubt because I had been snatched from death, my parents continued in good spirits. My mother ordered in a dozen oysters for my father to start his supper with, a sure sign that he was in favour because she much disliked opening oysters. It certainly seemed a diabolical thing to do to a bivalve, levering it open like that and breaking its back, and as for squeezing lemon on it, only a particularly nasty person could have thought that one up. But I always watched in case there was a pearl inside, preferably a black one.

While my father was eating his oysters, tipping up their shells and slurping them back raw in the way that had been invented for eating oysters, my mother remarked that she had thought of asking Frank and Nellie to dinner while they were in London.

'Not another intimate little dinner party. I hope?'

'Well . . . just Frank and Nellie. We haven't seen them for ages.' Aunt Nellie was my godmother.

'Black tie?'

'For you, yes. But you know Nellie would get Frank into a white tie and tails for breakfast if she could, and it's years since she's been seen in anything less dressy than black lace and ermine.'

My father groaned. He liked to spend the evening in his felt bootees and Jaeger cardigan, reading a French novel.

Though my mother was usually far from finicky, dishing up the food into whatever came handy and not always getting all the slugs washed off the salad, occasionally it came over her to dress up, ask somebody to dinner, and serve the food up on the right things she had been given as wedding presents—cut glass and silver, special plates to eat dessert off instead of hand to mouth. They always ate like that at my grandparents and very occasionally my mother reverted to type for an evening. This meant taking the prettier things out of the china cupboard where they had been put away. Convalescing after my tonsilitis, not

65

yet back at school, I enjoyed going into the china cupboard, a walk-in windowless roomlet normally kept locked.

'Why are you making this special fuss for Aunt Nellie and Uncle Frank? And what is that dish like two dishes one on top of the other with holes in the top one?'

'A watercress dish. It's Worcester. I make a bit of a fuss for Nellie because she enjoys display—she was quite poor when she was young.'

'Will you be using the watercress dish when they come to dinner? But she's rich now, though, isn't she?'

'No, it's a tea thing. Yes, they're rolling.'

'Is that why you asked her to be my godmother?'

'Not altogether. We got on well when we were young. She liked coming to our house, her own was very cramped, crammed with lodgers. She had to share a room with her mother.'

'Where did her father sleep, then? Did he have to share with one of the lodgers?'

'She hadn't got a father. Her mother ran this boarding place on her own. Frank was one of the lodgers and he married her. She was very pretty in a dark, sparkling way.'

I remembered what she looked like. She was still quite pretty, fairly small and pigeony. She was warm and bubbly and she spoke in the up-and-down trilling kind of voice I had heard on the stage on our occasional visits to the theatre but not among human beings. She called people 'my deeear', as if there were more e's in the word than usual. My father called this 'Sybil Thorndike articulation'.

My mother always addressed her as Nellie because that had been her name when they first knew each other, but I knew Aunt Nellie didn't like this much because she often said, in a particularly rich voice, 'Call me Eleanor.' But my mother went on calling her Nellie just the same.

Uncle Frank had always been called Frank but never said, 'Call me Francis,' in a thrilling voice.

He had become rich by expanding his family dyeing business, buying up other little businesses shop by shop, joining them together under different names all over the country until he had a dyeing and dry cleaning empire at

66

his command. Not a splash of oil on a sleeve or a dribble of egg down a waistcoat anywhere in the United Kingdom but it helped to make Uncle Frank richer.

They lived in Scotland and had an address that I liked because it was very short. It was simply:

Tayside,
Perth.

I liked short addresses. The only other short one I knew belonged to a friend of my cousin Dudley Arnaud, and it was:

Gothic House,
Maidstone.

My brother and I agreed that some addresses could be quite embarrassing, particularly the sort that had a name but needed a number, too, to identify it, such as:

'Sebastopol',
57 Florence Terrace,
Crimea Road,
Ugleton Wastes,
Near Hockshead,
Pinborough,
London SE 43.

My brother had once seen a house called 'Ebenezer'.

'Can you even think of a worse name for a house than "Ebenezer"?' he challenged me.

'I think a house called "Diarrhoea" would be worse,' I suggested, and he agreed with me.

But Uncle Frank and Aunt (call me Eleanor) Nellie were fortunate in their address. 'Tayside, Perth', could not be bettered.

They arrived by taxi. Aunt Nellie came in in a swirl of furs.

'My deeears!' she exclaimed, embracing everybody. She hugged me and kissed me on both cheeks. She smelt of very nice scent.

'What about a kiss for me?' This was from Uncle Frank. I looked up at him. He was just as I remembered him, rather pink and a little too fat with a potato nose and scarcely any hair. He kissed me. His eyebrows were very fair and could hardly be seen against his pink, bulgy forehead.

'My deeear child!' Aunt Nellie produced a cardboard dress box. 'I bought this for you in Paris, I know you will look sweet in it.'

I doubted if I would look sweet in anything. We opened the box, lifted the tissue paper and looked in. Inside could be seen the front of a folded dress, dark grey, made of a very smooth, dense, almost glossy woollen stuff, like the grey cloaks sometimes worn by mounted officers on ceremonial occasions. Down the front of it was gold frogging. Aunt Nellie took the dress out of the box and shook it and held it against me.

'I knew it! Just perfect for her with those eyes and all that dark gold hair!'

'In daylight her eyes are blue,' my mother muttered in a tone that did not express intense gratification. Years after it was too late, she said that as a child I had been a pleasure to look at, with a beautiful head of hair and the expression of an angel. But then I was not to know that. I never looked in a looking glass. All I saw of myself were arms and legs thickly covered with long golden hairs that my brother laughed at and measured with his ruler. I took it for granted that I was plain and then forgot about it.

Aunt Nellie hugged me again and said she wished she had a little girl like me. I was slightly embarrassed. My mother said it was very kind of her to remember me; and put the dress back in its box. I was told to go up to bed. If I was awake I could come down later in my dressing-gown while they were having dessert.

I had a dark red dressing-gown with a cape collar scalloped in white round the edges. It had two pockets and a silk girdle which, if I cinched it very tightly, would go twice round my middle.

Downstairs they were all in evening dress sitting round the table in candlelight, eating fruit off the proper plates for dessert. I wondered if my mother had been given the candles by Mr Morris—she liked Mr Morris—or if she had paid good money for them. Reject candles were quite good enough. I could not tell the difference between the rejects and the shop ones. There was the silver épergne in the middle of the table, loaded with white and black grapes as well as apples and pears, and there was also a big pineapple. Personally I preferred pineapple chunks out of a tin, but the real thing was all right and had a more exotic look than a tin would have had by candlelight.

Aunt Nellie smiled at me and said a few ridiculous things about little people and shut-eye, then they forgot about me for a while. I was given a few pigs of orange, neatly de-pithed, which I walked round the table eating while I reviewed things. I supposed I had not been given grapes because of the stalks and the pips. There would be plenty of fruit left over to eat tomorrow. My mother was in light green with bare shoulders and ear-rings and the diamond watch my grandfather had given her. It was halfway to her elbow because the gold bracelet was too big for her wrist. Her fingers were sparkling with rings. I passed behind my father's chair, noting his neat black head and the way his hair grew as if made to measure behind his ears. His head and neck came out of his shoulders in exactly the way I liked. Some soldiers had heads and shoulders carried like that, and so had some statues I had seen. I passed lingeringly behind his chair, round the corner of the table on his right, where Aunt Nellie (call me Eleanor) was sitting. Her dark hair was curly, naturally curly, my mother said. It looked crisp. She had a tortoiseshell comb in it. She was wearing a deep pink evening dress and a collar of pearls. She threw back her head and laughed ringingly at something my father said as I passed round the table. Uncle Frank sat lower and more humpily than my father. He had a little ridge of pink flesh with short hairs on it coming over the edge of his collar. He was fatter than my father but his shoulders were not so broad. His ears, which also had hairs growing out of them, stuck out a little from his head but not very much because he was fat behind his ears, connecting with the ridge above his collar. There was scarcely any hair on his head except for a fair fringe about ear-level. Uncle Frank was ugly.

Because he was ugly, with everything about him slightly off, nothing altogether right, I suddenly felt jangled and angry. As I passed I hit him with my open hand on his bald head. He made a gulping noise as if swallowing a grape

69

whole. Everybody looked up. My father, sitting opposite, looked up at the instant of the slap and saw my hand. There was consternation. My mother bent upon me her ice-burn look, rose from the table and took me out of the room. As we left I heard Aunt Nellie (call me Eleanor) murmuring something about overtired little people and my father making excuses . . . I hadn't been well . . . The door shut.

In the hall my mother demanded sternly to know what had come over me. In her beautiful dress and jewellery she appeared unusually imperious. I began to cry.

'His head is so ugly,' I explained between sniffs. 'His head is not like Daddy's.'

All at once her eyes changed. The sternness went out of them. She looked at me speculatively.

'No, it isn't, is it?' she said slowly, as if she agreed with me. Then she said:

'Go to bed now. You're over-excited. Goodnight, darling,' and she gave me a kiss and a little push towards the staircase.

I went to sleep and did not hear the guests leave. I woke up to hear my parents coming upstairs to bed, talking quietly to one another. (My bedroom door was always left open in case I had nightmares, that my screams might be heard.) Passing my door they were laughing a little and I heard my mother say, 'Call me Beatrice!' as her dress rustled and they went laughing through their bedroom door and closed it. I went back to sleep.

*　*　*

'So you hit Uncle Frank over the head because you thought he was ugly?' my brother remarked. 'You should watch that, you know:

"Inhabitants of domiciles of vitreous formation
Of lapidary projectiles should never make jactation",'

and he gave me a couple of routine wallops which I did not resent as they were not altogether unjustified.

At Sunday dinner they were talking about Aunt Nellie and Uncle Frank.

'So ironical they've no children, with all that money.

70

Their children could have had anything on earth. And when you think of all these huge families of children there are about, with not enough money to keep them in shoe-leather . . .'

'I thought Nellie was looking uncommonly well, seems to have got over completely that operation she had a couple of years ago,' remarked my father.

'What operation?' I asked. My mother replied, not altogether unexpectedly:

'She had to have all her insides out.'

Just as I had thought. All that hugging and little-peopling me was a sure sign of the absence of insides.

'When shall I wear that dress she brought me from Paris?'

'When do you think it should be worn?'

'Well . . .' I hesitated.

'Exactly,' said my mother. 'When you come to think about it, there is really no occasion when a child of your age could suitably wear that dress. It is a dress for a shop window.'

'Oh, I don't know,' my father said. 'Little French girls often wear very shop-window sorts of dresses.'

'Yes, and look at them—pale and undersized from staying up till all hours wearing dresses too stiff to run about in. That dress is far too elaborate and ornate for a child; it is an old woman's dress but for the size. I can't imagine what Nellie was thinking about, but of course she was always inclined to overdress, that was her weakness, only her good looks let her get away with it.'

'It would do as a party dress,' I suggested.

'It is far too warm for a party dress. You know how hot you get at parties and how much you hate them, even in a muslin.'

I could not deny that this was true. Evidently the stylish grey and gold-frogged dress was not for me.

'Will you give it away, then?'

'Who to? It is not a suitable everyday dress. It obviously cost a lot of money. If I gave it to Mrs Allen for one of her children, it wouldn't do, it would seem to mock their poverty. At best, all the other children would be jealous.'

I could see that, too.

'Do you know any Americans?' I asked my parents.

71

'I know a couple. I play golf sometimes with a chap in American Cotton called Bertorelli, and there's Bunfish —you've met them, Bea—he's the London manager of Connecticut Assurance.'

'Have they any children?'

'The Bunfishes have two boys and a younger girl a bit smaller than you . . .'

'. . . An affected little beast. Appallingly spoilt,' put in my mother. 'What's all this suddenly about Americans, anyway?'

I explained.

'You see, I read in a magazine somewhere that American funerals are different from ours. Dead Americans are left in open coffins till the last minute so that everybody can come and look at them and they are made up like actors and actresses with powder and rouge and wear their best clothes instead of being buried in their nighties or wrapped up in a sheet like dead people here . . .'

I could see that the attention of my family was wandering. Often they did not listen to me properly.

'Well, what about it, then?' said my brother languidly, reaching for the celery.

'Well, I had this idea. Listen, everybody. I have just thought that Mother could give that grey dress with the gold trimmings to Mrs Bunfish for her little girl to wear when she dies—it would look just right to be dead in, very dressy indeed and she wouldn't be running about in it.'

'No, she certainly would not . . . It is an interesting idea but I fancy it might not be well received by the Bunfish parents,' my father said.

'It's a dotty idea. The child may not die for years.' As usual, my brother was dismissive of my highest flights of intellect.

'Mother could point out to Mrs Bunfish that there was a hem for letting down to allow for growth . . .' I muttered.

'Growth before death—a good advertising slogan for Connecticut Assurance.' My brother pushed back his chair. 'May I be excused? I have some homework to do.'

Homework was always my brother's excuse. I would take it out on him by writing an entirely fictitious but sensational report about Midge Morris and a friend meeting two Dulwich College boys on the Common and accepting chocolates from them.

I never saw the dress again.

Since my mother never threw anything away, my guess is that it was unpicked and cut up to make ironholders. An ironholder was a circular pad of several layers of cloth, bound round the edges and crisscrossed with machine stitching to hold it all together. It was used for handling the hot flat-iron, the smoothing iron of the song, that my mother dashed away with at the end of a successful washing day, the iron that was spat on with a hiss to test its heat then dashed over the garments and finally clanged down on the wrought-iron stand that kept the ironing board from being scorched. Ironholders often had a loop sewn on to them so that they could be hung up handily on a cup hook.

The grey dress had been made of such excellent quality, dense, smooth stuff, it would have been perfect for ironholders. And as for the gold frogging, what could have been more conveniently to hand for making the loops?

* * *

Really thick clothing was commonly worn in the winters of those years. The heavy woollen cloth used for the ankle-length overcoats known as ulsters, if seen in section, was easily a quarter of an inch thick. Children's winter coats were heavy too, thick at the button holes on cold mornings. Skirts and woollen dresses for everyday winter wear were all much thicker than any to be found today, and though absurdly cheap by end-of-the-century prices, they were in their day relatively expensive and were expected to last. They did not wear out readily. Clothes that children grew out of before they were worn out were handed down. Happy was the child, in this respect, who had no elder siblings of the same sex.

I had no sister to inherit clothes from, but to make up for this my coats and dresses had very deep hems indeed, for letting down. Everything was bought a size too big 'to allow for growth'. Surprisingly, my boots and shoes were always very smart indeed, of fine box calf or willow calf, fitting perfectly my broad feet. The reason for this was that my mother claimed that her own feet had been spoilt by ill-fitting footwear when she was a child and she blamed my grandmother for not keeping watch on the unhampered growth of her children's toes. She often pressed down with a thumb on my toecap to make sure there was still enough space for my big toe in there.

Because clothes were so heavy and lasted so long, people naturally tired of them after a couple of winters. It was then that the dyeing vats of Uncle Frank came into action, and over the years had transformed his bank balance from red to the deepest black.

There was a protocol about dyeing. It had to be proceeded with step by step in an orderly ritual. One impulsive wrong decision and you could be trapped in a black coat year after year. This could be particularly galling if the black period coincided with a period of no deaths in a family. Equally, an unexpected death could cut short the bright youth of a light grey or fawn-and-green tweed, condemning it to a long after-life of unchanging black. For black, in dyeing terms, was irreversible. The sequence of dyeing was from light to dark as irrevocably as day darkens into night, but with no following dawn. Black stayed black.

Consequently there was much thoughtful discussion among wives and daughters about whether 'my lilac' (so pretty, yet so useful for half-mourning) should be dyed a strong light blue or a somewhat deeper green. After that there were still a darker blue or a sunless pinewood green or a dried blood effect to choose from, before night began to fall on nigger brown (as dark brown was called then), leading into the final blackness where all woollen coating ended.

My mother, however, was not the convinced dyer that some of her acquaintances were. For one thing, she usually had on hand various coat-lengths and remnants considered bargains at the sales, which she made up with the help of a visiting sewing-woman. This was more fun than having old clothes dyed. However, a limited amount of home-dyeing was undertaken intermittently, a do-it-yourself enterprise made possible by Dolly-Bags, which worked on the principle of tea bags. For years after my infant attack of measles,

74

a set of old curtains, dyed dark green in haste 'to protect my sight', lay about in the boxroom. There was also a set dyed red when my brother and I had chickenpox, in accordance with the folk wisdom of the time that light filtered through red minimised the risk of pockmarking. Home-dyed curtains were characterised by lighter streaks, whether because they emerged from the dye that way or faded easily in sunlight, is not on record.

Uncle Frank had already made a fortune out of dyeing, and from then on was to make an even larger one out of dry cleaning. Dry cleaners were known, and made use of, but gingerly. Very special clothes like evening dresses, too delicate to wash, or disaster victims such as a light suit hit by a shower of mulberries in a sudden summer squall —such special cases were sent to the dry cleaners. But most clothes, if not washable, were sponged and pressed. The boom years of the dry cleaners were yet to come.

Because clothes were so thick and lasted so long and seldom had any cleaning more radical than being breathed on by steam and then pressed more closely into themselves with a heavy iron, most people past their first youth smelt of old wardrobes. That was the basic smell. At the top end of the range it was somewhat redeemed by the cleanly odours of soap, eau de Cologne and spirit shampoo, at the bottom, tainted more or less faintly with urine. The strongest smell came from navvies in corduroys on trams, coming from work, but for all its rankness that smell, at least in short, sharp bursts, was to be preferred to the aura of funny smells that hung about a lot of ladies.

Miss Dickenson was my headmistress. My mother went to see her and took me with her. What the meeting was about I do not remember. Very likely it had to do with my rate of growth out of the gym colours of my previous school and the nearness of my appearance at gym dressed like the others, in chocolate brown and blue. When the meeting was over we went out of the front door instead of by the basement tunnel the pupils used for their comings and goings. There was a flight of steps leading down from the front door. The two stood there chatting for a moment. Miss Dickenson was not remarkably old. She was about forty-five, not bad looking, with quick, dark, hard eyes. She always wore a blouse and skirt. Her skirt was black. She was saying:

'. . . and we have been fortunate in keeping the school exclusive. We have no daughters of tradespeople here.'

My mother gave her the keen interested look that later in life I was to recognise in the eyes of successful barristers.

'How do you know?' she asked. 'How do you know that my husband is not in trade? Because you see him going by every morning in a bowler hat with a rolled umbrella and *The Times* under his arm doesn't necessarily mean that he is "something in the City" . . . something respectable in the City, that is. For all you know he could be running a rag and bone business from Paternoster Row.'

Miss Dickenson stirred uneasily. I could tell she was embarrassed and, though I had no liking for her, I felt slightly sorry for her. My brother and I knew how killingly embarrassing our parent could be.

Miss Dickenson drew me against her. Being on a lower step than hers, my face was crushed against her skirt. She laughed in a jerky way, a clockwork laugh with no power behind it. She seemed to be addressing me.

'Your mother will have her little joke, won't she? She knows well enough that all your friends here come from nice families.' And she added, 'And you and I are great friends, aren't we?' as if that made her family a nice one, too.

'That was awful,' I said to my mother on the way home. 'She squashed me against her skirt and it was smelly.'

'It probably needs steaming and pressing. Black doesn't *show* the dirt.'

'Steaming would make the smell worse. Unless it was her, too, underneath.'

'She did look a little drawn. Perhaps her insides were playing up. Ladies' insides sometimes do.'

It occurred to me that it might be time for Miss Dickenson to have all her insides out. The effect would be to make her suddenly love children very much, a distinct benefit to her younger pupils, hunched over our French verbs. Picturing Miss Dickenson gushing into the classroom, all warmth and love, a laugh came out the wrong way and I snorted.

'Don't make that disgusting noise,' my mother said. 'If

your nose is blocked, use your handkerchief. And come here, your hat is all skew-whiff; that woman must have knocked it sideways when she squashed you.'

And my mother settled my penitential fur hat squarely on my head.

'That's better,' she said.

(*Si vieillesse savait* . . .)

5

When inquisitive older persons inquired of my mother what religious instruction her children were receiving and whether they attended Sunday school regularly, she would reply that no, they did not attend Sunday school at all because she herself had not enjoyed Sunday school as a child. As for church-going, her children had been baptised into the Church of England and she had felt that she owed it to them to see that they were introduced to the services of that church. Accordingly she had taken them to church from the time when they were in decent control of their bladders until the age of five. After that they were old enough to judge for themselves.

Her instinct was true. The splendid rhythms and cadences of the Anglican ritual have resonated unforgettably through the echo chambers of my memory from those days to this. *Remember now thy Creator in the days of thy youth, while the evil days come not* . . .

Though we were not forced to go to church, our Sundays were not without their burden of duty. We were expected to accompany our mother on the weekly walk across the Common to visit our grandparents for tea. We went half willingly, half unwillingly. The general background to these visits was one of habit and tedium, but there were compensations of a material kind.

The house was a substantial Victorian one with two entrance gates and a sweep-around drive. It was covered with creeper that was not, however, permitted to straggle. A flight of steps led up to a storm porch, closed in winter, and the front door. The brass door furniture was brightly polished. In summer a striped awning shielded the paintwork from the blistering action of the sun. There was a brass bell-pull with echoes in the depths of the house, followed by the approaching footsteps of the parlourmaid.

We would say, 'Good afternoon, Alice,' in answer to her greeting. Off the hall there was a room scarcely ever used, half study, half library, where we would leave our coats and hats. After that we would go on to the drawing room which was at the far end of the hall. There, almost always, my grandfather and my two aunts would be sitting, he in his armchair, the two aunts very often at opposite ends of a large sofa, with papers and magazines scattered between them—no sewing on Sunday. Sometimes my grandmother would be there too, but as often as not she would be away on some domestic trail of her own, rootling in the linen press or checking that there was still fish and milk in the two saucers left for the refreshment of Ben, the blue Persian, on the landing at the head of the back stairs.

We would make the round of our seated relations, who would each proffer us a cheek to kiss. They did not kiss us. Grandpa's cheek was covered in carefully clipped white whiskers, what would now be known as designer stubble. He had a neat white moustache but his chin was clean-shaven. He had a head of thick white hair and strong, even features, with a chin like granite. His grey eyes were bright, keen, intelligent and merciless. Grandpa was immaculate. Everything about him was clean and fastidious. His well-kept hands were shapely. His speech was impressive—when Grandpa spoke, people listened. His articulation was crystalline. He never hesitated for the right word. All in all, Grandpa was a well polished specimen. It was hard to believe that he had started life in a miner's crowded cottage in Nottinghamshire and had had no schooling after the age of eleven.

With her father's example before her, it was not surprising that my mother held the teaching profession in such low esteem. If with no further education beyond his own unsupervised reading, a child of eleven could go on to make a comfortable fortune and, except for an ignorance of field sports and the classics, pass for a gentleman born, why torment bored adolescents with years of unnecessary schooling?

As well as being a shrewd business man, Grandpa must have been a consummate actor, aping his social betters in speech and manners whenever one crossed his path. That cannot have been often in a blackened mining village of the eighteen fifties. Did he once see passing him, on some country lane, an open carriage with four beautiful people in beautiful clothes on their way to a picnic? Did he hold open a gate in a woodland path for some divine lady riding side-saddle and did her nod of thanks fire his heart with ambition and change his life?

He had made his money. He had become a perfect imitation of a gentleman. And here he was in his own spacious drawing room on a Sunday afternoon with two unmarried daughters and the married youngest one, who constantly lowered the tone of the family, now entering with his only grandchildren, a bespectacled boy swot and a ruffianly little girl who answered back. Where were the beautiful people?

Grandpa shifted his head with an air of weary distinction to receive my kiss on his stubble. He did not love me and I did not love him, in fact I hated him. He aroused in me a strong antagonism. We were always sparring. Yet I admired his handsome head, his easy fluency, his unfaltering confidence in himself. We would look straight into one another's eyes and challenge one another silently, all through my childhood.

He was a man full of the sin of pride but he was no petty snob. He never turned his back on the remnants of his socially unredeemed family with the coal dust still on their backs. My mother used to tell me with obvious pleasure of a visit she had made there as a twelve-year-old, with her father. To this miner's cottage after his shift at the coal face she had seen a cousin return, a young man with blackened face and blazing blue eyes, fine white teeth gleaming as he smiled at her. Through the crack of a door ajar she had seen his back as he squatted in the tin tub in the back kitchen while his mother poured warm water over his head and shoulders and soaped him, and then poured again the water to rinse him.

'It was wonderful to see his great shoulders all at once coming up white under the pouring water, all the black washed off. And afterwards, when his head was dried and he came into the kitchen for his meal, his hair was as gold as a guinea.'

80

This early vision of male beauty had given my mother her first true thrill and she never forgot it. Her own father in youth would have been just such another blonde beast, but his skin had never been blackened by coal dust. At eleven he had gone to work in a tape factory and from there had set off on his quest for the beautiful people.

My two aunts on either end of the sofa, with a scatter of light reading between them, were called Ethel and Ada. There was a period, not so long past, when almost everybody had an aunt called Ethel. I even knew one or two who not only had an aunt called Ethel but were themselves called Ethel and were themselves aunts—Aunt Ethels, that is. There was something about the name that not only brought on aunthood but was somehow marriage-repellent. Ethels did not breed much. Perhaps that is why they have become comparatively rare.

My aunts had been christened Ethel Jarratt and Ada Shackell, names that my mother considered, and I was inclined to agree with her, a lifelong handicap. By the time she was born they had run out of unbecoming surnames so she was christened Beatrice Helena. Her more melodious name encouraged my mother, who was a martyr to romantic fiction, to identify as a Cinderella-type character with two Ugly Sisters. But her sisters were not ugly, though Aunt Ethel was borderline peculiar to look at and did her best to make herself less than lovely. Aunt Ada was fairly good-looking, quite tall with big eyes and high cheekbones, a Scottish face. She dressed well. They were a musical family and when Aunt Ada sang, people smiled slightly because the admired voice then was a rich contralto and Aunt Ada, as was said rather disparagingly, had 'a voice like a choirboy'. People said there was no 'feeling' in it, but I had a sneaking liking for the sound of it: it was clear and went up without seeming to care whether people listened or not.

Aunt Ethel did not sing. She had a delicate throat and a very quiet speaking voice. She played the piano, well enough. The piano was a fine one, a Broadwood grand. She was the shortest and dumpiest of the sisters, perhaps because she moved about very little. She was short-sighted and wore glasses with gold oval eyepieces. Her black hair was scraped back savagely from a high broad forehead. She had grey eyes with short black lashes, and a big chin. Late in life, looking through some old family photographs, it suddenly struck me that Aunt Ethel had looked weirdly like Lord Longford—could there be Irish blood in the family? I remembered names like Kate and Michael, tales of distant cousins too fond of the bottle, my grandfather's merciless grey eyes and his gift of the gab, my own mother's wild colonial ways. And my brother who grew up to look like President Woodrow Wilson, who came from Ireland.

All this has persuaded me that my grandfather's family, on his mother's side, were Irish navvies who came over to dig the canals and had settled in the Midlands. Our only claim to distinction is that we do not claim to be descended from Irish kings.

Although Aunt Ethel may have looked like Lord Longford in drag, she had been sought in marriage, though only by a curate. This offer had been refused. Her heart belonged to Daddy. Aunt Ada had received more than one proposal and had actually been engaged to one suitor called Ralph who had been, according to my mother, 'an organist at Balmoral', whatever that appointment meant. Unhappily Ralph had died of consumption. I pictured him as an emaciated dark young man, coughing blood over the keys as he laboured at the mighty organ, its vast golden pipes rising high as mountains, tremendous diapasons making the air shudder while down there, alone in the body of the kirk but for a few lords in waiting, Queen Victoria sat with tears on her cheeks, thinking about death and Albert.

With Ralph dead and gone, Aunt Ada sidestepped her other suitors and settled for life at home, where she was well provided for. Grandpa was generous enough with his womenfolk, so long as they did not stray into the arms of other men. In this respect my mother had offended and had not been entirely forgiven. When she returned Sunday after Sunday to the home of her girlhood, the air of the family drawing room did not glow rosier, it took on a bluish tinge.

The aunts always seemed to me quite nasty to my mother; I wondered why she kept on going there. But occasionally, when I was alone with them, some small thing would suddenly send them into a fit of the giggles and they would laugh till they cried, just like human beings. My mother did not bring out the best in them.

If the best had ever been brought out in Grandpa it must have gone back in again before I was born. He could not be said to be a mean or small-minded man but he was so cold, critical and joyless that his very presence filtered pleasure out of the air. Yet on the Bench he had the reputation of being the best of magistrates, unprejudiced, just and merciful. However, his family did not see him when he was chairman of the Bench. We saw him on Sunday afternoon and at Christmas and we did not like what we saw.

He was a Liberal of Radical tendencies. Consequently he had to appear tolerant, whatever his inward feelings may have been. Ridden on this loose intellectual rein, the various members of his family worshipped some in church, some in chapel, and might have voted for different political parties if women had then had the vote. It was in small, foody ways that they showed their liberalism and in this they were indulged.

There were some cousins of that generation, nieces and nephews of my grandfather, whose parents had stitched away so industriously in their tiny upholstery business that in a few years they had expanded into a chain of furniture shops and were short of nothing that money could buy. This Midlands family my mother visited as a girl. There were eight children, seven boys and finally a girl. At mealtimes each child would require, and would be given, potatoes done this way or that, nearly all different. One would want baked potatoes, his brother potatoes mashed, the next would ask for potatoes roasted round the joint, or for potato salad or fried potatoes or potatoes plain boiled or chipped or potato straws. The youngest, the darling daughter, could have *duchesse* potatoes if she wanted them, the pet. My mother said she felt quite sorry for the cook. But this tradition, handed down perhaps from our all but penniless great grandmother—doling out a raisin here, a lick of treacle there to spoilt though barefoot children—had carried on in a fragmented way to my aunts. It resulted in a great spread at tea, which was served at half past four on the dining room table.

There was of course the usual array of heavy silver tray, Queen Anne teapot, spirit kettle, sugar bowl and tongs —the great forgotten tea ritual. The room was furnished on mahogany and Turkey carpet lines like much of the rest of the house, solid but not particularly beautiful. But the china was fine. They were fussy about their china and had many quite valuable tea sets, some in use, some put away, which came to light when they were all dead. Because of this fine china I was, as a child, an unknowing china snob, refusing to drink out of anything that felt thick on the lips.

Aunt Ethel did not drink tea. She drank chocolate with cream. Aunt Ada drank tea at teatime but coffee at breakfast. Aunt Ethel drank chocolate with cream at all times. At tea various sorts of jam were always on the table— raspberry jam, quince jelly, damson cheese and (quite improperly at teatime) marmalade in its jar with a silver lid with a hole for the spoon. The marmalade was for Aunt Ada, who ate no other sort of preserve. There were macaroons, finger-shaped chocolate biscuits, sponge fingers, a Swiss roll, Fuller's walnut cake, Madeira cake, seed cake —all at the choice of one or other aunt and viewed with disgust by the other. At luncheon there was always a dish of rice pudding, made rather runny, for Aunt Ada. No one else touched it. And so on, at every meal.

On the mahogany sideboard there was the usual paraphernalia of silver, dominated by the inevitable ornate épergne laden with fruit. On a ledge under the mirror were always several silver bonbon dishes, each filled with different sweets which invariably included caramels, boiled fruit drops, chocolate peppermint creams and a kind of jellied fruit sweet dusted with sugar called jujubes. We could help ourselves as we wished from these dishes, though they were rather wasted on me because I was not as fond of sweets as children were supposed to be. The only ones I liked were acid drops, and when I crunched these up instead of sucking them, my grandfather would tell me that that was not the proper way to eat a sweet, as if there were a Manual of Correct Sweet Eating we were supposed to have read.

At one end of the sideboard was a glazed pottery jar with a tap in it, about gallon size. This was the water filter. It probably dated from the typhoid epidemics of the last century when tap water was still not above reproach. But by my day it was an anachronism. However, the parlourmaid refilled the filter jar as required and drew from it into a jug the filtered water for the table. As far as I knew the filter element in this contraption had not been cleaned or changed in years. Every now and then my grandparents would be laid low with an upset that was called 'one of the Mater's (or Pater's) turns'—a euphemism for diarrhoea, which in the light of later wisdom I would now put down to the occasional population explosion of bacterial nasties in the bowels of the filter. My two aunts were never affected by this disorder, probably because the one drank milk with her meal and the other, soda water; of course.

It will be noted that my two aunts addressed their parents as Pater and Mater. So did my mother. It was the custom of the time, never mind that those two words in Latin were the only Latin words they ever knew. However, my Aunt Ethel was spoken of as having been very clever at school and had even passed the examinations, the only ones on offer at that time, promoted by the College of Preceptors, who sounded to me a pretty grim body of people, easily irritated, with corrective rulers in their hands. Signs of cleverness in Aunt Ethel were limited to the possession of a small portable typewriter and some clerical work to do with a Sunday school and the Band of Hope. The Band of Hope had a somewhat negative aura for me. I knew it was in aid of not drinking alcohol but when one had not drunk alcohol, what then? Simply more not drinking, I supposed.

It would not have been easy for Aunt Ethel to be seen to be clever. Conversation at Sherbrooke Lodge (the name of their house) would have imposed limitations on the clever. The subjects of religion, politics and money were not to be mentioned. Except for a surprising liking for the theatre and a musical inclination, the family were cultural heathens, not *Kaleidoscope* material at all. At the same time a sense of social responsibility, of being pillars of something or other, weighed heavily upon them and prevented them from enjoying the simple earthy jokes that are within the reach of all and were the currency of our mealtime talk at home.

85

Naturally they could not gossip—that would be unsuitable—but they could mention in a neutral way the names of people they knew connected with the church, the chapel, the Band of Hope and the Orphanage. The Orphanage was a home for the orphans of the Band of Hopers, people who had actually died not drinking. My grandfather was a founder and benefactor of this charity, situated next door to their old home at Sunbury. I was taken once or twice, in extreme youth, to some teatime do at this place, where there were a lot of children in Norfolk jackets or pinnies. In fairness to the promoters of this establishment, it must be said that a number of the children reared there turned out very well indeed. One became the head of a powerful building and contracting firm whose name is to be seen to this day on billboards beside new motorways; another rose to be gynaecologist to royalty and delivered baby princes and princesses by the quarter-dozen, naturally appearing on the Honours List. Whether my grandfather influenced, or more likely hand-picked, these children, who can say? He held a certain magic for some people, though not for me.

Because of his connection with Liberalism and the decent housing of the (deserving) poor, a few more names could be dredged up for conversational purposes. Here it may be mentioned that my grandfather knew Lloyd George, but only just. John Burns he knew better and for longer. They were acquainted with a few people with new or minor titles, such as yanked-up property developers or the knighted builder of the Bank of England, but they had no real social life, just people coming in to tea; no dinner parties. My grandfather belonged to the National Liberal Club but as far as I know never entered it. He preferred the feminine ambience of his family. Once, on holiday, my aunts made the acquaintance of some people called Tankerville-Chamberlaine. This brush with high life, as perceived by them, so went to their heads that it was nothing but Tankerville-Chamberlaines for weeks afterwards, petering out only gradually, perhaps from a certain lack of responsiveness on the part of the Tankerville-Chamberlaines. (If the family still exists, my apologies if I have mis-spelled their name, which I only ever heard spoken.)

86

They often mentioned somebody called Sir Ernest Lamb
—and apologies again if there should be an *e* on the tail of
the Lamb. It was Sir Ernest Lamb this, Sir Ernest Lamb that,
not quite as bad as the Tankerville-Chamberlaines, but
pretty bad. Once when I was messing about in the hall at
Sherbrooke Lodge I saw through the frosted glass of the
front door a man come up the steps and ring the bell. As I
was by the door I opened it before the parlourmaid could
arrive.

The man, who was the usual daddy type, about forty
with a bowler and a thick dark blue overcoat, asked if he
could see my grandfather.

'I shall have to see. He may not want to be disturbed.
Who are you?'

'I am Lord Rochester.'

'Well, wait there while I find out if he wants to see you.' I
shut the door and, turning round, saw Alice the parlourmaid approaching. I told her it was all right, I was seeing to
it, and she went back through the green baize door.

Grandpa was seated as usual in the drawing room,
looking distinguished but not doing much. The aunts too
were in place.

'Grandpa,' I began.

He glanced in my direction.

'If you have anything to say,' he said, 'it would be better
manners not to communicate it across the length of the
room. Now, if you come quietly up to my chair and tell me
politely what it is you want to say to me, I may listen to you.
Don't rush,' he added.

So I rather dawdled across the fair distance between the
door and his chair by the fire. It was a big room.

'Now what is it?' he asked.

'I was in the hall,' I said.

'Well, what of it? What is interesting about that?'

'I had just come out of the library . . .'

'If you were in the library I hope you took care to replace
any books you took out, back in the right place. Which book
was it?'

'I put back the Dickens. I don't like Dickens. But this Lord
Rochester . . .'

'Mr Rochester is not in Dickens,' Aunt Ethel, the clever

one, put in. 'Mr Rochester is in Charlotte Brontë. In *Jane Eyre*, to be specific.'

'Lord Rochester is not in Charlotte Brontë. He is in the front porch, waiting to see if Grandpa wants to see him.'

'*Lord* Rochester! Waiting in the porch . . . ! Why ever didn't you say so . . . ?'

In consternation both aunts rose and made for the hall, Aunt Ethel leading by a short head. As my father had often remarked, Aunt Ethel was an irreversible case of duck's disease, and when she hurried, as now, it looked as if she was just coming into lay.

'Why did you not say at once that Lord Rochester was waiting?' my grandfather asked me with some severity.

'You wouldn't let me. You kept interrupting, asking what I was doing in the library.'

'Your manners are appalling. Imagine keeping Lord Rochester waiting like that.'

'You might not have wanted to see him. Sometimes you tell Alice that you are not at home.'

'Lord Rochester is different. I would always wish to see him. He is often here.'

'Well, I've never heard of him.'

'Of course you have heard of him. We have often spoken of Sir Ernest Lamb.'

'Sir Ernest Lamb, yes. But not Lord Rochester.'

'Sir Ernest Lamb recently became Lord Rochester.'

It was never explained to me how such a peculiar change of name could have taken place. But some time later, in a somewhat softened mood when we were alone, Aunt Ada said that Lord Rochester had not been cross at being shut out and made to wait, as he had several children of his own of about my age and knew what children were like.

* * *

As well as the usual Sunday afternoon visits, we always spent Christmas Day with my grandparents, and Boxing Day too until my father put his foot down. He hated it because it was a house where no smoking was permitted, except in the billiard room, where there were no comfortable chairs, only elevated wooden seating from which the game could be watched. After a good meal he liked to enjoy a cigar in comfort, not to perch alone on a hard-arse bench as if waiting for a train at some Godforsaken country station in the Midlands. The wooden seating round the billiard room was highly polished and slippery, with small holes punched through as on brogues. When I asked him what the holes were for he said they were for two-way ventilation.

Apart from these ritual visits I sometimes went to stay with my grandparents for a longer stay of a week or two. Why I was asked I am not sure because I do not think they were particularly fond of me. However my mother often said that Ada was good with children, it was such a pity she hadn't married and had a family of her own instead of being cooped up there with Ethel in That House. Instantly there would spring into my mind the scene, with sound effects, of the late long-haired Ralph (the Balmoral organist) at the Broadwood grand accompanying my aunt as she sang, in her choirboy voice, *Angels Ever Bright and Fair*, while their three flaxen-haired children crouched over a ludo board on the hearth rug, listlessly rattling the dice-box as they spat blood occasionally into the fire. This scene was set in my grandparents' drawing room from which all traces of grandparents and of Aunt Ethel had been wiped clean. It was a satisfying scene and the sadness brought on by the angelic music and the sight of my little cousins soon to die was a comfortable sadness. It was possible, I knew, to be moved to tears by some tragic death in a story or a poem and yet at the same time to be rather pleased. In real life it was somewhat different.

My mother had a little workbasket, the proper kind with a padded yellow silk inside lid. It was only about six inches cubed, much too small to contain her mending things, which spilled over into other bags and baskets. But she used it all the time. She never sewed but the little basket, worn with the years, was beside her. She told me sometimes about it. It had belonged to a school friend called Nettie Hewland. My mother had liked her very much.

Nettie became ill and stopped going to school. My mother missed her. She went to see her once or twice but was not allowed to stay long. After a few months Nettie died. She was twelve, the same age as my mother.

The little workbasket was new then and had been Nettie's favourite thing. Her mother said that Nettie had wanted my mother to have it as a keepsake. Since then my mother had used it all the time.

When she told me the history of the workbasket, as she would when I asked her, just for a moment she would stop sewing and look at nothing. Her eyes then would seem quite young and somehow helpless, unlike my mother's eyes. Then she would take up her mending again.

This sad story was not satisfying like the sad stories in books. It left everything torn off and painful, like a broken branch hanging from a tree with its leaves dying. It was not the story exactly. It was more what the story did to my mother's eyes.

Nearly half a century later, after her death, I found among her papers a letter dated 1888, written in a spiky hand and signed Mary Hewland. It had been much folded and refolded, with worn creases. It ended:

'. . . and our darling was fully conscious and knew us all to the end, when she fell asleep in the arms of Jesus . . .'

The faded ink was spotted here and there with watermarks.

The small workbasket was used and used, year after year, mended and re-mended with raffia, its yellow silk lining frayed away, its basketwork fragmented until it fell apart, literally in pieces.

A child's grief could last so long.

* * *

It is only fair to say of Aunt Ada that she was a generous aunt, though in a way so orthodox that it did not strike sparks of surprised delight from her astonished niece. Aunt Ada was free with her sixpences and the occasional half-crown, but Aunt Ethel never gave anything away except at Christmas and birthdays when giving was almost an obligation, like putting silver in the collection plate. Whether this stinginess, which was not a family characteristic, arose from parsimony or a plain absence of any wish to give pleasure, did not matter. She failed to give pleasure and seemed mean, all right.

Aunt Ada was generous with treats such as a pantomime matinée in winter or a summer trip to Hampton Court with ice cream (more of a rarity then) and cream teas at Fuller's in Windsor where we sometimes went. A cousin of my grandfather's lived there, Edward Atkins, an old and wicked man who had been a brewer and frequented cockfights. He lived with the remnants of his grown-up but oppressed family, most of whom had escaped and dispersed to the far corners of the earth. I am not sure whether he still had a wife or whether she had been done to death. The remaining family seemed subdued, speaking quietly as if something bad that everybody knew about but me was going on in some room that no one cared to enter. One of the sons was a hunchback, his deformity being said to be the result of having been dropped as a baby, though the unspoken implication was that his father, the wicked brewer, had dashed him to the ground in a fit of temper because his cock wouldn't fight. The house was unusual, too. It was a town house, right in the middle of the old part of Windsor, in view of the Castle. It seemed to be made inside entirely of polished wood, the colour of golden syrup (not spread but in the spoon) with floor, walls, ceilings and staircase all the same, like the Mormon Tabernacle in Salt Lake City. It felt shut-in, secret and ancient.

We did not visit the Atkins' house every time we went to Windsor. I think we had tea there once, dispensed in a furtive way by a middle-aged daughter as if the food had been stolen. There seemed to be a vague conspiracy in which my aunt had a part, something to do with 'getting away'. It was a bit like the poem my cousin Dudley's father, who was half French, often quoted with a sardonic smile: 'Tomorrow, oh tomorrow I shall go to Carcassonne.' What happened to the Atkins family I do not know. They were related to me only distantly. Wicked Edward Atkins I saw just once—white moustache, red face, angry eyebrows. His only recorded utterance concerned my grandfather, that pillar of society, that he was 'a good devil spoilt'.

It strikes me only now that the inside of their old house was the colour of a coffin.

But mostly our visits to Windsor meant a look at the Castle followed by tea, with cream buns and walnut cake and chocolate éclairs, at Fuller's. There were always Eton boys about, top-hatted, the young ones in bumfreezers and starched white collars almost as wide as their shoulders. I was accustomed to this garb as it was the regular party or stiff Sunday wear of the young boys I knew, but I thought it was a penitential way of dressing for school and everyday. While I was looking at a small group of Etonians being treated to tea by an aunt-and-uncle type couple, a false move with my pastry fork sent the better half of my cream bun skidding to the floor. As I bent to retrieve it from under the next table, which was unoccupied, Aunt Ada made tushing noises, remarking that surely I was not thinking of eating it and what would those Etonians think of me, grubbing about on the floor for fallen cream buns.

I said that what the Eton boys thought didn't matter and boys ate food off the floor or anywhere else they could get it. Anyway, the floor at Fuller's was pretty clean.

Aunt Ada started in then about the wrong way my mother was bringing her children up.

'I remember coming to your house unexpectedly at teatime once, and there were the two of you with the loaf on the table, *not even cut bread and butter*, knifing up marmalade from a seven-pound jar. I really don't know what your mother can be thinking of, it is not as if she had not been decently brought up herself.'

She looked at me speculatively.

'When you go to bed tonight, I think I'll put your hair in curling-rags again. You have nice enough hair but I like to see it in sausages once or twice a week at least. Does your mother put it in curlers? I suppose not.'

I shook my head.

'She tugs out the tangles, that's quite enough.'

'How is it you get it tangled so often?'

'I don't know. It blows about. Sometimes Percy puts burrs in it.'

'Was Percy the boy with the bad teeth and the Cockney accent that you brought back a few weeks ago when you got lost? I was out with the Mater but your Aunt Ethel told me about it.'

'Yes, that was Percy. He can't help his teeth.'

People couldn't help their teeth. My brother and I had

good teeth, Percy had bad teeth. It was the luck of the draw. I remembered the occasion when we had called in at Sherbrooke lodge.

We had been wandering about on the far side of the railway line, taking turns on my scooter, unthinkingly going further and further into the maze of small streets looking each much like the next in the neighbourhood of Clapham Junction. We were off a bus route and suddenly realised we did not recognise any of the street names and were slightly lost. We kept walking on, getting somewhat tired and thinking about dinner, when I recognised the name of the street we had just turned into.

'I've been here before. This road is not very far from my grandparents' house. Once we get there we can get back home easily.'

I led the way to the house, went up the steps and pulled the bell. When it was answered we marched straight into the dining room, where Aunt Ethel and my grandfather happened to be, he reading the paper, she seated at the writing table in the window. I explained to them that we had been slightly lost but after a while I had realised we were in grandparent country and so we had made our way to their house.

Nothing much was said. I sat down on a sofa, Percy beside me. We were a bit tired.

My grandfather asked Percy a few questions. What was his name? My grandfather could not call to mind having met his father. How long had he known me? (My entire life: there had never been a time without Percy.) Where did he go to school? And so on.

A kind of blankness set in. Nothing was said. I could see we were not going to be asked to luncheon, as dinner was called in that house. Not even a biscuit was offered. It was something to do with Percy. Aunt Ethel said at last,

'Hadn't you better be getting along? Your mother may be worrying about you.'

So we got up and went. After all, Percy had gone there expecting nothing, but I had been expecting luncheon. We walked back, wheeling the scooter. When we reached the Common I said that as we still had a mile to go, we might as well eat our iron rations. It was my habit at that time to carry, strapped to the rear of the footplate of my scooter, an Oxo tin containing several coloured skeins of floss embroidery silk (things of unspeakable beauty), a Bible I had been given on my birthday and a paper bag of jam sandwiches.

Sitting on a bench on the Common, Percy and I shared the jam sandwiches. It was rhubarb jam. We did not on that occasion engage in crewel work, nor did we read the Bible. The sandwiches did not fill us and we hurried home.

It appeared that soon after this incident my grandfather cross-examined my mother about the children with whom I associated. Before the arrival of Percy with his mouthful of bad teeth it is doubtful whether he had given the matter a thought, but now it had become part of his duty.

'He started by saying he often wondered where Phyl had picked up that Cockney accent and supposed it might be because she spent so much time in the kitchen with the servants instead of with her aunts when she was at Sherbrooke,' she told my father.

'Anyone in their senses would rather spend time with Alice and Millie than with Ethel and Ada. I would myself,' he said. 'They are nice cheerful girls and really quite pretty.'

'The Pater will never have a plain girl in the house, we all know that; it is rather unfair but that is how he is.'

'He might have started by booting Ethel out into the snow and clearing the decks for a fresh intake of pretty girls,' he suggested.

'You are always so down on Ethel. It is mostly that scraped-back hair and those glasses,' interceded my mother with a touch of smugness.

'And that chin like the prow of a battleship doesn't help. Personally I'd scrap the head altogether. Plus everything from the neck down,' he added.

From loyalty to her family my mother tried to salvage a few spare parts from the wreckage.

'Ethel has beautiful little hands and quite small feet. She takes fours, in some fittings three-and-a-halfs.'

'Did you know she has fifty-seven pairs of boots and shoes? I counted them all set out on that rack in her dressing room.' I was pleased to be able to contribute a hard fact to the conversation.

'As many as that? I knew she had a lot,' said my mother.

'Vain, too, and mean as dirt with it. Why doesn't she give the first fifty pairs away to the Band of Hope and tell them to patter off home? The woman isn't normal.'

'Will! That's enough . . . Well, I told the Pater I wasn't going to worry about a Cockney accent at her age, no doubt she'd grow out of it in due course just as he had grown out of Hucknallese.'

'How did he take that?'

'As a compliment, I fancy—you know what he's like. Then he asked whether all the children she went about with were as common as Percy and I said well no, actually, Percy was unusually adenoidal and scruffy but he and Phyl had always known one another and what did it matter if they got on well together? What did Percy's father do for a living? he asked then, and I said he was a clerk at the builders' yard but was not in line for promotion as he was well over fifty and in bad health. Do you know what he said then?'

'No idea.'

'He said he was not in favour of his grandchildren spending much of their time among unsuccessful people because failure was catching, if you didn't get away from it it got you.'

'Old sod never said a truer word. Nasty way of putting it but perfectly true. If you're born without money or influence, as he was, you need a powerful head of steam through your brain and bloodstream to get you anywhere. Set of sound teeth does no harm, either. Poor little Perce.'

'Grandpa is horrible,' I muttered.

'Don't speak of your grandfather in that way!' my mother exclaimed crossly. 'And you are certainly in no position to criticise him, you are very like him in many ways.'

'No! I'm not!'

'Yes you are. I notice it often.'

'How am I like him?'

'You're both cocky, critical and verbose.'

'Your mother means self-reliant, discriminating and articulate,' suggested my father sardonically.

'No I don't,' she snapped.

After she had said that about my being like my grandfather, I looked at him more closely, trying to see what she meant. I could not see it. I would look straight at him, wondering about this, and he would look straight back, defying me. I liked to imagine what he was thinking.

At Christmas, when my father sneaked off to the billiard room for a smoke, I sometimes followed him to keep him company.

'I hate Grandpa, don't you?' I confided as I leant up against him on the slippery seating and crunched acid drops in the forbidden way. A bright fire burned in the grate with spurts of blue flame. The air began to be fragrant as my father pierced the end of his cigar and lighted up. When men smoked cigars their mouths, whatever shape they were before, turned round in shape like babies' mouths.

'I might like him better if I saw less of him, but as it is I see the old so-and-so every day.'

For my grandfather was the big boss of the building society where my father worked, as well as being some sort of overlord of building societies in general, their association as it was called.

Sometimes, when I was staying at Sherbrooke Lodge, I would go in the car with my grandfather to his office, which was at the top of Ludgate Hill, right under St Paul's Cathedral. The chauffeur would wait while I went in and had a word with my father who had arrived a good deal earlier, by train. He was in a small office downstairs, the walls of which were surprisingly tiled throughout in decorative green ceramic with a raised pattern of leaves and flowers like lilies. When I was very small and asked my father what he did all day in the office to earn a living, he said he cut the stamps off used envelopes and it would be a great help in keeping the wolf from our door if I would assist him in this. He would produce a bundle of envelopes and a pair of scissors and I would work away at cutting out the red penny stamps until it was time for me to be driven back to my grandparents' house.

Grandpa had a big room to himself upstairs. It had a Turkey carpet and an enormous oval table that was used for board meetings. His own writing-table was at the far end, right next to a small bow window that overlooked the general office below, so that he could look down like God

96

and see if any of his creatures were doing wrong. The main office was like a bank. I liked Mr Phillips the cashier. He had a copper shovel with a steel tip for shovelling coins. When I went through the office on the way out he would always shovel up a heap of sovereigns and spread them out in a sweep of gold, like cards being dealt, on to the mahogany counter behind the grille. Perhaps Grandpa was spying on us while this happened, though I never heard anything about that.

But now I was older and knew that my father did more at the office than cutting out postage stamps. I knew what building societies were for—borrowing money from some people to lend to other people to buy houses, and keeping something back in between the two deals to pay my father's salary. He said that though people talked about the Building Society Movement as if it were something religious like Methodism, it was really no more than a set of pawnshops for houses. That is, people put their houses in pawn to the building society and if they paid up they owned their house all right in the end, but if they failed in their payments the building society would take possession of their house just as if it were a watch or a set of pots and pans. There was nothing specially virtuous about the building society movement: it provided a useful service at a realistic price, that was all.

'But there was a time,' my father remarked, climbing down from our dress-circle seat above the billiard table and easing off the ash from his cigar into the fire, for there were no ash trays provided . . . 'There was a time when the building society movement nearly came to grief and might have passed into nothingness, but for your grandfather.' He climbed back beside me and I settled down again against him.

'The idea of paying in money to a club to buy houses had been going on in a small unorganised way for nearly a hundred years, but about the time I was born the thing began to take off in a much bigger way and an Act was passed dealing with building societies. Then it was full steam ahead for a number of years. Your grandfather had always been quick to see which way the wind was blowing and he had jumped on the wagon early on. He was in charge here in 1892, I think it was—about ten years before your mother and I were married—and everything was rolling along nicely when suddenly the news broke that the Liberator Society had gone bust for several million. Now the Liberator was not technically a building society at all, there had always been an element of fraud about it, but the public took it to be one and started a run on the true building societies when the Liberator put up its shutters.'

My father looked down sideways at me.

'Am I boring you?'

'Not yet,' I said. I knew my father thought that almost the worst thing in the world you could do to people, this side of mayhem, was to bore them. I was not quite bored but it was a near thing.

'Good . . . Well, as you know, building societies don't, any more than banks, keep on the premises anything like all the money that has been deposited with them. Most of it is out at work buying houses. But of course depositors have the right to money on demand, up to certain limit, only in the ordinary course of things they don't all want it at once. If they did, the money wouldn't be there. It is a kind of gamble, a calculated risk, with banks just the same as building societies, that most of the time most of the money will stay comfortably on deposit.

'But when word got round, as it did very quickly, that the Liberator had gone bust and was not paying out, there began to be a run on other societies in the City. One of them was here where your grandfather was in charge. The staff were in, but the doors had not yet been opened for the day's business when a crowd began to collect outside.

'Your grandfather checked with the cashier the amount of cash actually on the premises. He told him he was going to let the depositors in and that the first two or three should be paid off at the normal pace for paying out, but after that the cashier was to drag his feet a bit, checking every passbook painstakingly against the Society's records and counting out the coins at a snail's pace. Then your grandfather went to the door, opened it wide, stood on the steps and addressed the crowd.

'He'd be about my age then, but his hair was already white, he'd gone white before thirty. He must have been a fine figure of a man, I'll give him that, and I suppose the white hair gave him a certain *gravitas* . . .'

'What's *gravitas*?'

'Weightiness. A kind of dignity . . . And you know, he must always have had this rather impressive voice and way of speaking . . . He stood on the steps and addressed the crowd. They would be nearly all small depositors, nothing like the sums we handle today, and mostly they would be working men who would be getting late to their jobs. Your grandfather told them that the failure of the Liberator had absolutely nothing to do with this building society, which was perfectly solvent and ready to pay out all depositors in full. However, with such an unusually large number of customers to deal with, order must be observed. Would they please form themselves into an orderly queue and file in one by one? They would then be paid off according to their demands. Then he stood aside to let the first two or three enter and hurry to the cashier's grille.'

My father heaved himself off the seat again and down to the fireplace.

'All those spondulicks and not a bloody ash tray in the house, it's unbelievable . . .' he grumbled . . . 'Well, as I was saying, these chaps filed in with their passbooks and were paid off and went away down the steps, putting their little grabs of sovereigns and silver away in their pockets; and then some others came in one by one and were paid off, but it took a long time, and others followed them and emerged after a bit, all fully paid off, gold and silver in their hands, and the word went round and time went on, and their mates thought of the wages they were losing in lost hours at work as St Paul's tolled out the quarter hours. Gradually the crowd thinned out and split off, muttering it wasn't worth losing interest on their deposits as well as a half-day's work, it seemed all right, must have been a rumour, this building society was paying out to all comers and that gent that came out on the steps and spoke to them, no panic about him, took it easy, not a care in the world . . . must have been a rumour . . . And in no time at all the word ran round the City that it was business as usual at the building society, and they all quietened down and the crisis was over.'

99

'And everybody lived happily ever after,' I added.

'Well, more or less. That episode certainly added to your grandfather's reputation in the City, and he soon landed some juicy directorships. Not but what he deserved it. And though I can't stand the man, I must say he is meticulously honourable, never did a dirty deed in his life, I'm sure of that—too much in love with himself to lower himself in his own eyes. The moment war was declared, did you know? he stood up at a board meeting and said he was going to renounce half his salary for the duration and invited the directors to do the same! Only time I've known him show any sense of humour—irony, more like. The money-grubbing old bastards didn't know which way to squirm, they were practically peeing themselves, the choice was awful—take a cut in fees or be branded as unpatriotic. They all toed the line in the end, the sheer power of his personality unnerved them. The supreme egoist, if ever there was one, your grandfather.

'And that is the story of how he saved the building society Movement with a capital M. By the way, if ever anything describes itself as a Movement, be it the building society Movement or the Labour Movement or the European Movement, be sure there's some cant in it somewhere, with pickings for the hangers-on. Never trust a Movement.'

'Not even a watch movement?' I suggested brilliantly.

He looked at his own watch. 'Come on,' he said, 'we've been away too long—ice will be forming in the drawing room. And as for movements, the only movement worth having is a good bowel movement.'

'And how *are* the bow-els?' I asked him as we proceeded chuckling together out of the billiard room.

'Oh, *there* you both are,' remarked Aunt Ethel from her corner of the sofa. Grandpa did not even look up.

'Daddy was telling me about how Grandpa saved the building society movement when the Liberator crashed,' I explained. It was an early attempt at tact, and it worked. My grandfather turned towards me with an expression of unusual geniality, a look only a few degrees short of blood heat, such as an elderly cobra might bend upon its tiny hooded grandchild.

100

Rather like those 'sleeping policemen'—unseen humps built into private roads designed to dislocate the necks, by roof impact, of drivers approaching at unseemly speeds —there were certain arrangements at my grandfather's house which had the effect, designedly or not, of checking the Christmas enthusiasm of the young. No delighted member of the family rushed with cries of welcome to answer the bell when we arrived at the front door, which was invariably opened by a maid. The one concession to blood ties was that we were not announced but were expected to make our own way to the drawing room once we had left our outdoor clothing in the library. Here, at Christmas, would be ready on a table the presents we were to receive, wrapped up and labelled 'To' and 'From'. No givers were present, only the presents and we the recipients. It was understood that the string must be unknotted and wound into neat coils and the paper folded before the presents could be fully examined. These were usually acceptable enough, once it had been noted that I had a strong detestation of dolls. According to our age, my brother and I were given well-made toys, pen and pencil sets, board games, Meccano, drums and whistles, footballs and tennis racquets, leather writing cases, scrapbooks and autograph albums. One year I was given a large, splendid paintbox by Uncle Jack, with three rows of paints, each in its small square porcelain tub that lifted out, and many camelhair brushes.

After no more than a brief glance at our new presents, for not everything could be carried, we had to shoulder our own burden of offerings and proceed to the drawing room where Grandpa, Grandma (if she had managed to tear herself away from the linen press) and both aunts would be in place, as if pinned there since our last visit. Only Grandma would look up and smile at us. She was a small, thin, wrinkled old lady with a fine aquiline nose and plenty of energy, who had given up on her two formalised daughters and liked to spend her time with things she could see the sense of, such as jars of chutney and damson cheese, hampers of clean laundry, her canary, the Cox's orange pippins in the cellar apple room, her parrot, her two cats and her dog.

We would walk round the room saying, 'Happy Christmas and thank you,' to each seated figure in turn, and planting a kiss upon each cool or whiskered cheek. We would not be so much as glanced at except by Grandma, who would give us a warm kiss before slipping away to see to things, such as a bone for Paddy. As we kissed, so we would bestow, easing our botched-up parcelled offering into limp hands. We would be thanked in a toneless parroty way, as if the form had been memorised from an English phrasebook for foreigners. Our parcels were not opened. Soon the gong would go for Christmas dinner (*not* luncheon for once) and by the time we returned to the drawing room after the meal, the presents we had given would have disappeared. We heard no more of them. They might have been shredded and engulfed by a waste disposal unit, had such refinements existed then, for all the news we had of them.

Since I would have spent most of the gas-lit evenings between Michaelmas and Christmas planning, making, botching and unbotching and finally wrapping up and labelling presents for all the relations and friends on my list, it fell a little flat not to know how they were received. For lack of feedback the giving impulse weakened. Less and less interest went into choosing presents for my aunts, and as for my grandfather, it is a hard thing for a small child to choose a Christmas present in the shilling range for an old man who has everything but love and does not smoke. Grandma seemed content to receive frequent needlecases made of cardboard covered with cretonne, bent double and lined with leaves of flannel tied on with coloured cord saved from last year's calendars, but Grandpa was another matter.

There had been the Christmas when I was about five, when I had made a notebook for my grandfather. Several pages had been cut with scissors out of a ruled exercise book, folded and cut again to make smaller pages. These were pierced along the spine with a thick needle and sewn, with immense labour, into a cover of thick yellow cardboard and behold! a new notebook for Grandpa to take notes in.

This gift, wrapped in brown paper and string, had been

presented and received in the usual way—the one-way kiss, the phrasebook thanks, followed by the total disappearance of the offering. I heard no more about it, but my mother was summoned by her father to account for the peculiar wretchedness of this present, at once valueless and badly made. As I heard much later, my mother let fly at her parent with both barrels of a righteous anger, not scrupling to draw the comparison between the image of the great and good benefactor he was careful to present to the children at the temperance orphanage and the cold, joyless old nitpicker his own grandchildren knew him to be. Imperviously, my grandfather instructed her to tell me to come up with worthier presents in future. It is not surprising that she failed to pass on to me this discouraging message. Consequently I continued cobbling together clumsy and worthless presents for him Christmas after Christmas, unaware that each offering would have been taken as an act of defiance.

My poor mother, the soul of loyalty to both factions of her family, had much to put up with as piggy in the middle. One year, when I had more pocket money than usual, I stubbornly refused to bother with presents for my aunts. Evidently nothing pleased them, for whatever was given to them very likely went straight into the dustbin. It was disheartening.

'Here is three-and-six,' I said to my mother. 'Buy something with that if you must, but don't ask me to think about it.'

My mother, starved of co-operation, ended up by buying a china dog which I never even saw.

This purchase, so uncharacteristic of my mother's normal shopping instincts, must have been undertaken in a moment when she was 'not herself', torn apart in a consumer's schizoid panic between warring loyalties. I understood that the china dog, which I disdained to look at, was repellent to a degree. Yet my mother, a keen shopper, bought it. Let psychologists make what they will of the abhorrent china dog, which was wrapped up and labelled with my name as the giver.

Barring the homemade notebook, this was the one present we ever heard mentioned again.

'. . . and she gave me a china dog,' exclaimed Aunt Ada in bitterness to my mother . . .' a china dog *not fit to put in a servant's bedroom!'*

This remark, repeated at home by my injured mother, became a catchphrase. Anything disliked or rejected, be it a pair of scuffed tennis shoes, a note sung flat, or a lump of unchewable gristle, was thereafter described as being 'not fit to put in a servant's bedroom'.

Once, when my father came home after a board meeting, he was grumbling about the unpleasant habits of one of the older directors.

'Old Paul was at it again—coughing and spluttering over everybody, blowing his nose like an elephant trumpeting, and then, if you please, walking over to the fireplace to shake out his handkerchief in front of the fire to dry off the snot; stood there with his back to the rest of us a good couple of minutes. I longed to kick his baggy old backside.'

'He always was quite a repulsive person,' my mother remarked, 'and he won't have improved with age.'

'Face like a rhino, too,' he added.

'Not fit to put in a servant's bedroom?' I suggested.

'Emphatically not,' he replied.

6

If there were bells and sirens I do not remember them. It was November 11th, 1918, Armistice Day. We children crowded on to the front steps of the school and knew that the fighting was over. There was an air of painful rejoicing. The little Belgian pupil teacher, a refugee of about twenty, burst into tears and ran away along the road to the shops, and ran back again with a paper bag full of Allied flags which she pinned on our coats, laughing and crying and hugging us. Perhaps it was her tears that made the celebration poignant and silenced in my memory the bells and sirens, as if a bloodied hush had fallen over Europe.

The walking wounded from the military hospital wore bright blue jackets and trousers of a hairy flannel that was not pressed or tailored like a uniform. It had a cosy look about it, more like a bed jacket. Their shirts were white and their ties were bright red. They were hatless. They humped about on crutches or on two sticks. They wore an arm in a sling or were minus a leg or bandaged round the head. Some showed no visible signs of injury. On fine days they lurched and hirpled about the Common. Most of the benches would have two or three wounded soldiers in their hospital blue, resting, when the sun was shining. When they looked up as I scudded past them on my scooter they did not look sad. They smoked cigarettes and seemed contented enough. But these were the ones who were not going to die.

For many months after the war ended the military funerals from the hospital went on coming, though at longer intervals, down the road past our house. The soldiers, the limbers, the sound of hooves, the coffin draped in the flag, still passed. Still the Last Post sounded for these stragglers. These were the soldiers who had died late of their wounds, for whom there had once been hope but it had faded. I was

105

aware that these latecomers who came last to the Last Post had died slowly: just up the road from me.

The living soldiers began to come home from the war. These were not the same as the ones who had gone away. They looked older and duller; their hair was not so bright. At the beginning of the war, when I was small, there had been several young subalterns who had come to the house to say goodbye to my mother before they went away to fight. Some had worn beautiful tightly fitting leather leggings with the colour and gloss of conkers. One had a sword.

He had unbuckled it and laid it on a settle in the hall before he went into the drawing room to pay his farewell respects to my mother. The door was shut. I was excluded. My mother's farewells to these young soldiers were always private affairs. I went up to the sword where it lay in its sheath on the settle. A real sword was thrilling. I withdrew it partly from its scabbard and felt the edge with my thumb. It was not as sharp as I could have wished, used as I was to my mother's razor-sharp dinner knives. While I was fingering it the drawing room door opened and out came my mother and the young soldier, both a little pink. She pushed the sword back into its sheath and drew me slightly away from it, but not crossly.

'Is it sharp enough?' I asked the tall, yellow-haired soldier, as he was buckling it back on. 'If it isn't, Mother could sharpen it for you, like our knives.'

He laughed at this. You could see he was happy. You could see he loved having a sword to wear. Just for a moment you could see he was not quite a man yet, only a big boy like the scouts who sometimes made dens of branches in the field. He was still a big boy as he went down the path to the gate, but as he closed the gate and turned back to us and saluted, he became a soldier.

At the end of the war, suddenly, I remembered him, half a lifetime away. I asked my mother:

'That soldier who came to say goodbye at the beginning of the war, what happened to him?'

'Who do you mean? There were quite a number.'

'He was a one-pipper with yellow hair. Tall. He had a sword.'

106

'That must have been Colin Cowper. What a good-looking boy he was! . . . He was killed in the autum of 1914. He was only twenty.'

I saw the sword drawn in his hand, saw him hit and saw him fall, saw the bright sword fall from his hand, point down into the mud, and be lost like a spoon in a jar of jam. There it had fallen and there it lay still, rusted, the bright sword.

The soldiers who came back were not the same as the ones who went away.

Uncle Jack came back from the war. He was my mother's brother. I liked him but had not often seen him because he had been away at the war for so long. He always gave me presents at Christmas but was seldom there himself. My only memory of him was watching him walking towards me down a long corridor in my grandparents' house, where at the top of the main staircase the landing widened. Between two doorways there was a console table supporting the white marble bust of a lady. She was cut off short just below the shoulders and was not wearing any clothes, so perhaps that was why she had been cut off short, either that or a scarcity of marble if there was a war on when she had been made. I was wondering about this when I saw my uncle in uniform walking along the corridor towards me and the staircase. He was a slim man with big, rather sad blue-grey eyes, not keen eyes like Grandpa's and my mother's but eyes that looked at something further off. As he passed me he ruffled my hair with his hand and said,

'Hello, Poodle,' and passed on down the main staircase.

That is all I remembered about him, yet he seemed a known and familiar figure. I asked my mother why Uncle Jack looked sad.

'I expect the war made him sad. Because he was in the Territorials he was in it right from the beginning, in a West Riding regiment. He worked somewhere up there, as a land surveyor . . . He was a wizard with animals, always had been, got on with every sort of animal as a boy, even used to take a pet snake into church and offered to fight the verger when he was ordered to take it outside . . . He was particularly good with horses, so when he joined his regiment he was put in charge of the horses they used for transport. This

107

was not a smart cavalry regiment, you understand, the horses were used for hauling everything that was needed from base up to the front. There were convoys of them, hauling guns, munitions, rations, spares of every sort —more like a train, really but over any sort of difficult country . . . ruined farms, seas of mud, bomb craters and shell holes to be got round somehow. Poor Jack . . . he loved his horses so much, and when they were wounded he had to shoot them. That must have been a kind of hell for him, seeing his horses and mules mutilated and having to shoot them. I expect that is why he looks sad.'

But as I was to learn later, there were other reasons.

It was understood that in my mother's family Uncle Jack and Aunt Ada had always been very close, a pair in the middle separating the eldest, Aunt Ethel, the pampered swot, and the youngest, my maverick mother. Surprisingly, it seems that in their youth these middlemost brother and sister had been a lively and attractive pair—good-looking, carefree and not overburdened with brains. According to the standards of the day they were good sports, ready to take on 'anyone for tennis', adept with scull or pole on the Thames at Sunbury, whirlers at the waltz on ballroom floor or ice. They twanged away on banjo, mandoline and guitar in what would now be a small jazz group. In addition, Jack was better than average at various manly sports and was an admired amateur rider. So they were popular and usually asked out together. It is true that time had wrought its change in them, saddening him and stiffening her into formality, but they stayed companionable through thick and thin, in spite of his working away in Yorkshire before the war and seldom home on leave during the four years of its duration.

Uncle Jack was a bachelor in his late thirties when the war broke out. It was his sister whom he escorted to *Chu Chin Chow* and the other wartime shows when he was home on leave. But it was seldom indeed that he came home. Aunt Ada waited anxiously for him and worried about him while she did her voluntary stints serving tea and wads to soldiers, or rolling bandages with other ladies of leisure. She took it for granted that after the war he would return to live in London, perhaps even at home, where there was plenty of room for him to have his own quarters. A directorship was being kept warm for him and no doubt a partnership would soon become available in one of the larger estate agents or property companies where his father was in a position to exert influence. The old companionship between brother and sister, which had survived the separation of his years at boarding school in Germany, as a young surveyor in Yorkshire, and this hideous war, would thrive and flourish again in all its easy good humour.

* * *

My mother's preoccupation with well-fitting footwear for the young was painfully justified when she was advised to go into hospital for an operation to correct a distorted big toe, brought on—she swore—by her own mother's greater interest in fledgling sparrows, wandering hedgehogs and stray cats and dogs than in her children's growing feet. While it was impossible to deny the superior attractions of pet animals to the smelly feet of children, I could not help pointing out that Aunt Ethel had managed to grow up with a pair of small and undistorted feet. How was that?

'Ethel was so wrapped up in herself and her feet, always wanting to go into shoe shops and try on shoes, she would have noticed if her big toe had been pushed out of true by so much as an inch.'

'So would most of us.' I remarked. 'Don't you mean a millimetre?'

'There were no millimetres when we were young,' said my parent dismissively, 'and it is only to be expected that somebody who collects fifty-seven pairs of shoes must have an abnormal interest in feet and would be always looking at them. I had better things to look at.'

Such as your face in the looking-glass, I thought, but did not say. My mother was distinctly good-looking and decidedly vain. Everybody in my family was rather vain but I had been brought up to be plain and in a way this was a kind of relief, it let me off a lot of hooks, such as wasting time sitting in a good light at a dressing table examining my face in a magnifying mirror and sighing. A lot of ladies spent time doing this and it seemed to me a boring thing to

109

do, much more boring than watching the ladies doing it.

It could be conceded that Aunt Ethel, with a face like Lord Longford, might well give up on faces and turn to feet, thereby forestalling the onset of bunions.

While my mother was in hospital having her big toe seen to, and later during her hobbling convalescence with friends at Scarborough, I was sent to stay with my grandparents at Sherbrooke Lodge. My paternal grandmother, meanwhile, came up from the country to keep house for my father and brother and tut-tut over my mother's latest intake of untrained domestic help, now being released from the women's forces and the munitions factories.

Except that my aunt kept brushing and combing my hair and doing it up in rag curlers, I had an enjoyable stay at my grandparents'. I realised that it was only necessary to humour my relations according to their individual kinks to have quite a good time. My grandfather liked to be asked the meaning of long words and to be listened to while he went on about a writer called Robertson who had lived a hundred years ago and had warned everybody about the dangerous ambitions of the Prussians. He also spoke about another author who warned of the Yellow Peril, an explosion of pig-tailed Chinamen who, actually increasing at an exponential rate of growth in spite of all that incessant flood and drought could do to them, were due to overrun the world at some date in the future not yet announced.

My grandmother was easy to get on with. This was the grandmother who declared she had seen snakes hanging from the trees in Little Switzerland near Brattle Place. Her bent little body scuttled round the house like a mouse as she chattered unceasingly about whatever came into her head, hopping about across time, from a tiny bed of pansies she had tended as a child to the coming of the Kingdom of Heaven, and back again to the disgraceful way my grandfather's shirts had been ironed. She spoke of Joseph and his coat of many colours not only as if she had lived next door to Joseph, but had patched his coat. All the Biblical characters were everyday people to her. She had taken strongly against Abraham for his cruel treatment of the ram in the thicket and said it was just what you would expect of a man

110

with a beard like that, she had always disliked a beard on a
man. Dirty. Eggy. Old Mr Pike had come to dinner and
drooled soup down his beard: 'Wipe your beard, man, wipe
your beard!' my grandfather had been driven to exclaim in
disgust, and who could blame him? She would never sit
down to table with a man like Abraham. It seemed they
lived on mutton, the children of Israel, hardly had time to
get outside their kitchen door but they had grabbed hold of
some wretched sheep and were slaughtering it. We were
having pheasant for dinner tonight, she only hoped that
new cook who had just come out of the WAACs was up to
game chips. Her Madeira cakes were terrible but with
practice she might improve. In the Army they ate nothing
but bully beef and bread and plum-and-apple jam. Her
father had been in the Army. He had worn the kilt and had
died in the Crimean War. His name had been Heughan and
so had hers been of course before she had married my
grandfather and she was not sure it had been a change for
the better, but at least he had not got a beard, she would
have cut it off in his sleep. She had several scissors in need
of sharpening but the knifegrinder had not been round for
some time, he must be about due, the cross-eyed woman
who re-caned chairs had been round a couple of weeks ago
but there had been no work for her; it is children who break
up cane seats, always standing on chairs and jumping up
and down on them. The old nursery could be made over
into a dining room for Jack if he came back to live at home,
he already had his own bedroom and sitting room, those
rooms would easily convert into a service flat for him if he
wanted them. Ada seemed to take it for granted he would
be coming back to live here, didn't seem to realise a man
might want his freedom from the family, a man could be
eaten alive by his family, look at Ethel and Ada, echoing
each other like two parrots: 'Isn't that so, Ethel?' 'Yes, Ada,'
and, 'Don't you agree, Ada?' 'Yes, Ethel,' siding with each
other against their own mother.

'Your mother was the sharp one and she got out, a good
thing for everybody, they were always quarrelling, girls are
always jealous of one another, playing up to get their
father's attention, and of course it suited him, sitting there
like a cat lapping up cream. Now where has Smoke got to? I

111

don't want him getting into Mr Scott's garden again, he jumps down from a branch in the chestnut on to the wall and there is broken glass on top of it, let's go and see . . . ah, there you are, Ben, what have you done with Smoke?' Ben, the blue Persian, followed us out.

Mr Scott lived next door in a big house behind a high brick wall. He had an electric brougham and a footman who sat beside the chauffeur. The equipage would glide away in perfect silence, leaving no trace of odour on the air. Mr Scott moved in a mysterious way. An ordinary cat like Smoke who climbed up a tree in Mr Scott's garden might well turn into a Cheshire cat and vanish.

When I stayed with my grandparents I slept in Aunt Ada's dressing room which opened out of her bedroom. When she was dressing or changing I would often drift in and out. She did not, like her sister, possess an unusual number of shoes, but she took trouble over her clothes. She always wore silk stockings, except for country walks, and all her underclothes and nighties were of silk. What were really special were the numbers of kimonos she had. These were of very heavy silk, elaborately embroidered from collar to hem with complex patterns, often with dragons coiling round. They were composed of every colour of the rainbow, light blue, gold, midnight blue, blush pink— everything but green which Aunt Ada considered unlucky and would never tolerate in clothes or furnishings. They were gorgeous to look at and luxurious to handle, heavy with the sumptuous weight of the silk which very slightly squeaked or crunched when squeezed, as only silk and snow can do.

These exotic garments had all been presents from her cousin Valentine, one of the sons who had got away from the wicked Edward Atkins and his closely panelled house in Windsor. From time to time he arrived back in London, always from places to the east on the map. I had seen him once or twice. He was big, dark, smooth and stylish. His work, which was said to be banking, seemed to keep him ever on the move. He sometimes turned up unexpectedly. He wrote to my aunt from outlandish places with strange postage stamps.

She had on her mantelpiece a small glass bell filled with

112

layers of coloured sands from the Isle of Wight. White sand and grey sand, yellow sand and brown sand, as well as sand almost red. I liked to look at this glass bell and wonder about the beaches on the Isle of Wight, supposing them to be divided into bays, each bay with sand of a different colour. I had heard that on the Isle of Wight you could never be more than four miles from the sea, yet in the paper recently there had been a bit about an old lady, well into her eighties, who had lived on the island all her life but had never set eyes on the sea. It followed that she would never have seen those bays, each of a different colour, scooped out of the white cliffs, edged with the blue sea. I looked again at the bell of sands, then away towards the dressing table, where my aunt was seated, doing something to her face, powdering it perhaps. I strolled across and stood by her, looking at her reflection in the mirror.

To my surprise I saw that my aunt was crying slightly, dabbing at her face with a handkerchief, not powdering her nose. She was being very quiet about it.

Occasionally my mother cried. My brother and I had grown up with it. Over the years we had come to understand that our mother's tears were all-purpose symbols of her grief/disappointment/sadness/dismay (but never anger) at our bad temper/rudeness/ingratitude/selfishness. These tears were stored in a convenient reservoir from which they could be dispensed at will by the millilitre. Our reaction to them had gradually altered from contrition to disregard and finally to derision. Now when our mother turned on tears we laughed at her and finally, acknowledging that the tactic was obsolete, she would laugh too.

But my aunt's tears were different. She was not making a fuss. She was trying to conceal her tears. Standing beside her, I said nothing.

Finally she said, 'Would you mind if I went away to live in Russia?'

Russia! I was with my brother in a sleigh, sped by galloping horses over the snow. On either side the boundless forest rooted itself in silence. But what was this weird howling behind us? Wolves! and the pack was gaining on us, bared fangs gleaming . . . I gave my brother a stealthy push and the sleigh sped on, lightened . . .

'I would come and stay with you in Russia,' I replied. 'When are you thinking of going?'

'Oh, I don't know, I haven't decided anything yet. But Val has asked me again to marry him, he wants me to marry him and live with him in Russia . . . but I don't know.'

'Don't you want to marry him?'

'I don't know what I want.'

'You could have the Russian national anthem played on the organ at your wedding.' Of all the Allied national anthems we had learned to recognise, this was the one whose wild minor surges swept me away to the other country.

'I don't think they play that any more, not since the revolution. Anyway, weddings are not the place for national anthems and we would want to be married in England: if at all,' she added.

An uneasy thought struck me. If my aunt and Valentine Atkins married in London, was I not, as an only niece, in danger of being roped in as a bridesmaid? In a flash, as before drowning, I saw the gruesome procession of events —the many fittings, the tight curling-rags the night before, the shining sausages of hair to be kept unruffled, my own face under a chaplet of flowers being bidden to simper time and again at the photographer. I was simply not bridesmaid material.

'As you are both so old,' I suggested, 'you might prefer a quiet wedding at a register office.'

'As I am so old,' my aunt retorted, 'I am getting too crotchety to put up with any more asinine remarks from young idiots, so run along now and wash your hands and tidy your hair before tea.' By now her tears were dried and she was putting her face in order.

On my way out I noticed the bell of sand from the Isle of Wight. It had somehow lost its magic and was only a glass ornament with layers of sand inside. The steppes of Russia called to me now, the endless melancholy versts where always the wind sang in a minor key.

The next Saturday I walked across the Common to my own home to see my other grandmother and my father and brother. Annie my mother's current trainee from the slums of Battersea, let me in.

114

'Hello, ducks,' she said. 'No motor-car and shover for you today, I see. Been chucked out by His Nibs or what?'

'Grandma was out in the car at her bonnet makers or something, so I thought it would be a chance to walk. They didn't want me to, they gave me sixpence for the bus, but I walked instead.'

'You'll spend the bus money on sweets, eh?'

'I'm a bit sick of sweets, when they are always there you don't want them. You can have threepence to get some for Madge and Ernie if you like.' Madge and Ernie were her youngest siblings. I counted out the three coppers into her red palm.

'Thanks ever so, ducks.' She winked at me and spat on the money.

'And better not call me ducks,' I added quietly as my grandmother came downstairs.

'How are you, darling?' She kissed me warmly on the mouth and then on both cheeks. She had slightly Frenchified ways, picked up from all those French chefs and their wives that she and my Grandfather Betts had known. She was tall, with the sort of face seen on cameo brooches. Her figure was full and stately. She wore a lot of petticoats and when she hurried away along a platform to catch a train she was rather like a hen scuttling towards thrown grain. The next thing to say was how I had grown.

'How you have grown! But of course we don't see you often. How I wish we were not so far away from Will and you children.'

'I wish Grandpa had come with you.' I liked my Grandfather Betts. He had a twinkle in his eye behind round gold spectacles.

'He would only have been another man to look after as well as your father and brother. Hilda will keep an eye on him.' Hilda was my aunt. 'And between you and me,' my grandmother said, lowering her voice, 'Annie is only good for the rough. She has no idea how to serve up a meal decently or answer the door to a visitor. She quite embarrassed me yesterday, when a lady called who was kind enough to bring a dozen of new-laid eggs, thinking no doubt that your mother might be home by now. I got there just in time to find Annie practically shutting the door in her face. Can you imagine what she said? She said: "Thanks, m'm, the missus'll see you right soon as she's ahter orspital."

'Well of course I asked who it was. It was a Mrs James, quite handsome and very well-dressed, and I apologised as well I might but it was awkward for me; after all, Annie is not my maid or one I would ever have engaged, but your mother . . . I think I made it right with Mrs James though she wouldn't come in, said she'd just come by to drop in the eggs. Naturally I had to lay it on a bit about what a kind thought it was, such a generous impulse and new-laid eggs were always so welcome a gift, more especially if one had been convalescing . . . and so on. I think she went away smoothed over but I must say it was embarrassing. Why, I wonder, does your mother always pick such young, uncouth maids?'

'I think they are the only ones about who are not able to better themselves,' I explained.

'Who is Mrs James, by the way?' Grandma asked.

Who was Mrs James? Mrs James was a handsome lady with a high colour and hard blue eyes, known for her extreme gentility, which it must have taken all her powers to maintain in the face of Mr James's over-active drives. He was a smallish man with a slightly yellow skin and flat dark eyes that made him look a little bit like a Chinaman. They had lived in a road near the Common as long as I could remember. Then I began to notice that Mr James was getting to look more and more like a Chinaman. Something seemed to be happening to his cheekbones and the slant of his eyebrows. I mentioned this at home but they brushed it off, saying that I stared far too much at people's faces, it was rude and made people uncomfortable.

But suddenly Mr James got to look so much like a Chinaman and to carry on in such outlandish ways that he was put away in our local lunatic asylum.

'Mrs James lives near the Common and her maid Hannah keeps hens down the garden. Mr James looked like a Chinaman and went mad.'

'What?'

'He went mad and was put away. But after a bit he came home.'

116

'He recovered, then?'

'Not exactly. It was just for the weekend.' Come to think of it, it was extremely odd that a person could be mad for five days, then unmad and well enough to go home, then mad again on Monday and ripe to be put away again till the next Saturday. There should be special calendars for lunatic asylums printed Sunday, Madday, Tuesday, Wednesday, Thursday, Friday and Saneday.

'Well, go on,' my grandmother urged me. People like to hear about other people going mad. It sort of cheers them up that it is not yet Madday for them.

'He came home for the weekend but on the second night,' (the Sunday night, I thought—of course, Madday dawning!) 'he must have crept downstairs very quietly, not waking Mrs James, and fetched tools from the shed down the garden beside the henhouse, because the next thing, the neighbours next door were woken up to terrific thumps and bangs on the party wall, the house shook and a picture fell off the wall, there were shouts and grunts from the James's side of the wall and more crashes and thumps like an air raid getting nearer, and when they called the police it was Mr James with a crowbar and sledgehammer from the garden shed. He had thrown everything out of a built-in cupboard beside the fireplace and was trying to break through into the house next door, he was nearly through with bricks prised out and tumbling everywhere, so the police came and then people from the lunatic asylum and put him in the special jacket they keep for very mad people and he was taken away and hasn't been seen since. He must be looking completely like a Chinaman by now.'

'I don't know what you mean about looking like a China-man. Some mad people look quite English.'

'Yes, and some English people look quite mad, have you noticed? English people going about outside?'

'Here comes your father. I'll go and help Annie dish up. I've made him steak and kidney pudding, he always liked that.'

'Enough for me too?'

'Enough for all of us,' said my grandmother in a tone of satisfaction. 'Plenty for everybody, with apple tart to follow with *egg* custard. Mrs James's eggs, poor lady,' she added.

117

My father was pleased to see me. My mother would be home in a week. He had had a letter from her from Scarborough.

This visit to Scarborough had a touch of romance about it. I had often been told that in the days when my Aunt Ada had been engaged to the dying Balmoral organist Ralph, his younger brother Nelson had been in hot pursuit of my mother, who was then eighteen and a part-time student at the Guildhall School of Music. She and Nelson had played and sung duets and things together. He had not been dark like his brother but fair as an angel. Nelson had been absolutely perfect, fair, musical, protective, attentive and so much in love with her he had almost burst. He had brought her flowers. But for some reason my mother had not agreed to marry this perfect lover—why I could never understand—and she had never seemed able to explain. Instead, she had married my father who looked like a cad and fell so far short of perfection in every way except in looking like a cad. Every now and then, when the two had a disagreement, my mother would disinter Nelson from the grave of buried love and hint at how much better off she would have been in the care of this perfect man than with my father, who was totally lacking in romance and foul-mouthed into the bargain.

By chance, after many years she met up with Nelson again. He no longer lived in London. He was married now, with a son. My mother let it be known that no doubt Nelson had shaken the dust of London off his feet in an effort to free himself from the clinging associations of a romance that was never to be, and as for his marriage, it was to be expected that every girl in sight would have thrown herself at him, after he had lived through a long period of hopeless grief. I calculated, however, that with a son so big and old he must have married somebody almost as soon as my mother refused him, but she brushed these figures aside with a brief reference to being caught on the rebound.

She had met his wife who, she said, 'had been pretty'. They kept vaguely in touch, Christmas cards were exchanged. Then it was suggested that she and my father should join Nelson and his wife on holiday somewhere. My father showed no interest at all in this idea but said why not

118

fix up to go away with these people after she had her foot operation, it would be a change of air for her and he could not get away from the office for a holiday at that time.

'Won't you be jealous?'

He looked at her in amazement.

'What? Jealous of that warbling runt? Good God, no!'

So off she had gone to stay with Nelson and his wife on holiday in Scarborough. She was due back next week and soon after that Grandma Betts would return to her little house in the country and I would come back from Sherbrooke Lodge to live with my own family again.

But now I had to go back to the house of my maternal grandparents. I managed to beg a lift from my brother on the step of his bicycle. In those days bicycles were still fitted with a step on the near side of the back wheel. This was a vestigial relic from the days of the penny-farthings, which were impossible to mount without a step up. Since the step was only the size and shape of a steel finger it was an agonising ride, with the whole weight of the body bearing down on this tiny support. The left foot was severely punished. Nevertheless this painful ride was greatly sought-after by younger children from their older brothers, who enjoyed showing off, freewheeling at speed down steep hills, perhaps in an effort to shake off finally their pestilential siblings. The practice was quite dangerous but no one seemed to bother about it. Children hurtled about in total ignorance of crash helmets. If RoSPA was in existence then we had not heard of one another.

My brother cast me off a short distance from our grandparents' house. He did not wish to be seen.

'Nice to have you out of the house,' he remarked kindly. 'Why not stay away?'

I ignored this. 'That was funny about Mrs James and the eggs, wasn't it?'

'You mean, both of them so crushingly genteel that she couldn't ask to be paid for the eggs and Grandma had to assume they were a present for fear of offending?'

'Yes.' Mother often bought eggs from Mrs James. They were never a present.

'Shall I tell Mother?'

119

'No. Let Mrs James find a way of letting it be known that is perfectly genteel.'

'Did you know Val Atkins wants to marry Aunt Ada and both go off to Russia together?'

'*Russia*, is it, now? What do you think he does for a living?'

'He's supposed to be something to do with banks.'

'Banks my foot. Russia's gone communist. What do they want with capitalist banks? Val isn't a banker.'

'What is he, then?'

'An armaments agent, of course. Isn't it obvious? Watch where his letters come from. Wherever in the world trouble is, Val writes letters from. Chap's a gun-runner.'

I pondered this. It might be true. My brother was very clever and knew things. Often I hated him very much and wished he would die, but he was worth keeping in with because he had interesting ideas and knew things.

'Do you think Aunt Ada knows he sells guns?'

'Certainly not. She's an ass, knows nothing of the world. Happy to believe he is sent scuttling round the world from branch bank to branch bank specifically to hand out notes and silver from behind a grille. How does she think he makes his money? She must be an ass.'

'Is he rich?' He looked rich. He had that smooth look.

'Val smells of money. You must have noticed it.'

Yes, I had noticed it. Not exactly a smell but something that sorted out the rich people from the others. I had not known it before but now I recognised it.

It was in that sort of way that my brother was clever. He knew things, and sometimes passed them on to me.

When my mother came back she was still walking a little awkwardly but was pleased with her new straightened toe. I asked her what Scarborough was like and she said it was bracing. She showed me a picture, taken by a beach photographer, of herself and Nelson and his wife, sitting on a seat on a promenade. They were heavily wrapped up and their eyes were screwed up, making them look wrinkled.

'You look much older there than usual,' I said.

'It was the light. The sun was in our eyes. It was taken on the one really sunny day, but there was a wind.'

'Is that Nelson? I thought he was bigger and thinner than that.'

'Nelson has become a little plump. And he wears glasses now, which makes a difference.'

'Of course . . . Did you like the hotel?'

'I wouldn't call it a hotel, though it called itself a private hotel. It was more a boarding-house.'

'What's the difference?'

'In a proper hotel there are separate tables, in a boarding-house people often eat at the one table.'

'Like Brattle Place?'

'Yes. At this place there were separate tables but otherwise it was more like a boarding-house.'

'How?'

'There were a lot of sauce bottles about, brown sauce and ketchup and stuff with dried trickles running down the outside, and the tablecloth wasn't changed every day, either. And there was this extraordinary way of serving cheese and biscuits at the end of a meal, not a normal cheeseboard at all, just little cut-up cubes of mousetrap Cheddar the size of sugar lumps served in a saucer like sweets. Never seen anything like it. But Nelson and Enid said they had come across it before.'

'It wasn't a very good hotel, then?'

'Not really.'

'Why didn't they go to a better hotel?'

'I don't think they can afford it. Nelson has had some business setbacks lately, poor old boy.'

It was not necessary to ask whether Nelson had been let down by a partner. It was a near certainty. My brother had pointed out to me that losers ten to one had had a partner who had let them down. It had become a catchphrase between us, but a secret one.

'You wouldn't put up with a hotel like that if you went with Daddy, would you?'

'No, I wouldn't. But then he'd never book in at a place like that.'

'So you're not sorry you married the old cad after all, instead of Nelson?'

'Not altogether sorry. And not only because the old cad

121

takes me to better hotels . . . but don't tell your father that, his head is quite swollen enough already.'

And she flashed me one of her sudden, radiant smiles, that made her for a moment young and beautiful.

That Christmas there was an exchange of presents between my mother and Nelson's wife Enid. The gift mother received was a boudoir cap. Much in vogue at the time to conceal the morning array of curlers, a boudoir cap was basically shaped like a shower cap but with a frill. This one was an elaborate confection with panels of silk and lace with a ribbon to draw it in to fit the head, like something worn in a nursery rhyme, but the frill drooped so that only the lower half of my mother's eyes could be seen. The effect was killing. We persuaded her once to put on her boudoir cap when she was wearing her sacking apron to hearth-stone the step, and we rolled about nearly dying of it. When she looked at herself in the glass she was overcome too, and all four of us streamed with tears of mirth.

After this a Christmas card or two was exchanged between mother and Nelson ('and Enid') but then the friendship seemed to lapse. As so often, a longer silence followed the reunion than had preceded it.

According to my mother, as a girl she had had many admirers. She had known a family called de la Mare and had been pursued to the mistletoe by one of the sons who was called Bert. There had been another son called Walter. As my interests widened, I asked her once what Walter had been like.

'Walter? Can't say he made much impression . . . oh, yes, I do remember once at supper at the Bedbrooks, he chased one of the girls round the table with the bread knife. He was upset about something or other, I forget what it was.'

'Did he show you any of his poetry?'

'Poetry? Did he write poetry? I don't remember.'

Perhaps if she had been the one who had been chased round the supper-table with a bread knife she might have called to mind that Walter de la Mare also wrote poetry from time to time.

Not long after my return home from my exile at Sher-brooke, I came into the kitchen where my father was cleaning his shoes ('no woman ever cleans shoes properly') and my mother was knocking up a cake. They were talking about a wedding. My mother, noticing me listening, looked up and said:

'Did Ada tell you about this?'

'Yes, she told me,' I replied in all good faith. But as they talked on it seemed it was another wedding altogether they were talking about.

'And a Thames Valley divorcée, into the bargain,' my father remarked.

'It'll have to be a register office. The Pater won't like that.'

'And three children. The eldest boy's sixteen.'

'He'll soon be off. Boys of that age don't take kindly to stepfathers.'

'What are you talking about?' I interrupted. 'I thought it was Aunt Ada's wedding you were talking about.'

'Ada's wedding!'

'Yes, one day I found her crying to herself and she said Val Atkins wanted her to marry him and go out to Russia with him, but after all she doesn't *have* to marry him so why should she cry about it?'

My mother looked thoughtful.

'Poor old Ada. It wasn't Val she was crying about, she'll never marry him anyway. She must have been crying because Jack is getting married. She will miss him so much.'

'Nothing to cry about,' said my father sensibly. 'He'll only be at Richmond. She'll see more of him there than she has for years.'

'Not Ada. It's all or nothing with her, always was. She monopolises people. Painfully loyal but has to gobble her loved ones up, always been the same.'

My father chuckled.

'Now we know why old Jack's home leaves were so few and far between. Half the time when his anxious family were thinking of him answering the call of duty in the mud of Flanders, there he was cosily tucked up in . . .'

'Will!'

'I wonder how long he's known her.'

'Years, it seems. They knew each other before the war and she got her divorce when the youngest boy was three and he's seven now.'

'Was Jack . . . ?'

'No, he wasn't. It was cruelty and desertion.'

'He told you all this when he took you out to lunch?'

'He seemed to want to talk about it. Said he couldn't get near Ada, she kept bursting into tears and locking herself in the bathroom. He was very upset about how she's taking it.'

'What I can't understand is why he left it so long.'

'The war, I suppose.'

'All the more reason for getting married. At worst she'd have had a war widow's pension.'

'She's thirty-six and very pretty.'

'Thames Valley divorcées are always pretty. They need to be. Does she breed dogs? They often do. It's a sort of cover.'

'As a matter of fact she does have two Airedales, a dog and a bitch called Major and Mynah. Jack mentioned them.'

'That explains it, Jack's marrying her for her dogs. It's a case of *couvrez-vous Monsieur*. How are your parents taking it?'

'The Mater doesn't care. Pater hasn't said anything to my knowledge but I don't suppose he's jumping for joy.'

'Never will say anything either, I bet. Just sit there breathing out frozen vapour for ever. Horrible old spoilsport. But, good for Jack! Never thought he had it in him. Quite the dark horse. When's the wedding?'

'As soon as they can arrange it, in a month or so. He asked me to be there, I don't suppose any other member of the family will go. They'll see to it that the car won't be available that day to take the Mater, or they might lock her in the linen press—I've known that happen, when she was having the change of life and being more outspoken than usual—if visitors were coming that they wanted to impress, they'd lock her in the linen press.'

'Didn't you let her out again?' I asked my mother.

'I couldn't. Ethel had the key.'

'You could have bashed her. You are stronger than her.'

My mother let this pass. I guessed then that she had helped to push her angry mother into the linen press and lock her in; she had been party to this act of *lèse-mère*.

I wondered how it would be if I managed to push my own mother into the linen cupboard when she got on my nerves but I saw at once it would not work. A mere airing cupboard with shelves would not accommodate a redundant mother. By the time my mother was old enough to have the change of life perhaps we should have moved into a bigger house with a walk-in linen press.

Soon after this my brother fell off his bike. It was an ignominious fall. He fell off an all but stationary bike. During my absence he had taken up with a desirable fifteen-year-old from the other side of the Common. Her name was Winnie. Now the two of them had cycled together to Richmond Park. At some stage they had alighted from their bikes and were walking. My brother did the chivalrous thing and pushed both bikes. This was somewhat tedious so, being something of a cycling virtuoso, he remounted his own machine and proceeded along beside her at walking pace, wheeling her bike by one hand beside his. It was a minor case of *La Belle Dame Sans Merci*. He nothing else saw all day long. He could not take his eyes off the girl. She sauntered along. He rode at walking pace and wheeled the second bike and looked at her as she walked beside him. The wheels of the two bikes converged, clashed, locked, and my brother was thrown to the ground. He had a bunch of keys in his trousers pocket and on them he fell in a muddle of pedals and handlebars.

How he laughed off this incident at the time will never be known. He arrived home and entered into a hushed colloquy with my mother. They went into the bathroom and shut the door. The bunch of keys on their ring had consisted of a Yale key and another house key, a locker key and a railway key for opening locked carriage doors, and the key of the drawer where he kept things he did not want me to know about. All these keys in a bunch he fell on in Richmond Park.

'Any blood?' I shouted through the bathroom door. My brother had never been a rough, scrambling boy. Unlike mine, his knees had never been a mass of scabs. A fiction had grown up between us that as he had never even had a nose-bleed, the fluid that ran in his veins and nourished that giant brain was not red blood at all but the sort of colourless ichor that lubricates the insides of snails.

'Bleeding at last?' I jeered. My mother opened the door

125

an inch and told me to go away. She was in the condition known to readers of *Woman's World* as 'white to the lips'.

'The poor boy has hurt his *thigh*,' she said, in heavy italics, as if a thigh was something special. There had been none of this note of high tragedy when I had recently sat on a drawing-pin. It had simply been pulled out of my thigh with no more ceremony than if I had been a noticeboard.

It was plain that he had been showing off to Winnie about the way he was in perfect control of both bikes though scarcely moving. But I could have told him that you can't expect to ride one bike while wheeling another at point one miles per hour and keep your eyes on a girl at the same time, without risk of falling off on to your bunch of keys and damage to your thigh, however protectively italicised.

In spite of his grievous bodily harm my brother refused to call on the healing skills of Dr Biggs. My father, with some ribaldry, agreed that in a case like his the condition of the bowels was immaterial and neither the brown nor the red medicine was likely to avail. Only time would tell. However it was not long before Dr Biggs's brougham was again drawn up outside our front gate.

After asking what seemed to be the trouble, Dr Biggs asked how the bow-els were. My mother reassured him about my bowels and said that an itchy rash on the back of my neck seemed to be (and indeed was) the trouble. She lifted my heavy mane of hair for him to inspect the rash. Some business followed while he changed spectacles, then he said,

'Ah . . . a firm diagnosis is not possible at this juncture. We must wait and see how the condition develops. Meanwhile, bed rest would be advisable, with a light diet and, of course, isolation from other children. I will send round some medicine this evening. And keep the bow-els open till my next visit.'

(What, all the time?) Feeling perfectly well, though itchy, I was bundled away to my bedroom and told to undress and get into bed.

Usually I enjoyed a few days in bed, as so often happened in the winter when the wheeze was on me. But then, though I pretended to be iller than I was to prolong my absence from school, I was genuinely a little ill, with a thick

126

chest and a slight fever. Now I did not feel ill at all and the bedclothes made my itching neck itch worse. I stuck it for two days, then defied doctor's orders, dressed and came downstairs.

I sat at the dining room table, scratching and reading. The pendant gas fitting with its red silk shade cast its light onto my book. Absorbed in the story, I hardly noticed my mother come up behind me, part the hair over my neck and examine the rash.

'My God, child! You're alive!'

This terrible exclamation shocked me into full consciousness and understanding of its revolting meaning. I was alive with crawling head-lice, teeming with hatching nits. I was a pariah child, a leper.

I burst into tears.

Having a dirty head was a disgrace. Children from clean homes were not supposed to have dirty heads. Time the great leveller had not yet ushered in the era of periodic lousy heads for all children, from clean and dirty homes alike, and their instant redemption by chemical pesticide. De-lousing then was a lengthy process of washing in quassia chips (whatever quassia chips may have been chipped off) then combing through every strand of hair with a fine tooth comb to draw the presumed dead lice down to the end of the hair, then dousing the head in paraffin . . . more washing, combing, paraffining. My hair was as thick as a sheepdog's and long enough to sit on. The process was a misery. I wonder now my mother did not cut my infested tresses short to the head and so lighten her labours, but I suppose she was either proud of it or too ashamed. Out of half an ear all my childhood I heard people going on about my splendid head of hair, but I hated it. It was a cause of pain and now of shame—misery.

I went about smelling like an oil lamp. The paraffin treatment, however, imparted to my hair a spectacular brassy gloss which was much admired. Its source was not revealed.

It was to be expected that the reputation of Dr Biggs as a medical wizard was not enhanced, in the eyes of my father, by this episode. But my mother was active as ever in his defence. Dr Biggs was a very able doctor.

'He brought both the children into the world.'

'And is quite likely to see them out of it again if they are unlucky enough to pick up spotted fever—you bet he'd prescribe a good wash in quassia chips and conscientious toothcombing.'

'Perhaps his sight is not as good as it was,' she suggested, trawling for excuses.

'Then he should get his specs changed or retire. Does he think it's not sound medical practice to diagnose head-lice before you can see the whites of their eyes? Child's head must have been squirming like an over-ripe Gorgonzola.'

'It was,' agreed my mother ruefully.

I knew what an over-ripe Gorgonzola looked like. We had a microscope. It occurred to me to wonder why my mother had not spotted my teeming head before ever Dr Biggs had been called in. It dawned on me that it was not Dr Biggs that my mother was defending. She was defending herself. My capable mother had missed a trick. Her shame at my infestation had not been because of what the neighbours would think; she had never given a toss for the neighbours. Her shame was at herself that she had not spotted what the conscientious mother she deemed herself to be, should have spotted. Like her imperious and disdainful father, my mother had a sin of pride.

'It was mostly my neck that itched,' I ventured, trying to make it better for her. After all, we had been in it together over many shameful days, suffering as every louse was drawn down its yard of hair to the bitter end. She flashed me a grateful look.

'Your hair looks simply lovely now, darling,' she said.

This was the second compliment my mother had paid me. The first had been when I was five years old, blowing experimentally on my mouth-organ. Then she had said:

'I must say you don't make the atrocious noises on a mouth-organ that most children do. You pick out quite musical little phrases, almost a pleasure to listen to.'

From my mother, a compliment every five years was not bad going.

The source of the infestation was traced to Annie, our rough diamond from Battersea. She was released to better herself but instead married a young man who was willing to make an honest woman of her.

7

It must have been getting on for the summer after the Armistice that sugar came off the ration. Marion Morris and I went to the grocer's and bought a quarter pound of pieces sugar in a blue bag. This was a soft brown sugar like sand with a taste we just knew but had never had enough of.

We did not touch the sugar till we reached the field. This was a planned celebration. We climbed the big old pear tree that yielded hard, sharp, uneatable pears—a perry pear tree, I suspect—and settled on our special branches. Mine had another strong branch running parallel a little in front and above it, like a narrow table. There was a small hollow at the right-hand side which I thought of as an inkwell. Marion had a slightly inferior but still esteemed perch within reach of mine.

We opened the blue bag carefully. We each shook a helping into a palm and licked it off. The flavour was unspeakably delicious. We took a second helping, which we chewed over and gulped. Then the same again. And more. Till it was all gone. A wonderful feeling crept over me and evidently over Marion too, for we began to giggle so much we had to get down from the tree. There we lay on the ground, rolling about, shrieking with laughter. Yet there was no joke in sight. Nobody had said anything funny, yet we had to roll about and laugh and shriek.

There is no doubt about it. We were drunk, plain intoxicated with the unaccustomed charge of sugar into the blood. It was a great sensation, full of bliss with no hangover to follow. Later shots of alcohol could never touch that first taste of intoxication at ten years old. It could never be repeated.

One day I went to Marion's house to call for her. It was some time before the door was answered. Cathie came to

129

the door and said in an abrupt way that was not like her that Marion could not come out today. She shut the door at once. Screams were coming from upstairs. It was Mrs Morris carrying on in her mad way again. I hoped it was not Marion she was screaming at. It was high time Mrs Morris got shut up in the linen cupboard to cool off. It would be worth taking out the shelves if necessary. The sheets and towels could be neatly stacked under a tablecloth on a spare bed, quite easy to get at, and the house would be much quieter. Mrs Morris could be let out from time to time to go to the lavatory. If they followed this procedure whenever Mrs Morris started screaming, life would be better for them. Unfortunately I felt I could not make this useful suggestion to Marion. Except for that early lament about how her mother had burnt her Bulldog printing set, she never spoke of her mother at all. Come to think of it, if I had a mother like that I would never speak of mine.

Cathie's young man was home from the war and they were going to be married. They were happy about that but she was distressed because in the last weeks of the war he had been hit in the arm by shrapnel and would probably always have a rigid elbow.

My father had seen her at the station and they had walked across the Common together.

'Cathie was upset about his arm. Luckily he has a safe office job to come back to but he was such a keen cricketer and that is over for him now. She kept saying, what is the purpose of war?'

Grown-up people were always asking what was the purpose of war. Any child could have told them. The purpose of war was to kill as many of the enemy as possible so that you could take whatever they had that you wanted. It was so obvious. Yet grown-ups were always asking each other what war was for. They should know by now.

'She was talking about you,' my father said to me. My mother was not present. 'She seems so fond of you. She said that since Marion had got to know you she had been a different child, so much brighter and livelier, and rosier, too. It was lovely, she said, to see Marion with her hair untidy and getting into mischief like other children. She had been rather a sad little girl till you came along.'

130

I was astounded. Accustomed as I was to being considered a bad influence, here was someone who was next thing to a parent being actually pleased at seeing the child of the family led into mischief. I wondered if it had reached her ears that her next-door neighbours had come back from a holiday to find their back door keyhole glued up. Marion and I had been feeding their kitten, which we decided they had neglectfully abandoned during their absence, so we had arranged reprisals. Could Cathie be approving of this sort of thing? If it made Marion rosier and happier, apparently yes. That must be why Cathie's eyes always dwelt upon me so kindly, as if she liked me.

At this time Marion and I were engaged in academic research. We were investigating the origins of the species. Though we had an inkling, admittedly sketchy, of how babies got out, we were unable to discover how they got in. Unlike the children I have read about since, we suffered the terrible disadvantage of never having been talked dirty to. Marion had always been under the wing of her big sisters, and as for the small boys who had been my companions, they had been pure in word and deed, if you do not count peeing competitions. In fact they had never talked about anything except to boast to one another about how good they were at things they were bad at.

Years later my mother was to tell me that when she had asked me, at the age of five, whether I knew where babies came from and I had said yes, she had considered further information on the subject superfluous. I am satisfied that she invented this conversation. The fact is that she, like most parents, had found the details of human reproduction, recounted in cold blood, so improbable and so plain ridiculous that she had squirmed away in embarrassment from a description of those ludicrous activities in which she must have engaged.

Marion and I were thus thrown upon our own resources. We decided to consult the article on Reproduction in the *Encyclopaedia Britannica*, of which we had a set in the revolving bookcase in the dining room. It was an old edition, the ninth, which had been thrown out of my grandfather's library, to land, years before my birth, in our house. Some of the essays had been written by people like Lord

Macaulay who, even in 1919, had been dead long enough to become part of history. The light of antiquity lay also upon the science sections of the venerable encyclopaedia. It is doubtful whether anaesthetics were in common use when these were printed. The article on Reproduction was about as intelligible to Marion and myself as the Rosetta Stone.

The lack of information was doubly galling. Not only had I hoped that these arduous studies would explain clearly how babies got in, but I had hoped to précis the information for use in the personal encyclopaedia for which I was beginning to gather material and expected soon to throw together. The old Ency Brit's tortuous investigations into the sexual mores of glutinous lower animals baffled me.

'There's not much there you can pick out to put in your encyclopaedia when you write about reproduction,' Marion remarked.

'I shall have to keep it short. I shall say something like "Birds reproduce by hatching eggs. The higher animals do it in ways appropriate to their species."'

'That sounds very good. Shall we look again at the article on Medical Juriprurience?'

'You mean Medical Jurisprudence. Yes, all right. But it will only be that old stuff about contusions and punctured wounds and impacts on the base of the skull.'

'There is that bit on poisons,' she said hopefully.

'Babies getting in has something to do with people being married. How could poison come into that?'

We had no idea.

* * *

By now I had parted company with Queen's College and attended, as a place of last resort, the school run by Mrs Stroud in the house opposite ours. It goes without saying that I bore with me from Queen's College, and still wore, the brown and blue gym outfit I had not long enjoyed, having finally grown out of the navy and reseda green tunic and blouse of my previous school. But now I was ten and so immunised against public opinion that I felt able to wear my noticeably wrong gym colours almost with panache, to the

132

point that when at last I grew into my new (navy and scarlet) outfit I hardly noticed the change.

Not that Mrs Stroud was a woman to bother about a little thing like school colours. The school swirled with the diversity of the human genetic pool. This was a private house. The ground floor was occupied by Mr and Mrs Stroud and the small daughter who had replaced that Molly who had died of black measles when we were both six. The pupils, of all ages and sizes, mostly girls but including a sprinkling of tiny boys, were packed into the first floor and the attics, that ran from front to back of the house. The place was crammed. A few small children were given lessons in the school kitchen, also on the first floor, where dinner was served to a dozen or so of girls who stayed in school for the meal. A cheerful charwoman called Mrs Wingrove dished out the food. For some reason I ate there once and remember hot boiled potatoes and cold beetroot. There was no room to move. The only game possible in the eleven o'clock break, which perforce had to be spent in the classroom, was Sardines. Nobody gave a thought to the fire risk. The undertaker's was conveniently placed next door.

The top class was in the main front room, what would now be known in estate agency terms as the master bedroom. Every square foot was packed with desks in rows, desks of all shapes and sizes, ranging from large comfortable desks to the left of the front row down to small cramped joined-up desks intended for young children, to the right of the back row. Those at the top of the class occupied the left front desks, the dunces the back right-hand ones, near the door. In case of fire the dunces might perhaps escape, the giant brains up front would certainly perish.

In this top class I was on my first day installed, without benefit of examination. We were told to sit anywhere we liked, a test of ability would soon sort us out into our proper places for the week. A smiling Mrs Stroud entered, looking as if she really enjoyed the new term beginning, and everybody beamed back at her, for she was greatly loved. She unfolded the *Daily Mail* and began dictation from the leader.

The system of priority—that is whether one got to sit at a

133

good desk in the front row or at a thigh-nipper at the back—depended entirely upon one's ability to spell correctly. The leading article in the *Daily Mail* was read out at dictation speed. The next day the corrected exercise books were returned, marked, and according to the number of spelling mistakes recorded, so the order of desk precedence was established for the coming week.

Since I happened to be good at spelling (though at nothing else) I never had to shift lower than the top three front left-hand desks during my year or so at Mrs Stroud's school. The other two top contestants were also about ten or eleven. It was an absurdity that the first three rather splendid front desks, with their ample writing area and padded seating, should be lolled in by us youthful lightweights while the abhorred four-seaters in the back row were stuffed to capacity by fat and nubile seventeen-year-olds who could barely spell their own names. Their fleshy tophampers and hindquarters overflowed on to the cramped writing surfaces of their tiny desks and pressed against the iron framework of their benched seating like a bulging trawl of codfish. They squashed giggling against one another's overheating flanks.

The greatest good humour prevailed. The fat older girls, who must have spent years failing to spell 'receive' and 'conspicuous', bore no resentment at all against the juvenile prodigies in the front row who took 'recidivists' in their stride. One of the big girls lived over a sweet shop. In the press of eleven o'clock break, from her cattle-crush in the back row, she would give out lumps of French almond rock to be passed hand over hand like crowd casualties for us to enjoy as we queened it at our comfortable desks in front.

I cannot call to mind any lessons that could be called lessons at Mrs Stroud's school. Sometimes, after the *Daily Mail* dictation, she would read to us from a small book of etiquette, with useful hints on how to start a letter when writing to a bishop and how it was not nice to blow the nose too obviously but at all times it was better to blow than to pick the nose (particularly when writing to a bishop). Mrs Stroud had been to Italy and was cultured. When we did well she would exclaim '*Eccelente! Eccelente!*'. She gave piano lessons in her own, downstairs, part of the house.

I never attended any lessons that were not conducted personally by Mrs Stroud, though in the heavily populated hinterland of the school there were other classes, less advanced than ours. In view of the educational standards of my own class it is hard to imagine even deeper abysses of ignorance, but such classes, lower than mine, did exist and one of them was conducted by Miss Snead.

Miss Snead was the sort of person you have to look at when they pass you out of doors. She would be in her late forties, tall, thin and rectangular. Her face was a yellowish brown, with dark eyes and black hair above a high forehead. Seen from the front she appeared to be a sketchily articulated series of oblongs, some longer and thinner than others, the head almost square. But these rectangles were not in parallel with one another, nor did they move to the same rhythm.

There was a touch of wryneck about Miss Snead—the head a little tilted to one side, the face on yet another plane, the lower part pushed forward, the lips stretched in a contained smile over uncountable false teeth. She was like a cluster of metal mirrors set at different angles, jangling together as they flashed uneasy light into the eyes of strangers. She could have scared crows.

We three or four at the top of the class, who knew what a verb was, dubbed this pushing forward of the lower face over a tight smile, sneading. *I snead, thou sneadest*. Our young elastic faces became adept in the skill of sneading. Passing Miss Snead on her way to or from school, we would slightly snead at her by way of greeting.

Miss Snead was a few days absent from her class at school. A rumour began to circulate. Somebody's parent had been overheard to say that Miss Snead had been found wandering the Common with nothing on. She had been taken care of.

This rumour was neither confirmed nor denied. But Miss Snead was never seen again by any of her pupils.

We did wonder whether our sneading at her could possibly have urged her to throw off her clothes and take to the Common, but after all she had been sneading at us for ages and we were all right: so far.

* * *

Mr Stroud, the optician, kindly brought back from his shop some dozens of smoked-glass lenses. These were for us to look through at a dramatic eclipse of the sun expected shortly. Each of us was handed one lens: a treasure. It was not framed. It could either be held up to one eye, the other eye being shut, or daringly held screwed in by will-power, like a monocle.

We were packed into the small front garden as tightly as folded sheep, the tallest girls the hindmost. It was morning, with the sun more or less opposite, above my own house across the road. At the appointed hour we were told to hoist lenses and look at the sun. A shaving began to be cut off it. The cut bit deeper into the body of the sun. The air grew somewhat darker. Might this be how the world would end?

Beside me there was a tinkle and a kind of gasp. A precious lens had been dropped and had broken. It had been dropped by the tall pale thirteen-year-old at my side—Edna, a girl it was always being hinted about that everybody should be nice to, something to do with her mother that was never explained. In the increasingly un-natural light of the eaten-up sun I could see tears shine on the edge of her eyelids. I slipped her my lens and continued to look at the eclipse with naked eyes. There seemed to be a few small black dots on the uneaten part of the sun. When later in the year a disturbance in the weather was attributed to some newly discovered sunspots, I was convinced that I had been the first to discover them. Later still I learned that to look at the sun with the naked eye can be a dangerous threat to the eyesight; yet cats do it all the time.

On account of the rumour, never explained, that Edna needed extra kindness because of her mother, she came back to tea with me once or twice. Everybody said: 'Poor Edna.' Her mother looked hot all the time and made me feel hot too. Her name was Mrs Cratchett, spoken of by my father as Old Mother Scratchead. She was not particularly fat but seemed so because her clothes were too tight. She always wore a costume (known now as a suit) of thick black woollen stuff that looked hot. She wore a black hat of thick felt. Perhaps she was in mourning but if so the mourning had been going on an unusually long time. There seemed to be no Mr Cratchett. Mrs Cratchett had a shiny red face and

136

small brown eyes like goats' pellets but less restful. She seemed about to explode with anger just contained. She had a smell all her own. It was possible to unravel this into three common smells which, plaited together, were unique Mrs Cratchett. The first smell was of thick black clothes that had been dyed black a long time ago and had not been back to be cleaned since they were dyed. The second smell was a faint echo of pub sawdust as one passed the door, lightly tinctured with smell number three which reminded me of the spirit-lamp under the tea-kettle at five o'clock tea in my grandparents' house, but was not so nice. These three smells, made one, accompanied Mrs Cratchett on her over-heated plod through life.

Edna came to tea once or twice but was too sad and lank and dull to be asked back again, even for kindness; particularly as nobody ever told me what I was being kind about.

* * *

The beginning of the end of the world was ushered in by a flicker of lightning and a rumble of thunder like no other thunder I had heard. For this was the thunder I had been steeling myself for months to expect, the sound of the approach of the last night of the world.

I was out on our road in the dark. Nobody else was about. There were lights in the houses still but soon these would be put out by the towering tidal wave coming up from the south which would overwhelm them. People and houses and trees would be tumbled together over and over, like pebbles in the backwash of a wave.

This form of extinction was slightly to be preferred to the incineration by subterranean fires which was to follow.

I had come from a small tea party to celebrate the eleventh birthday of one of the girls from school. It was December 11th, the date I had been dreading. At about six o'clock we were turned out. I had a quarter mile to walk to my own house. Then had come the lightning flash and the clap of thunder heralding the end of everything. Evidently I was to perish alone. Not that it mattered. We all had to go.

137

When there was no hope it was each man to his own fate. Being alone, I should not have to pretend to be brave. I could scream if necessary.

It was a few months since I had spotted in the newspaper an inconspicuous item about some soothsayer who had prophesied that the world would come to an end on December 11th. When I mentioned this prophecy to my family they showed little interest. People were always prophesying the end of the world, my mother had said, but they had never got it right yet.

'Of that day and hour knoweth no man,' she quoted. So I said no more about it. Nevertheless, though December 11th was still a fair way off, the date implanted itself in my mind like some miniaturised time bomb, which by the end of November was ticking audibly.

I did not mention my fears to Marion. A mad mother was quite enough, without having to accommodate the end of the world as well.

The overwhelming tidal wave became extremely vivid. Its toppling crest towered over our house. The air began to thrum with the driven spume of it.

Yet there was nothing to be done. It could not be spoken of. It must simply be endured. I called to mind my mother's description of a tooth being pulled . . . 'a terrible pain that was over as soon as felt'. Would the end of the world be like that for me? And for my family? Marion? Umski?

When I had been asked to Dorothy's birthday tea party on December 11th I did not want to go. I did not want to go out anywhere that evening, assuming that the world had not ended earlier in the day. But I could not think of a good enough excuse, nor could I call upon my mother to supply me with one for she was not a party to my fears.

Consequently here I was alone out of doors on the last night of the world, with the end of the world beginning with a flicker of lightning and a rumble of indescribable thunder.

I found I was hurrying. I had not intended to hurry. My intention had been to meet my fate with calmness and dignity, like Charles the First, but the fact was I was running like hell. I hauled up my (recently acquired) latch key from its cord round ny neck and crammed it into the keyhole of our front door. I went in. I threw off my outdoor clothing and entered the dining room.

All was calm. All was bright. Under the light of the red silk-shaded gas fitting my mother sat at the table darning socks, with Nettie Hewland's worn little workbasket beside her. In the armchair sprawled my father in Jaeger cardigan and felt bootees, smoking and reading the evening paper.

My mother looked up.

'I thought I heard thunder,' she said, 'but you seem to have escaped it . . . How was the tea-party?'

'What tea-party?'

She looked at me suspiciously.

'I hope you've been to Dorothy's to tea and haven't been running about in the dark with Percy, ringing doorbells?'

Ringing doorbells indeed! As if that was a proper way to spend one's last hours.

'Of course I went to Dorothy's.'

'Well, you did seem to be looking for excuses not to go . . . How was it?'

'Just the usual tea-party. Too much icing on the cake.'

'You had better go up to bed early tonight. You look over-excited. You can read in bed if you like but nothing hair-raising, I don't want you waking us up with one of your nightmares.'

'I don't feel like a nightmare tonight.'

And somehow this had become true. The panic was over. The world was not going to end after all. We had come near to it but at the last moment had sheered off. Somewhere another world was ending, ours not yet. The overwhelming wave was gathering but not for us.

The ordinariness of the quiet scene settled me. After all, the warmest, brightest fortnight of the year lay just ahead. No hard work would be expected of us at school in the last week or so of the term. Then there would be Christmas presents to wrap up and despatch, paper chains to make . . .

I thought about the Belgian refugee child all those years before, who could not make paper chains as they should be made. With the war over, if she had not fallen on the fire and died she could have been back in her own country by now, making paper chains in the peculiar Belgian style, all in the one colour. I had been glad to be rid of her at the time but now I saw it was a pity. She had been a sort of casualty of war.

On holiday once in the country we had walked through a churchyard, reading the inscriptions on the gravestones. On one I had read: *Remember the dead in your joy.*

It was a relief that the world had not come to an end but sad to think of the people who had been stopped short while the world was still going on, sad to think of the dead wounded soldiers left behind broken in their graves after the bugler had gone.

Perhaps before I went to sleep that night I would make up a prayer for the dead with some splendid words in it like *transcendental* or *marmoreal*; though it would be hard to do better than *remember the dead in your joy.*

* * *

Meanwhile Uncle Jack had married his Thames Valley divorcée and was living with her in her untidy, pretty little house in Richmond, embowered in its small flowery garden. My mother and father had attended the subdued register office wedding but no other member of the family had been present. They had retreated behind a deeply refrigerated decontamination area. Was this because he had married a Thames Valley divorcée?

'Nominally, yes,' my father replied, 'but the fact is, Ada would have been more upset if he had married a beautiful blameless virgin of twenty, and as for your grandfather, he would have begrudged Jack his lovely twenty-year-old, so really the divorce isn't the main thing, only makes an excuse to justify frigid behaviour that comes naturally.'

Thus I had acquired overnight a new aunt, tentatively known as Aunt Luke (for she had been enterprisingly christened Lucretia) and three ready-made cousins. These were Stephie, about my age, a very pretty girl, all blue and gold, a younger edition of her mother, and a seven-year-old angel-faced boy called Kim. There was also Oscar, a surly, burly, acned hulk of nearly seventeen, quite unlike the younger two. It was not long before he fulfilled my father's prophecy and made off to work his passage to Australia,

140

fortified by the contents of two piggy banks, three Post Office savings books, his stepfather's gold cigarette case and a couple of his mother's rings, of no great value but readily negotiable. It was confidently expected that he would do well in Australia.

Although there was no contact beyond the briefest formal meeting, just short of an open breach, between this new family and my mother's people, my mother herself put in some quick footwork to establish friendly relations with Aunt Luke, thereby stalemating Aunt Ada who found herself cut off with no news. Locking herself in the bathroom lost its meaning if there was no one to hammer on the door. Through certain intermediaries, some of them on the wrong side of the green baize door, my mother let it be known at Sherbrooke Lodge that Jack was very happy and she was seeing a lot of him and his new wife, who was charming.

Aunt Luke was not bad at all. Her house was comfortably mismanaged, smelling strongly of dog, with delicious bought-in delicatessen meals handed out at all hours. I spent a weekend there once. Uncle Jack must have been there, yet still the only memory I retain of him is of that slim soldier with sad eyes coming along the corridor towards me, ruffling my hair, passing on down the staircase. Aunt Luke never seemed to cook or do anything dull. She groomed her Airedales, picked flowers, took little snifters. Her two pretty children were lightweights, pickers and grazers, obviously not brought up on the Irish stew with dumplings, the blackcurrant pudding, which had built me up to be pounds heavier, inches taller and many points (Miss World Standard) less prizeworthy than eleven-year-old Stephie. I liked my new cousin well enough for a weekend or a holiday, but on a day-to-day basis she would be rather dull because she never seemed to wonder about anything or want to know why. She could not play chess but was fun when we ran about Richmond Park with the dogs.

After a while the resistance at Sherbrooke Lodge weakened somewhat. A stilted teatime visit or two from Jack's family followed, always one-way, to my grandparents. Neither grandparents nor aunts ever called in at the flowery little house in Richmond but to some degree the first affronted hostility was relaxed. There was even a Christmas when both families, my own and Uncle Jack's newly made one, were all bidden to spend the day at Sherbrooke Lodge, when a somewhat theatrical charade, of our being one big happy family, was put on. It did not take. The Christmas gathering was not in following years repeated. Evidently my grandfather decided that he was more at home with genuine grandchildren of the blood, however little loved, whose known faults he could enjoy criticising.

So, after a year or two, Uncle Jack and his acquired family seemed to be fading gently out of sight. We sometimes had news of them through a hairdresser friend of Aunt Luke's in Richmond, where my mother had taken to going to have her hair done and where she occasionally took me, too, to have the ends of mine singed. While it was understood that we were on perfectly friendly cousinly terms with Uncle Jack's ready-made family, it no longer happened that we met.

* * *

My father had been friendly with an old gentleman called Mr Winsford. I do not remember him but at some time he must have met my brother and me because sometimes he would send us presents of books, and when he died he left us his microscope.

He would have been something of a scientific dilettante —my father spoke of his collection of birds' eggs and butterflies, all labelled and filed away in their cabinets. Microscopic sections of all sorts of plants and insects were preserved between slides and these we inherited when Mr Winsford died.

He had appointed as executor my father who, when the house was being cleared out, brought home various bits and pieces, among them a glass tank framed in iron which became my aquarium, a modest affair of goldfish, tadpoles in season and water snails. It stood outside on the by-the-lilac in all weathers and its denizens survived for years, though the ice had to be broken over them in hard weather to let in oxygen. Breaking the ice was my job, faithfully performed.

Among the curiosities that came our way at this time were about half a dozen very large sea shells. They were never identified so I do not know their name, though I suppose they were a kind of gastropod from tropical shores. They were superb conches, beautiful spiral shells as big as a baby's head, their colour a lustrous mother-of-pearl. To me they were glorious objects. I set them out at intervals on the wide window-sill in the dining room and would admire them at meal times. They were not, however, in tune with the interior-decorative perceptions of the time—this was 1920 with its tendency towards stark lines and black and orange décor. Shells were out, they were Victorian. My mother, naturally, had no inhibitions of the kind; she was no slave of fashion, and if a child enjoyed an unmodish display of huge seashells in the dining room, why not? There was no harm in it. Only recently I had been invited to choose new wallpaper in my bedroom and had not been restrained in my choice of enormous red roses, much the size of the shells, climbing a trellis. This would have been considered in awful taste among people who knew what was what, but I did not know what was what and my mother did not care.

In the changing light towards the end of a summer day my eyes would rest on the prodigious nacreous shells and be satisfied. They were supremely beautiful and the sea sang in them. I felt they were my shells.

The microscope was kept permanently set up ready for use on a table by the French windows in the drawing room—probably another asethetic *faux pas*, come to think of it. Here we would repair to examine in detail any object that took our fancy—a nail paring, fallen petal or morsel of food from a plate, such as a sugar crystal or a crumb of cheese.

Cheese then was not as cheese now is. It came in wedges, cut from a round. The milk it was made from had not been pasteurised. It was allowed to ripen. It was not uniform from cheese to cheese. Individual processes of fermentation took place in it and gave it flavour; sometimes too much flavour.

143

My brother liked very strong cheese. Such cheese, near the middle, if steadily scrutinised by the excellent sight of youthful eyes, would sometimes appear to move among its own inwardness. A subliminal, scarcely perceptible turbulence could be seen to be at work within the crumbly middlemost structures of the stuff. If a particle of this slightly seething substance was placed under the microscope it came up revealed as a compact mass of living, squirming cheese mites. Curiosity satisfied, my brother would return to the dinner-table and finish off the rest of the living heap quietly heaving to itself on his plate.

My love-affair with the microscope did not last for ever. It received a jolt after which I brought to it only such occasional offerings as seemed scientifically necessary, instead of every fly-blow or smidgen of scurf that caught my eye. Messing about in the field where cuckoo-spit was everywhere on the seeding grasses, I separated one of these blobs of foam to get at the grub which always nestled in the heart of it. I hurried home, in at the French windows with my booty, which I smeared off carefully on to a glass slide and set in place under the eye of the microscope. It was a brilliantly sunny day and I had some difficulty getting the thing into focus—rainbow colours shot in sideways. I twiddled the knurled knob. Suddenly, there it was, in full focus, a pallid, damp, magnified mite of a thing with legs that . . . but there was no time to look at it—even as I watched the creature changed colour, browned, shrivelled and was consumed, as if under a grill. It had burned to death under my eyes, incinerated by a deadly beam of sunlight that in all innocence, twiddling away to get it into view, I had focused upon it. I had operated a death ray and in the same instant had been shown what went on at the receiving end. I was deeply shocked and never looked again through the microscope on a sunny day.

But having a microscope of our own, something not in the gift and beyond the power of parents, was a status symbol. None of the children I knew had a microscope at home, let alone boxes and boxes of exotic slides. The microscope was an asset, something to be shown to Thackthwaite when he came to tea.

My precocious brother was now sixteen. As packed with

brains as hormones, he had been for some time in the Eighth, the top form at St Paul's. He often spoke of a friend he had there, another brainy boy who sounded much more interesting than my brother. This boy was Thackthwaite.

Henry Hopkinson Augustus Thackthwaite was his full name. Its robust Englishness was, however, deceptive. For many generations past—so the tale went—the males of the Thackthwaite family, then living in Dover, had crossed the Channel and plundered France for their brides. They had a settled preference for French women. Having secured the bride of his choice the male Thackthwaite would return with her to England where he would beget upon her sons who, in their turn, would revert to France for their mates. There is no record of how these French girls settled down in this foreign land and one can only guess at their struggles to pronounce their own name: Meesees Sacksweat. Their sons, of course, grew up to be perfectly bilingual, with useful French connections, well equipped when their time came for the ritual marital swoop across the Channel.

My brother assumed that in due course Henry Hopkinson Augustus would seek a bride in France. But now he was coming to tea with us.

It was true then and perhaps is still, that boys and girls who went to the great public day schools in London—Westminster, St Paul's, Merchant Taylors and so on—were like as not to make friends who lived at widely separated addresses. In the holidays, hour-long tracts of suburbia might stretch between buddy and buddy. Spontaneity was out and meetings had to be arranged.

My brother set it up that Thackthwaite was to cross London to have tea with us and play tennis.

The timing was cunning: my parents were away. Several times a year they went for short holidays on their own, no doubt glad to be rid of us. One of the good grey widows who were to be found in those days, but who now have dyed their hair and gone skittish, was brought in to keep house and supervise whichever untrained maid was putting in time with us on her way to bettering herself. There could not be a better moment for introducing a sophisticated school friend, free from the embarrassment of shaming parents who could not be relied upon not to put a foot in

145

it by filling the house with lights boiling, or audibly wondering how toilet rolls could possibly be got through at such a rate. There had been a plague of fleas in the neighbourhood not long before, and my brother may have feared that our mother might refer to this degradation in the presence of his guest. It was best that the parents were safely out of the way.

As for our house, though it was far from stunning and not really a credit to us, it would just about do, my brother must have concluded.

Thackthwaite arrived. He was a stocky boy of sixteen with dark hair and swarthy, rather greasy skin with traces of spots past. His teeth were good. His face was puckery and toad-like, quite ugly really, but I liked it. They went off to play tennis at the local club and I tagged along too. Thackthwaite's flannels were very yellowed and rather shrunken-looking. This was surprising because my brother was a choosy dresser, who was most critical of the sort of laundering that left flannels yellow and felted and was dismissive of those who wore them; yet I was aware that he held Thackthwaite in high esteem. I meant to ask him about this later, but forgot. Naturally I was not asked to play. I ran about retrieving tennis balls. Then we walked back to tea.

On the way they talked about Freud and psychoanalysis. This was very advanced at the time. Not many people had even heard about Freud, let alone boys of sixteen. I asked them what psychoanalysis was, but they ignored me. I could not look it up because I did not know how it was spelt, never having seen a word beginning with 'psycho' in print, in newspapers or anywhere else. The present jostling crowd of psychopaths and their attendant psychotherapists had not then come out of the woods.

Tea was ready for us in the dining room. Thackthwaite sat opposite me, his back to the window. We talked and ate, and though it was enjoyable in a way, I felt that something was not quite right. The room seemed somehow impoverished. Thackthwaite said something and as I looked up from my plate at him and beyond him, suddenly I got it. But for a bowl of roses, the windowsill was bare.

'The shells have gone!' I exclaimed. 'Where have the shells gone?'

My brother said nothing. Thackthwaite looked up inquiringly. I explained that there had been six beautiful pearly shells there, each one as big as two fists, and they had gone. Where could they have gone?

My brother suggested that Mrs Restall, the temporary housekeeper, might have taken them away to clean them.

'But they were perfectly clean,' I protested, 'they were like pearls.'

'Their outsides, yes. But maybe their insides needed cleaning out. Like ears.'

I rushed out to the kitchen to confer with Mrs Restall. She knew nothing about it. She seemed to remember the shells were in place yesterday, when she was whisking round with a feather duster, but she wasn't sure. She had certainly no intentions of cleaning out their insides, she was not looking for work. Kitty might know something about it but she was out, it was her afternoon off. (Off to look for a better place, no doubt.) I rushed back to the dining room. The boys were just finishing their meal and talking about Einstein. I broke it up by inviting Thackthwaite to come and look at the microscope.

We went into the drawing room and looked at some head-scratchings under the microscope. The boys rootled through some boxes of slides but in no time at all were talking about polariscopes and refractive indices.

'Come and look at the aquarium,' I urged. We went out through the French windows. There it stood on the quarry tiles, lightly dappled with the shadow of the lilac leaves. I showed Thackthwaite my two water snails named by my father Nostalgie and Boue, and the very small frog, no bigger than a shilling, crouched on his raft of cork. The goldfish, I explained, were temporarily on holiday in the rainwater butt where I had recently transferred them for a deep dive while part of the water in their aquarium was being changed; but this had been done now and we could fish for them and put them back in their home again.

'Come over to the water butt,' I invited him. The water butt was beside the remnants of a rockery and received rainwater from the gutter of a garden shed. I offered Thackthwaite my small battered aluminium saucepan so that he could fish for a few. He was, after all, a guest. It was not as difficult to catch a goldfish as it sounds, for mostly they swam near the surface. Thackthwaite caught three and deposited them in the bucket of water provided, then politely gave the saucepan back to me. I caught the last two. I was leaning over the butt, peering in at some minute wriggly figure-of-eight worms, when something among the weathered stones of the old rockery beyond the butt caught my eye.

There, stacked closely together, lightly speckled with splashed mud from the last night's rain, were my shells.

I was delighted. 'But how on earth did they get there? Who could have put them there?'

I picked one up and showed it fondly to Thackthwaite.

'Isn't it beautiful? We think it is the shell of a gastropod.'

'A stomach-foot,' said Thackthwaite gravely. 'Yes it is very beautiful, it is rather marvellous, really.'

'Help me carry them back to the house,' I said. 'I must get this mud washed off them and then back on the window sill. I can't imagine what got into whoever moved them out here.'

I was aware of my brother looking at me very hatefully as Thackthwaite and I gathered the shells together and went into the house by the back door. My brother strode over to the aquarium and tipped the goldfish back in.

Later I said to my brother:

'You moved those shells, didn't you, you beast? Why?'

'Can't you see why? They are absolutely awful. Thackthwaite would have thought we were impossible people. I had to move them before he came. Then of course you had to go and mess it all up.'

'But Thackthwaite thought they were beautiful! He said so. He said it again when we were in the scullery, washing them. He liked them very much.'

My brother sighed.

'What is beautiful beside a water butt is not necessarily beautiful on one's dining room windowsill,' he explained, wearily.

No wonder he grew into a man of taste and away from me.

As for Thackthwaite, as far as I know I never saw him again. As far as I know.

Only now, as I write, I remember a summer afternoon early in the Second War. I was staying in a country house in Berkshire. There was a lovely old garden there, lost among fields. Stephen, the son of the house, arrived on a visit of a few minutes, just passing by, to pick up something from his room to take back to the airfield where he was in training with the RAF. He had with him two boy officers and an older one in his thirties. There was a great bank of lavender in the garden, spreading behind the airmen in their blue uniforms, like the beginning of space itself. The older officer and I caught each other's eye with a sort of mutual curiosity but did not speak; all four men were only there for a moment. The older one was stocky and rather swarthy with an ugly, agreeable toad-face. Then they were gone.

Within a year the son of that house, Stephen, aged twenty, was dead, shot out of the sky. What happened to his three companions, nameless to me, was not for me to know.

* * *

That was the only time Thackthwaite came to tea. There may never have been another likely occasion when my parents would have been safely out of sight and it is also possible that my brother calculated that my own inescapable presence was a grave social hazard in itself.

After Thackthwaite left school he qualified as a doctor at Guys hospital and then, increasingly remote and only by hearsay, was said to be in Vienna, studying under Freud. My brother lost sight of him. But long afterwards, when the Second War was over, we heard that during that war Thackthwaite had been a hero, parachuting into France to liaise with the Resistance. With his impeccable French and all those contacts in France he would have melted into the background perfectly, like a toad in a wood, a mud-speckled shell on a rockery.

In books on the history of that war I have sometimes seen his name in footnotes, with reference to his reports from those dangerous safe houses.

His name is in the archives but he is dead.

He died without a son to follow him, in the Star & Garter Home at Richmond.

As far as I know, I never saw him again. But I remember him. I remember him as a kind, rather ugly boy in yellowed tennis flannels, who had a toad face and thought my shells were beautiful, really rather marvellous.

*　*　*

It was at about that time that another boy of sixteen came into our lives and stayed there. We met him at Brattle Place, on what was to be my last visit there. He was on holiday with his mother. His name was Clifford. He had a father, a shadowy, even shady commercial traveller of Welsh origins who was rarely seen and was to melt away in a few years with the family bank account in an inner pocket. What he travelled in we never knew. It could have been a line in other people's cheque books. But his wife was on an entirely different plane of being.

She was a dedicated Fabian and looked the part, with her serious grey eyes, wide intellectual forehead and her air of a pained saint always looking for the good in people and not finding much. Such a woman is not likely to provide a good table and Mrs Jones, for that was her name, was no exception. I had early observed that people of idealistic left wing tendencies did not seem to enjoy food much, let alone provide it for others. They drank a great deal of tea and ate shop buns at their gatherings, and at home they were often lentil and bread-and-jam people.

It turned out that Clifford and his mother (and father too, when he was there) lived across the Common within easy walking distance of us. Mrs Jones taught in adult education. She was no cook, in an age of few convenience foods, and Clifford, in the holidays—he went to a Quaker boarding school—came close to being starved. They were not well off, he had no spare pocket money for pork pies and bars of chocolate.

On his return to London Clifford at once crossed the Common to see us. He smelled food. It could have been steak and kidney pudding. If it had been boiling lights or fish heads I do not suppose Clifford would have minded, it

150

was food. He was invited to eat. He ate. Clifford was hooked. He came back and he came again. He could no more stay away than a stray dog can stay away from an overturned dustbin.

Having come for the food, he had to learn to like us. It was only civil. He never approved of us but somehow he learned to like us. He came for the food and stayed for the company, conveniently long enough for the next meal. The rich succulent juices of our baked meats, the fruit pies, the ever-present crock of cream, tempted him sometimes from the true Fabian path where he had been trained to go and he began to laugh at the wrong jokes. He was hooked, corrupted by the steak-and-onions of an uncaring capitalism.

Half a head shorter than my brother, Clifford had inherited the thrifty Welsh gene that economises on necks. In feature he resembled his mother, though with a more hopeful expression and a more outdoor look. The light tan came from being so much in the open air, walking from his house to ours. He had a way of holding his head slightly back, lips parted, as he entered our front gate, something between glad-hailing mankind at large and sniffing the air for cooking smells.

Seeing him arrive, my parents at table would groan slightly and mutter that-boy-again. It was against my mother's instincts not to feed generously anyone in need of nourishment, yet her strong and lifelong prejudice against educationists made her boil inwardly at the thought of Mrs Jones, away forcing time-elapsed lessons on grown-ups (of all people) while her child had to knock on doors in search of a square meal. She could be perceived simmering as she laid another place for Clifford.

Clifford was an extremely well-read boy. He too knew about Freud. Wandering in and out of rooms and the garden, feeding yellow pansies to the tortoises, cutting photographs out of magazines to add to the material I was collecting for the encyclopaedia I was planning to write, I would hear Clifford explaining to my brother how necessary it was that a son should learn to loathe his mother. Once I overheard my brother pedantically remarking that the word *mother* derived from the same root as the word *meter*, that is, one who measured out the food. When I repeated this to my mother she snorted derisively, beating all the harder at the cake she was knocking up. My mother always spoke of knocking up a cake. She was a somewhat slapdash though tasty cook and sometimes her cakes did look knocked up compared with some other housewives' finished products. But Clifford was always ready to eat them.

* * *

Because Marion and I were now at different schools, though only half a mile apart, we did not often see each other except at weekends. At New Year she came to my house, and while I was showing her my Christmas presents she said:

'They're sending me to boarding school next term. To Eastbourne.'

This was a bombshell. Next term was almost next week.

'Why?'

'Well . . . Daddy said it was time I left Queen's College, I had learned nothing there. You know Midge left at Christmas? She's seventeen now and according to Daddy as ignorant as when she first went there. And . . . Mummy's not well, in fact she's worse . . . Daddy thinks boarding school would be the best place for me, now I'm thirteen . . .'

'Do you mind?'

'In a way. Not altogether. Now Cathie's gone, it's sometimes not very nice at home . . .'

This was an understood thing. Without Cathie, home life at the Morris's could have become less than stable. Marion went on, 'And you and I will see each other almost as much as now, in the holidays, anyway . . .'

The road where Marion lived had not had the funerals of soldiers going down it, day after day, year after year. She would not know that people who came to say goodbye did not come back. There was no need to tell her. Those who went away thinking they would come back went away happier.

'I'll write to you. Shall I give you my address?'

'Put it on your letter . . . As you're going to a new school you can have that pencil case you've always wanted, the one with all the lilac-coloured pencils. None of the pencils have been sharpened yet.'

'Oh, thank you!'

'Goodbye, then,' I said.

Not long after Marion went away to boarding school, Mrs Morris died in circumstances somehow mysterious but never explained. The distractingly pretty sister Midge married, at short notice, a young man she met at the tennis club. He worked in a bank and, almost at once after the marriage, was transferred to a Brighton branch.

The house the Morrises had lived in was put up for sale. Mr Morris went to live in a flat near Battersea Park. So the family was broken up.

For quite a long time after they had left it, whenever I passed their house, without thinking I would turn my head to look at it, but of course they were not there any more. Sometimes I would see Cathie at the station or on the Common. She lived on the other side of the Common now. Whenever she saw me she always gave me the warm look that people give you when they are thanking you for something that has really pleased them.

The time with Marion was over. That small flawless friendship stretched itself, yawned, curled itself up and fell quietly asleep. Without pain it died in its sleep to be drifted over and over with many falls of leaves.

* * *

In the holidays now there was Clifford to talk to and play games with. He was always there hanging about, waiting for the next meal. Of course he was older than I was and knew more, but I liked that. I liked to be with people who knew things and could make sense of what was going on. The difficulty was that being so much younger I often bored people like my brother or Thackthwaite or Clifford, and they told me so. But I was catching up on them all the time and when I was the author of an encyclopaedia they would listen to me because I would know things, too.

But at the moment, it seemed, I knew nothing. My easy-going father, perhaps alerted by Marion's departure

153

to boarding school, decided it was time for me to get some serious education.

'We must see about getting you into a decent school,' he said.

'I like it at Mrs Stroud's. I don't want to leave.'

'I can see you're happy there. All the girls seem to be. But when it comes down to it, I'm not sure Mrs Stroud knows enough to teach anybody anything.'

'She plays *The Rustle of Spring* beautifully. And she speaks Italian.'

'How much Italian does she speak?'

'I'm not sure. But she often says *eccelente*.'

'And *fortissimo* and *con brio* and *macaroni*, no doubt.'

'I haven't heard her actually use those words.'

Here my brother butted in. 'What about your maths? What is the answer to: How many girls, each twelve inches in diameter, can be packed standing into a room fifteen feet square (standing in the hearth permitted at your own risk)?'

My brother was dismissive of the attractions of the fat big girls who could not spell. He never asked me for reports on their movements as he had about the comings and goings of Midge Morris or the tragically beautiful Scott sisters. I was not sure which girl he had in his sights at the moment but I would find out and pull his leg about it. Perhaps Clifford would know.

8

The only thing I remember about the entrance examination is the interview with the High Mistress. Surprisingly, this was not conducted from behind a desk in an impressive study but upstairs, in a gallery above a hall of assembly where at one end there was a platform and an organ. All round the gallery were classrooms, empty now, with glass panels in the doors and glass giving on to the gallery. Beyond, through the far windows, sky and clouds could be seen.

The High Mistress sat at a small table obviously set up for the purpose of the viva. She was impressive, getting on for elderly, with white hair built up in front over what I knew must be one of the things one sometimes saw on dressing tables, a small framework of fragile wiring netted with human hair. She had a pale face with strong features on the lines of my grandfather's. Her eyes were a very light grey, almost colourless, so that the pupils seemed concentrated on what she was looking at: me. She was not frightening but very intent.

I had to read out loud from a book. It was something about sailors landing on a foreign shore, probably Phoenicians, people of long ago trading goatskins of wine for copper, something of that sort. After I had finished reading, Miss Gray (for that was her name) asked me the meaning of certain of the words. I remember only one. It was 'azure'. I looked across the gallery through the glassed wall and the windows of the classroom opposite to the sky with the clouds billowing across it, and described what I saw. As I looked down again from the sky across the hall I saw the light grey eyes of the High Mistress looking at me intently.

In due course the result of the entrance examination arrived. I had failed.

155

This news did not disturb me. I was quite prepared to settle for a pleasant, undemanding future in my comfortable top desk in Mrs Stroud's top class, taking from dictation daily the *Mail*'s leading article to the tune of Mrs Stroud's repeated *'Eccelente!'* This could go on for years, until I was an old as the fat big girls at the back of the room. However, my mother, that enemy of education, was piqued that a child of hers, without benefit of systematic schooling or even regular attendance, should not pass with flying colours into one of the most selective schools in the country. Without my knowledge, she made an appointment with Miss Gray to ask her why her child had been rejected.

How these two reacted to one another can only be imagined. All I heard about the interview was that my mother had asked in what respect I had failed the examination. Miss Gray, who had evidently done her homework, had told her that what had decisively failed me had been the maths paper, where my method had been all wrong. My mother asked if I had got the answers all wrong, too. No, my answers had mostly been right but my method had been wrong. Here may have followed a brief outline from Miss Gray on the primacy of method over the right answer in the education of the young. Nothing of this would have been received as common sense by my mother. A world in which it was accounted better to get the wrong answer by the right means than the right answer by any means was not a world in which my mother could safely hang her washing out to dry. She would argue that the weakness of the theory was that whereas the rightness of the answer was provable, who could say which method of reaching it was better or worse? She would have had something there.

Apart from an intellectual polarity that was total, it did not sound as if the two of them were altogether uncongenial to one another. After all, Miss Gray had been a Dubliner and it is just possible that what made them able to tolerate one another was a common Longford factor. Miss Gray appeased my mother to some extent by saying that she remembered me clearly as being totally lacking in self-consciousness and possessing an unusually large vocabulary, though it must be said that I was wanting in the elements of a sound education.

By this time my mother was set on my going to this school—anything hard to get, she wanted. Where could I go to be taught the restrictive practices that would lead me, if need be to the wrong end, by the right means? Miss Gray gave her the address of two lady crammers, sisters who had guided many educational strays back on to the Right Path. They were well qualified to put me through the whole programme of required orthodoxy.

The two learned sisters were the Misses Bebb. The younger, known as Miss Hope, came to our house at the invitation of my mother to talk things over and to meet me. Miss Hope was about thirty with gentle blue eyes, slightly inflamed round the lashes. Her front teeth stuck out a little and she had a noticeable moustache. After she had had a private chat over tea with my mother she asked me if I would show her my books. I led her upstairs to my bedroom where, in a small bookcase, were ranged some annuals of *Playbox* and *Chatterbox*, several volumes of the cases of Sherlock Holmes, *She* and *Ayesha* by Rider Haggard, a much-cherished Victorian paperback entitled *Miss Simmins in Search of a Husband*, and other matter of a similar degree of educational value.

Miss Hope Bebb eyed this collection without comment. The tea-time sunlight picked out the glossy hairs of her moustache. It occurred to me that what she had expected to see, all that interested her, were my schoolbooks.

What were my schoolbooks? Hastily I ran through in my mind the unimportant little heap in a corner of my Number One desk at Mrs Stroud's. There was a book of sums, though mostly arithmetic at Mrs Stroud's had been mental arithmetic. There was a French reader (something about a *moulin*) and there was a school atlas with the British Empire in red.

Miss Hope asked if I had done any Latin.

No. Though I knew the Lord's Prayer in Latin, picked up verbatim from my brother who used to gabble it from hearing it at prayers every day at St Paul's.

Miss Hope smiled a kind but faint smile. That was perhaps a beginning. Had I learned any algebra?

157

My brother had sometimes tried to explain algebra to me. He had told me too about things like surface tension and waves and ripples and the angle you had to hit a billiard ball to pocket it . . . and polariscopes . . . We had a microscope. Would she like to see it?

I led her away downstairs, away from my private library which I enjoyed so much but which I could now see was not quite the intellectual thing.

* * *

The Bebb family lived in a quiet terrace down Wrights Lane, off Kensington High Street. I went there on the 49 bus, a long ride that was a treat in itself. On the corner of Wrights Lane was a small café or tea room, always half empty. In the window there was usually a platter of Scotch eggs. I gazed at these slaveringly every time I passed them on my way to and from the Bebbs.

The Bebb sisters lived at home with their parents and a younger brother. There was a sister younger still, but she was away abroad somewhere. The elderly father was grey-bearded, neat and brisk, with sharp brown eyes. I had been told that he had been a Senior Wrangler, as had his father and grandfather before him, way back to the time when Senior Wranglers had been first invented. I understood now that Senior Wrangler was a Cambridge term for an outstanding mathematician, but it still sounded a quarrel-some word to me. Perhaps it was because he had this irritable title attached to him that I thought of Mr Bebb as being just on the point of flying off the handle. It is, however, quite likely that he was in fact in a state of constant high irritation brought on by the torment of a towering intellect forced into almost daily contact with the educationally subnormal such as myself. For sometimes, when I had lessons in the afternoons, I stayed to lunch with the Bebbs.

On these occasions, after morning lessons were over and before lunch was served, there was an interval during which the Misses Bebb disappeared from view, probably to help prepare the meal, for I never saw a servant in the house. Having descended from the schoolroom and washed my hands, I would wait in the sitting room till called to table.

As like as not, Clement, the Bebb brother, would be there already, seated at the grand piano, playing, but not playing with attention; ready to smile at me as I entered the room while his hands moved over the keys, expertly but not with attention. He doodled at the piano, sketching in phrases, snatches of tunes I half recognised, bits of Chopin, bits of Debussy, long torrents of classical music going down in cataracts to current hits that the errand boys were whistling. He seemed to be nearly always there, doodling at the piano. He was not old. He was like his father in feature but his hair was dark, not grey, and his brown eyes were not sharp but lively.

He must have joined us at lunch in the basement dining room but I do not remember him there. I remember him only at the piano, doodling music. I do not remember much about my meals there. The food was nondescript, cabbagy, adequate. No brilliant table talk occurred that stays in my mind. Perhaps it was too far above my head. What I do recall is the halo of unuttered annoyance, like a cloud of midges, above Mr Bebb's exceptionally brainy head.

Lessons took place in two small upper rooms furnished with table and chairs and school text books, the one presided over by Miss Bebb and the other by Miss Hope. One taught one set of subjects, the other the rest. Between them they encompassed the entire range of knowledge I had to acquire. I liked Latin best. Never having been taught any before, I came fresh to a fresh subject. Its lucidity, as taught by Miss Hope, revealed each step by logical step as I progressed. Everything else, except English grammar, which it seemed we had all been speaking at home anyway —everything else had to be picked out of the seething vat of encyclopaedic know-all that was my sum of knowledge, shaken out, displayed, unpicked and put together again in forms more acceptable to decent educational practice. I found I rather enjoyed this process. It was not as difficult as I had been prepared to find it. But outside lessons and homework hours, I never gave a thought to it at all. Lessons were all right but they were not the real world. Beyond lessons the real world bubbled and fizzed with interest.

159

From their window in the café in Wrights Lane, the sun-like yellow and white of the Scotch eggs in their nest of pink, lightly tanned sausage meat, allured me like the eyes of harlots.

'What's it like at the Bebbs?' my mother asked me.

'It's not bad. The other Miss Bebb has a kind of foxy look. I like Miss Hope better. Mrs Bebb is sort of grey and sad.'

'Poor woman. She lost a son in the war, an exceptionally promising young man. Miss Hope told me.'

'They have another son. He plays the piano all the time. Most of them have rather scurfy eyelids, where the lashes come through.'

'Most of what?'

'Most of the Bebbs.'

'Must be getting the wrong diet. Probably not enough greens or animal fat. You must take them some lettuces, there are more than we can eat in the garden.'

So I was sent off with a big bundle of lettuce, in all stages of development, secured with a webbing book-strap on top of the leather attaché case, stamped with my initials, in which I carried my homework. I greatly disliked this burden of green stuff which was received with an increasingly apathetic show of enthusiasm by the Bebbs. It was my pleasure to sit whenever possible on the front upstairs seat of the bus, which was of course open-topped. I liked to grip the brass rail close in front of me and steer the bus; as the driver's seat below was set in somewhat, I seemed on top of everything with almost a sheer drop to the street below. I felt in control. This coveted seat was naturally not always available, though I would watch as passengers left so that I could move up by stages and pounce if at last the front seat fell vacant. On really wet days the front seat was always free. Passengers crammed inside, standing if necessary, to avoid the rain. Not I. Hardened by my mother's rigorous régime, equipped with the high boots, oilskins and sou'wester she provided, I was happy to brave the storm, sit in the top front seat and steer my bus into harbour, my barque to Barker's.

'Plenty of room downstairs, Miss,' the conductor would say as he punched my ticket, 'no need to sit up here getting drowned.'

'But I like it here.'

He would jerk his chin up and flip up his eyes in a some-mothers-have-'em expression and leave me alone in the rain. The rain would drive on to the attaché case on my lap, darkening the leather, making it heavier. If there were lettuces on top, tightly strapped down, they would take the water after the manner of fragile battered greenery, in a sort of transparent wilt. When it came to unstrapping them, usually in the Bebb's hall, hidden waters would break from them over nearby feet.

Little as I liked my job of lettuce-bearer, I was wise enough not to mention my objection to my mother. She might have pointed out that with their scurfy eyelids the Bebbs were in real need of fresh greens *or perhaps animal fat* . . . only too well I could foresee the next move—a great greaseproof-paper parcel of gouged-out casually wrapped-up lumps of dripping of carbon-dateable antiquity, which I would be required to cart halfway across London as an offering to the amazed Bebbs. What could I say to them? Mother thinks it might help your scurfy eyelids? Or, We eat a lot of dripping toast and have never had scurf on our eyelids? Could I leave the parcel on the bus without the conductor spotting it and calling *Hi! Miss!??* If I left it on the bus, could I be sure that at their next meeting my mother would not ask them if the dripping had done anything for their scurfy eyelids? (Obviously not.)

No good drawing attention to the lettuce if it was likely to bring on the dripping. Until the lettuces went to seed, and a little after, I continued to bear my wilting bundles past the blooming Scotch eggs on the corner of Wrights Lane.

In the room with the piano and Clement playing the piano, where I waited to be called to go down to lunch, the curtains and the loose covers were a rather dark blue —what assistants in dress shops called French navy. This was the colour signalling culture and brains at that time —people like my family had linen loose covers patterned with big flowers and leaves which would naturally not be blue. Looking in through lighted windows I had observed that when a room had this light-dark solid blue upholstery there were usually low bookcases round the walls and very

161

thick, arty-looking pottery lamps and vases. If there were Cape gooseberries in the vases it was a sure bet that someone in the house was a schoolteacher—schoolteachers were usually hung up on Cape gooseberries, which they kept telling their pupils to paint, year after year. But such people, I could see now, were only imitators. They were imitating people like the Bebbs, who were the real thing.

There was no mistaking the genuineness of the Bebbs. The soundness of their scholarship rang like gold. Knock their heads and those brains would toll like bells, not a false note anywhere. Their dark blue sitting room was walled with books, not coloured books looking pretty on low shelves, but old as well as new books, books in foreign languages, books in Greek and Latin that had been *read*, scuffed, annotated. Dissect the brains of that family and you would find encelled there the history of the world, its music, its philosophy, its languages, mathematics and a good part of its science. The family was like a small university of the better sort. Ignorant as I was, I knew already the right, true ring of the genuine.

What was surprising was that this learned family should take in the likes of me—so ignorant, so ravelled in the head—and try to teach them. Why did they do it? It could not be very interesting. I was pretty sure that it taxed considerably the patience of the wrangly Mr Bebb to have all this mental dross mixing in with the pure family gold. Then why did they do it?

It must be for the money. It was incredible, but it must be so. This family, with all their true, deep learning, were not at all well off. They must all have done well at school, carried off every sort of degree with honour at Cambridge, yet here they were, cramming the educationally subnormal. Mr Bebb himself, it must be assumed, in some small book-walled corner of his own, was writing textbooks of mathematics for the improvement of the better sort of brain.

My mother would have said it was their own fault. Instead of stuffing their minds with useless education until their heads were stiff with it, they should have left school at fourteen and gone to serve in shops. By now they would

162

not have been the Bebbs, they would have been the Self-ridges. And no scurfy eyelids either.

In their dark blue sitting room with the books and the grand piano, there was an incongruous object mounted, like a stag's head, above the fireplace. It was a small, stout propeller, in bright steel, solid looking but not much more in span than a child's arms extended. One day I asked Clement about it.

'It was the propeller of my brother's aeroplane. He was in the Royal Flying Corps. He was killed in the war.'

'Was he older than you?'

'Yes. When he was killed he was my age now, twenty-four. He was very clever and promising, another Wrangler.'

'You're clever and promising too, aren't you?'

'Unfortunately not.'

'What was his name?'

'His name was Constant.'

'You all have names like that, don't you? Sort of virtuous names, like Honor and Hope?'

Clement laughed. 'Yes, we do, don't we? Mother's name is Faith, too. To distinguish the sexes we have adjectival males and nominal females.' He said this in the way that people speak when what they say has two meanings, one of which I never seemed to understand.

'Why do you say you're not clever and promising like your brother?'

'I'm too old to be promising.'

'But you said he was promising when he was killed at twenty-four.'

'To be promising at twenty-four one must have done something promising before that age. He had done ex-tremely well at Cambridge. I have done nothing. I haven't even got a degree. I left Cambridge . . . not with honour . . . in my second year. I tried to follow Constant into the RFC. But they never even let me fly.'

'Why not?'

'No aptitude. Wrong temperament. Insufficient stamina. I spent the war servicing aeroplanes on the ground and entertaining troops at the piano.'

'I bet you did that well.'

'Well enough to entertain. Not well enough to be a concert pianist.'

'You could have gone back to Cambridge after the war, couldn't you?'

'No thanks. Away from the family I could see that all it had been doing for generations was sit in dusty libraries smelling of rotting leather, writing books about books. No thanks. But now I'm back in the bosom of.'

'Why?'

'No job. No money. What else?' Clement lifted his shoulders in a tiny shrug, let his hands come down on the piano keys and lapsed into his rippling runaway musical doodling.

His sister Honor put her head round the door to tell me that lunch was ready. She did not glance at Clement. I wondered why the family always seemed to ignore him, almost as if he was not there at all. I liked him better than any of them.

It seemed that something was not being said out loud. I began to listen for what was not being said. It could be heard faintly, as an approaching drumbeat far away can be faintly heard in the background of a conversation. This family, while ignoring Clement, were all saying something silently. The ones who said it silently loudest were the eldest sister Honor and the wrangly Mr Bebb; but all of them were saying it. The drumbeat approached and above the hum of everyday I heard what they all were saying, over and over, in their silence. It was:

If one of them had to go, why did it have to be Constant?
If one of them had to go, why did it have to be Constant?
If one of them . . . if one of them . . . did it have to be
Constant?

One day the youngest sister, Prue, suddenly appeared. She had just arrived from Paris. In those days, to simple souls, Paris still had a certain air of romance attaching to it and some wisps of this swirled like smoke-rings around the arriving Prue. She was dressed rather dashingly in a light tweed, overchecked in red and fawn, with a two-inch red feather stuck randomly, like a trout fly, in her natty small tweed hat. She was very like her brother Clement but with a

164

wilder light in her eye, and her slightly reddened eyelids spoke more of smoky nights in bars than a family tendency to scurf. I was impressed. Here was another promising Bebb—Cambridge, the Sorbonne, now Bologna, Heidelberg after that. Her forte was modern languages, with a dash of politics and economics thrown in—so much her family had let fall. It was confidently expected that she would slip easily into some plum job in Geneva at the League of Nations. She was the only one who did not ignore Clement. While he doodled at the piano I heard her in there with him, both pealing with laughter.

Next day she was gone. No more laughter was heard.

They asked me again at home how things were at the Bebbs. I rather liked the lessons, I told them. I told them the Bebbs had the propeller from their dead son's aeroplane mounted on the wall above the fireplace.

'Hope it's properly fixed. Heavy things, propellers. Better keep away from that fireplace,' my father advised me. 'Have that propeller come down on your head, next thing you know you'll be blowing your nose through your arsehole.'

'Will! Must you?'

'Child had better be warned, hadn't she? The thing's probably only fixed with a couple of six-inch nails, one inch into flaking plaster, three into crumbling mortar between the brickwork of the chimney. I know what some of these early Victorian and small Regency terrace houses are like —woodworm, dry rot, brickwork never been re-pointed —we've had a few come up for mortgage, surveyors reckon they're a poor risk. And talking of surveyors,' added my father, 'have you seen anything of Jack lately? No? Well, next time you see him, take a good look. At last month's board meeting he seemed decidedly absent-minded, but at today's he was almost embarrassing. Doesn't drink, does he?'

'I shouldn't think so. In fact I've heard Luke complain she has to drink alone. What was the matter with him?'

'Some question about a disputed survey came up and he was asked for his opinion. He had to be asked twice, as if he'd been dreaming. Then he mumbled and bumbled and started fumbling through some papers in front of him in a shuffling sort of way as if the answer was there . . . his speech seemed slurred too . . . I covered up for him by chipping in with a few figures and stepping hard on the bell under the carpet for Simmonds to bring in the coffee and sandwiches. That broke it up. It wasn't of any importance, the point Jack had been asked about, and it wasn't brought up again, but still . . . As soon as the meeting was over he left. Didn't stay for a word with anybody. From the window I saw Luke was there, waiting outside in that little boneshaker two-seater she drives. He got in beside her but she stayed at the wheel. The way he climbed into the car, he looked really shaky.'

My mother looked rather worried, but said nothing.

Back at the Bebbs, I would sometimes ask Clement the name of a particular piece of music he was playing. He asked me if I heard much music—for this was, of course, years before wireless and the BBC. I told him about the oratorios my grandparents took me to at the Crystal Palace —*The Messiah*, *The Dream of Gerontius*, *Elijah* and one or two others. One of my godmothers—not 'Call-me-Eleanor'— was a rather grand old lady who had a box at the Albert Hall which she sometimes lent us for a weekend matinee. My father always went along to these concerts because they were free, but otherwise he did not really enjoy them.

'Do you enjoy them?' Clement inquired.

'Some of the pieces. Some music I really hate. I hate Gilbert and Sullivan.'

'Do you play the piano?'

'Only very badly. I've had two piano teachers and they both got cross because as soon as I know a piece I start playing it in another key.'

'You must have a good ear, then.'

'Oh, I hear it all right, but I'm ham-handed. When I play it sounds awful. But my brother has fixed that—he has done something to the soft pedal of our piano so that it is down permanently and I can't be heard in the next room. But it works both ways—if nobody hears, I can read instead of practising.'

Clement laughed. 'Yet you seem to like music?'

'Oh yes. Your music, but not the kind I bang out.'

'What music do you like?'

I told him how much I enjoyed *Sleepers Awake*, how it woke you up and made you feel strong. He knew it and he picked out some of it for me on the piano.

'There's a piece I heard once played on a flute. I don't know what it's called, I don't know where I heard it but I really love it. Only I can't quite catch it, it sings in my head like a ghost and it's gone. I only remember about a bar of it. If I whistle it do you think you would know it?'

'Try me,' Clement said.

One thing I could really do well was whistle. I whistled the few notes I knew. It sounded right, clear but not shrill.

'Again,' said Clement.

I whistled it again while we looked straight at one another. Again it sounded right.

Clement played the phrase on the piano.

'Gluck,' he said. 'From *Orpheus and Eurydice*. It's called in English "The Dance of the Blessed Spirits".'

And he played it for me.

The notes hit me on the heart. It was as if the ghost that had haunted my head came back into life with a heartbeat of its own. I stared at Clement wonderstruck as he brought the ghost to life.

Clement brought his playing to an end. He still looked at me. There was a pause.

'How old are you?' he asked.

'Twelve,' I said. 'Nearly twelve, anyway.'

'You are tall for your age.'

'Yes. I'm almost five foot six.'

He sprang up from the piano stool.

And at once we were rolling over and over on the carpet, laughing and wrestling. We were hugged tightly together with me underneath and for a moment stopped struggling. Looking up over his shoulder I saw the aeroplane propeller fixed on the wall above me. *Keep away from that fireplace*, my father had warned. I wriggled free.

'Constant's propeller might fall on us,' I said.

Clement got up. He was quite pink from exertion.

'I suppose it might,' he said.

When his sister Honor put her head round the door a few minutes later, ignoring him, to tell me that lunch was ready, Clement was playing a mazurka *con brio* and did not acknowledge his sister.

* * *

Towards the end of my spell of tuition with the Bebbs I sat again the entrance examination to the school where the right approach counted for so much. While awaiting the result I continued for a few weeks with the lessons, to keep me going on the chosen path. But now the pressure was off and there was plenty of time to look around, and scarcely any homework.

Near the bus stop in Kensington High Street an interesting display of human wreckage was always laid out for inspection and the receipt of charity. They sat on seat cushions or sections of mattress with chalked placards describing their hardships at their feet and a tin basin or upturned cap beside them. The boards read: *Blinded at Vimy Ridge. Toes blown off. Thank you.* Or: *Paralysed hips down. Four children under five.* Or: *Leg lost Passchendaele. Totally deaf. Sole support aged mother.* One read: *Total mental wreck. Thank you.* I liked the mental wreck best and sometimes put a penny in his basin. All of them claimed to have no pension. This seemed strange to me. What more did the War Office want by way of proof of disability—no head?

There was one very fat red man with a *Totally blind, sick wife, no pension* board beside him. He looked extremely cross and had half-closed eyes with some of the under, white part showing. I had never liked him much and went off him completely when one day out shopping with my mother I saw him outside the Underground at Piccadilly Circus with a freshly chalked notice beside him which read: *Sight destroyed Salonika. Severe internal injuries. Please and thank you.*

No mention of the sick wife. Worse still, he had been unfaithful to Kensington High Street. I was sure it only needed someone to nick sixpence out of his cap for his sight to be miraculously restored.

The Scotch eggs at the corner of Wrights Lane still rolled their golden eyes at me. One afternoon, on the way home I went into the shop and bought two at sixpence each.

'Here's a present for you,' I said to my mother on reaching home. 'One for you and one for me. We'll eat them together.'

They were delicious.

'I expect they would be quite difficult to make?' I suggested. 'I mean, cookshops have a kind of knack, haven't they? Slapping on the sausage meat just right wouldn't be easy, would it?'

'Nonsense,' said my mother vigorously. 'Half a dozen hard-boiled eggs, a pound of pork sausage meat and a few dried breadcrumbs and some good beef dripping or bacon fat, that's all it needs. This is very good but I'm not sure the sausage meat is pure pork—trace of beef there, I think. I could easily knock them up.'

And she did. Thereafter my brother, Clifford and I often had Scotch eggs to take with us on picnics. It is true they were a touch boss-eyed, after the fashion of my mother's rough-and-ready cooking style, with mumpish bulges of over-thick sausage meat, but all the better for that. The Scotch eggs in the Wrights Lane cookshop now eyed me in vain as I stode past them without so much as a glance.

Uncle Jack no longer attended board meetings. It was understood that he was suffering from some disorder of the nervous system that slurred his speech and made him shaky and unsteady. My mother had her hair done rather more frequently at the hairdressing establishment in Richmond run by Aunt Luke's friend Celia. I was not invited to accompany her to have my ends singed.

Word reached us that Mrs Milton had retired from keeping the boarding house at Brattle Place. She was so racked with rheumatism that uric acid crystals were coming out of her eyes. (*Out of her eyes? Uric acid crystals?* What could they be like? Demerara sugar? Chips of blue john? Mrs Milton mineralising like a stalagmite? No answer.)

A letter came to say that I had passed the entrance examination, I was to be admitted in September. Presumably I was no longer educationally subnormal.

Miss Bebb and Miss Hope expressed pleasure at my success. There was no mistaking the genuineness of their gratification. I had never seen them so animated. It was evident that an exam success did for them what a night out did for my mother. Even grey old Mrs Bebb favoured me with a quiet smile and the Senior Wrangler himself congratulated me, remarking that I was going to a school that sent more girl scholars up to Oxford and Cambridge than any other in the country.

This must mean that if I acquitted myself well I might in twenty years be where Miss Bebb and Miss Hope were today, that is, congratulating some educationally subnormal dope on having temporarily normalised under my tuition. As a career prospect it did not grab me more strongly than sitting beside a hatful of small change and the legend *Total mental wreck. Thank you.*

As usual, Clement was by himself at the piano. I told him I had passed the entrance exam and so should not be coming back for any more coaching. He doodled a bit on the piano, looking at me.

'So you're heading for success?' he said.

'I shouldn't think so. But I've learnt a lot since coming here.'

'What, specially?'

'Well, Latin of course . . . But the real thing I've learnt is that I shall never be able to write an encyclopaedia.'

'Were you thinking of doing that?'

'I have been collecting material since I was ten. What held me up was the difficulty of sorting it out. Geography blurred into History and History into Religion and Literature—there were no boundaries that I could see. Now I am twelve I see that the whole idea was absurd. Childish.'

'I think that's rather sad.'

'Not sad at all. Just growing up.'

'Will you be coming back to see us?'

'I shouldn't think so. In a way I should like to but the way things are I don't expect I shall.'

'Why do you say that?'

'Because I've seen that people who come to say goodbye usually don't come back.'

'When did you begin to notice this?'

'It came on gradually, from when I was about five right up to now. It's true, you know.'

'You were young to notice that that is how things are.'

'Fairly young, I suppose, yes.'

170

'Do you remember the people who don't come back?'

'Yes. I remember them all.'

'Will you remember me?'

'Of course I shall. If I live to be eighty I shall still remember you here playing the piano . . . playing "The Dance of the Blessed Spirits".'

'Playing it. But not dancing it,' Clement said.

For a moment we looked at one another across the piano. It struck me that those eyes with slightly reddened rims, common to the family, yet could be thought to be reddened from different causes. It was easy to see that Miss Bebb and Miss Hope and their father might be in want of fresh greens and animal fats and that the dashing Prue suffered from too many hours in smoky nightclubs. Only Clement's eyes looked as if he had wept the night before and might weep again tonight.

'I must go now. Goodbye, Clement.'

'Goodbye, my innocent.'

Going down the steps and away from the house I heard him playing. Fainter and fainter fell those perfect notes, as the ghost that had been called into life and given a heartbeat of its own, went back to being a shade again.

* * *

On holiday at Felixstowe that summer, I slipped while clambering over rocks and twisted my ankle slightly. Consequently I was less able to move about outside and found time to note my brother's interest in a young woman called Mabelle. When I say young, she was about twenty-five. My brother was seventeen, but being tall, dark, lean and blackavised he looked quite as old as Clement. His new horn-rimmed spectacles gave him an impressively intellectual look which evidently fooled Mabelle, who spent a good deal of time with him on a small balcony leading off one of the upper reception rooms. They talked earnestly together, and as I passed hobbling to and fro I often heard the word *psychology* mentioned. Mabelle had a highbrow look, backed up by employment at an art gallery in Windsor. (I took it for granted that my brother would have suppressed all reference to wicked Cousin Edward Atkins and his nameless sins in that same royal borough).

171

Mabelle had black hair that grew in a widow's peak on her forehead. She had grey eyes and wore amber earrings and a long necklace of amber beads. Somewhere in tow was a young man, called Teddy, with a stunned boneheaded look. Every now and then he would appear indoors from some outdoor sporting activity, glance over at the two in earnest talk on the little balcony and lurch away again like a punch-drunk boxer. Once, passing me on his way out, he was to be heard muttering under his breath 'Jesus Christ!' in a tone of total amazement.

Mabelle's name, though embellished in print, was pronounced like any other Mabel, to rhyme with *table*. My father was always very hot on people who did silly things to their names, like putting hyphens, substituting y's for i's or other gentrifications of that ilk. (This was still more than a decade before any young woman who wanted to be thought interesting announced that whatever her name had been before, hereafter she wished to be known as Ann. Anns sprang up everywhere, either on their own or coupled-up as Sally-Ann or Joan-Ann. The name, adopted with such hope, did nothing for these young women, who have been stuck with it ever since.)

My father's holiday frolic took the form of pronouncing anything that rhymed with Mabel as if it rhymed with Mabelle. Entering the hotel dining room he would say, in his clear baritone: 'Waiter! Now that the party by the window has left, I should like to move over to the Tabelle in the window.'

Once settled there, he would ask my brother whether he would be Abelle to join him in a round of golf after lunch, or should they hire a couple of ponies from the riding Stabelles? My brother, who cared for neither of these pursuits, would slink off again to some quiet corner to discuss psychology with Mabelle, with occasional interruptions from the poleaxed Teddy looking in to say, 'Jesus Christ!' My father's little game petered out pretty soon for want of rhyming material, though right at the end of our holiday he did manage to ask my brother to pick up from Reception a dozen luggage Labelles.

Waiting at home when we returned was a note from my new school giving a list of clothing and sports equipment required. No deviation from the norm was permitted. Gym tunics were to be so long, measured from the knee. The school seemed very strict. I had heard that all new pupils were subjected to a medical examination, too. I wondered if I would pass it. After all, it was not so long since I had been educationally subnormal, though unaware of my handicap. Could it be that some physical deformity, hitherto unremarked, might be brought into the light of day by a medical inspection? I was still limping slightly from my twisted ankle and also had a sore place on the ball of my foot. Much of the shopping was done in Kensington High Street. Hobbling past the familiar line of amputees with their trade descriptions beside them, I felt a touch of fellow feeling. I tossed a copper or two into the basin of *Total mental wreck* in case there happened to be a Fate or a Fury coming up from the Underground.

My awareness of physical handicap was kept up to date by the presence of our latest maid, Mavis. A pretty redhead, she was missing all the fingers on her right hand. She had been born like that. It was widely held in her family that if at the time of her birth the doctor had taken the time to run his penknife across her blind knuckles and 'open up the buds of her fingers', those members would have sprouted out with all the released vitality of plants in spring. By now she might have been a concert pianist. As it was, she managed remarkably well, peeling potatoes at express speed by pressing the tuber against her body with her square palm, while she scraped away with the peeler held in her left hand. Mavis was engaged to be married. Far from being depressed by her deformity she seemed to enjoy the attention it attracted. When the attention, from daily familiarity, waned, Mavis would turn to other ways of turning the spotlight on herself.

One of the visiting cats who had made its home with us and could not be dislodged was a fat grey half-Persian called Fluffkins. He had a good home up the road but would not stay in it. An outstandingly affable and stupid animal, Fluffkins was distinguished by a tummy covered with tight grey curls. From time to time I would snip a curl from his tummy to give to the occasional unbeliever who doubted the existence of a curly cat.

173

One morning my brother came downstairs with a bed-room slipper in his hand, complaining that he had found it sopping wet inside. It was established that the mindless Fluffkins had peed in it. My brother was disgusted but my father defended Fluffkins, pointing out that cats had mysterious optical powers and could not only see in the dark but could read the invisible *Gents* on smelly bedroom slippers. As a precaution, both slippers of the pair were washed out and up-ended to dry on the croquet box in the back yard.

A day or two later Mavis was seen up-ending a bedroom slipper to dry in the sun on the croquet box.

'What is this, Mavis?' my mother asked.

Mavis looked coy.

'Fact is, ma'am, I must have got out of bed in me sleep, not realising, like, and made water in me slipper instead of in the chamber. So I had to wash it out.'

'Of course,' said my mother, making nothing of it. She knew her Mavis.

Next day, down came Mavis, looking coy again, with a bedroom slipper in her hand. She washed it at the sink and put it to dry on the croquet box. My mother made no comment, as if nightly urination into footwear was now a settled thing in the household.

For several mornings Mavis repeated this performance, which was ignored. Before long she forgot to pee in her slippers and took to nicking small items of table napery, such as egg cosies, to furnish her bottom drawer.

My ankle had now recovered but I continued to hobble because of sharp pain on pressure on the ball of the same foot. I let it be thought that it was still the ankle that made me limp. Using the outside of the foot only I managed to walk without limping but could not run. I avoided tennis. Remembering my father, that strong handsome man, being turned down as unfit for military service because of varicose veins, I reasoned that a foot defect that slowed me to a careful walk would certainly block my entry to this selective school. As soon as the medical examination got as far as my feet it would be all up with me. No amount of Bebb burnishing of the brain would make up for a gross physical defect. I should be rejected as unfit. The next four or five years would pass back at the top desk at Mrs Stroud's, taking dictation from the *Daily Mail*'s leading article. Enjoyable as it had been at the time, I had now done with Mrs Stroud's. I did not want to go back there. Retreat into educational subnormality would be humiliating.

I examined my foot. On the ball of it, level with the big toe, was a callus the diameter of a pea. On pressure it stabbed like a knife. It was now early September. Time was running out. I directed prayers for recovery to a pantheon of deities from the Holy Trinity to Woden and Thor, on Wednesday and Thursday, in case.

Three days before term began I stepped out of a hot bath and my scab, my callus, my unclean affliction, fell off onto the bath mat. Wonderingly, I bent to pick it up. I examined it with joyous curiosity. The tiny disc of yellowed skin, softened by the hot water, was pierced in the middle by a thorn. The 'thorn' was a sliver of stone, a present from Felixstowe. Where the disc had stuck to my foot the skin was pink and young, like a baby's and perfectly free from pain. I was whole again.

The medical examination of new girls took place away at the top of the building. It was conducted by an old, old lady doctor in a cardigan. She was assisted by a young woman in a white coat. I was weighed, measured and scrutinised for curvature of the spine, required to listen to a watch ticking, read letters from a card, match up skeins of wool, squeeze a machine each hand in turn and blow into a bag.

'Now for your feet,' wheezed the old doctor, shifting in her chair. 'I see your arches are not as high as they might be. Go up and down on your toes a few times a day . . . That will do, you can put on your blouse again . . . Next please, Miss Tancred.'

It was over. I was scandalised. What a travesty of an examination! Not so much as a glance at the soles of my feet, I could have been covered with foot-leprosy for all that old she-doctor knew! Were all doctors like this old person and Dr Whhhen-and-Whhhatski Biggs, not looking at bodies properly and getting diseases wrong? Half an hour with the medical section of Pears' *Cyclopaedia* could teach a person as much about medicine as these old parties seemed to have learnt during years and years at medical school.

175

Doctors! . . .

Rejoining the new intake of pupils to the Middle Fourth, I was gratified to learn that nobody else had notched up so high a score *with both hands* on the squeezing machine. I did not then reveal that I was ambidextrous. For good measure, I showed them how I could flex the topmost joints of my fingers without bending the other joints and could also freely move my ears. These accomplishments were well received but I left it at that. This was a school, I could see, where brains counted for most and I had not so long come up from being educationally subnormal for it to be wise to push my luck. Some other time I might tell somebody how I had once been run away with on an elephant and had also been privileged to see a snake at the Zoo being sick, but now it would be as well not to overdo things. This school was very selective. I had better not forget that but for God's grace and an aged doctor on her last legs, I could well have been excluded, an untouchable with foot disease.

To my surprise, lessons at my new school came as no ordeal. The Bebbs had taught me well. After the carefree disorder of Mrs Stroud's top class, the serene and disciplined clarity of my present curriculum calmed like an armistice. Anything not understood was clearly explained. Reason ruled.

Not so on the playing fields. Except for tennis, I had never played any outdoor games with rules—beach cricket and rounders could hardly be counted. My previous schools had had no playing fields: if at all we exercised in a public gymnasium hired by the hour, and swam in the public baths. My present school had both these facilities on the premises. There were many tennis courts and ample playing fields. On these fields we played in their season hockey, lacrosse and cricket. There was also an abundance of games of netball.

There were no lessons in the afternoons, which were given over to preparation and to games. Out into the playing fields we went. There were three or four games mistresses, one or two quite young, one or two full-bodied forty-year-olds with buns of hair, and even one with pince-nez glasses. Up and down the field she jogged, one hand holding a whistle to her lips, the other steadying her bobbing bosom as her straining bra was tested to destruction.

What was she up to? Why did she whistle?

Nobody ever explained to me the lay-out or the rules of any of the team games we played. Whether any of the others had ever received instruction on these matters I never knew. It appeared that knowledge of these games, their rules, their finer points of advance and retreat, were supposed to come down to us by tradition, like standing up for *God Save the King/Queen* or bowing the head when prayers were said.

It was easy enough to get the general drift of these team games, that is, to score goals or to knock down stumps as the season indicated. More than that was never clear to me. I still do not know why at a signal everybody moves from one end of a cricket pitch to the other, or when the whistle blows two hockey players stand over the ball tapping their sticks together. Terms like 'slips' and 'cover-point' still mean nothing to me, though I played these various games for several years without ever falling into serious conflict with the whistle-blower or referee.

How was this achieved? Observing the drift of all these games, I cracked their code. There is only one code. There is no need to know the rules. Only two things are necessary: if the ball comes at you and you have something in your hand, hit the ball, the harder the better. If empty-handed, catch the ball. That is all. Simply hit the ball or catch the ball. That way nobody will ever find out that you do not know the rules of the game.

9

The little train I had to take to school left Clapham Junction at about 8.30 in the morning. It stood at Platform No. 1, where perhaps it had been sleeping all night. It was a steam train with not many carriages, as if tailored to the number of passengers it had to carry, because although every seat seemed occupied I do not remember ever having to stand. Its clientele was specialised and probably did not vary by more than the odd dozen. Now long defunct, the line ran between Clapham Junction and Addison Road and from the rarity of its service—no more than two trains morning and evening—might have been closed years earlier but for its use by the GPO clerks at the offices at Blythe Road. Except for the compartment in the very front of the train, by unspoken agreement reserved for the exclusive use of a few boys going to St Paul's, virtually nobody used the train except this small multitude of women clerks, and myself.

They were a drab pack of people. Mostly clad in various shades of sand and mud that did not actually show the dirt but suggested concealment of it, these women workers stumped or slouched on to Platform No. 1 to be engulfed by the little train. There they sat in facing rows in separated compartments. Among them, I was an alien form of life. Through imaginary grilles, they regarded me with the trained malignity of seasoned Post Office employees. Who, fumbling nervously for stamps or change across the polished wood, has not felt the crack across the knuckles of those toffee-hammer eyes? My presence among them was resented. I was not one of them. Silently they practised upon me those techniques in which many of them must have gained distinction in the Customer Repellence course necessary for their advancement.

I was not one of them. I was younger than them. I still

178

had, or seemed to have, a choice. They had none. Their antagonism was to be felt.

But there it was, I had to travel with them. There was nowhere else to go. Iron protocol barred my entry to the front compartment where the Paulines travelled, though in private life I was acquainted with one or two of them. I was an outcast.

There was however another apparent outcast. This tall, noticeable person stalked the platform until the last minute, only stooping to enter whichever compartment was nearest as the guard blew his whistle. At least six feet tall, in a felt hat and crumpled brownish tweeds, lean and long-headed with a thick, clipped, light brown moustache and unnerving, stricken eyes, this figure stalked the platform every morning, at once tragic and farcical, like a bereaved schoolmaster in a skirt. Who was she? Might it not be better to be clean-shaven? Another mystery with no answer.

Heavily avoided though I was by the boys at the front of the train who included, of course, my own brother, there were times when I was conscious of being a person of some consequence. These were when I arrived on Platform No. 1 in the company of a senior boy called Jack Buchanan who lived not far from us. Sometimes we happened to cross the Common together, travelled to Clapham Junction on the local train and arrived together on Platform 1. There we might stand talking till the train was due to start, when Jack would raise his hat to me and move up to the front. The kudos attaching to these encounters was incalculable, because Jack was the Captain of St Paul's, a powerful friend indeed for an unregarded twelve-year-old schoolgirl alone among a crowd composed of a few male chauvinist pigs, scores of embittered female clerks and a hermaphrodite. On the elevated plane where he had his classical being, Jack could afford to be seen with me without losing status. Less senior Paulines could not risk the contamination of being seen talking to a girl. It should be remembered that this was 1921.

All aboard the little train: off it puffed, stopping at three forgotten stations, crossing the river with a hollow, thrilling thunder. Here the light changed slightly, showing up the whites of the eyes of those few who glanced eastward,

179

seeking the escape route to the sea. Then the light would alter, the rhythm of the wheels flatten, the walls of the prison house close in again. At Addison Road the drab crowd left the train to spend the day totting up interest in Post Office Savings books in their uniquely illegible handwriting.

This only available train sped me to school half an hour earlier than I need arrive. Few people were about. There was space and there was peace. Sometimes one of the music staff would be at the organ playing, breathing the air of heaven over the unpeopled hall. The light then would hold the golden stillness of the first morning of the world. Soon the others would arrive and the plain day of the week begin, but for that quarter of an hour while I was alone there, I lived in the first morning of the world.

* * *

On Christmas Day that year we walked across to my grandparents' as usual, bearing unwanted gifts (not fit to put in a servant's bedroom). Uncle Jack and his family were not present.

'Your uncle has to take things very quietly at the moment,' Aunt Ada explained. 'He is suffering from nervous exhaustion as a result of the war. We all are,' she added.

My handsome aunt looked in the pink of health, though perhaps it was possible that she was suffering from delayed bandage-roller's wrist, three years after the cessation of hostilities. She had not fallen into the arms of Val Atkins after all. In the course of conversation it was mentioned that he was now in Argentina.

'What does he do for a living?' I inquired innocently.

'He works in a bank,' my aunt replied.

'They seem to move him about a lot,' my brother remarked.

'He is an organiser,' Aunt Ada said importantly.

By way of the sideboard mirror—a system of signalling we had perfected—my brother flashed me a look which conveyed the message that our aunt was a silly cow and Val was booking orders for bombs from anarchists.

For the first time we did not go back to Sherbrooke Lodge

on Boxing Day. Something had been arranged at last that let us off this obligation. My father was delighted, even accepting with affability the return of Clifford, come to rootle for nutrients in the family trough. He brought with him an anthology of noble passages in English literature.

It was a hardback, bound in pink linen. He sat opposite me at the dining room table with the book open before him on the red chenille tablecloth, under the red silk shade of the gaslight fitting.

'Listen to this,' he said. And he read aloud to me the passage from *Ecclesiastes* 12, beginning:

> *Remember now thy Creator in the days of thy youth,*
> *while the evil days come not,*

and ending:

> *. . . Then shall the dust return to the earth as it was: and*
> *the spirit shall return unto God who gave it.*

I was spellbound. 'Read that again,' I said.

When he had finished reading he looked up.

'Because the language is beautiful it doesn't mean it's true, you know,' he said. 'You don't have to believe that crap about your Creator.'

'Well, I shall remember Him all the same, in case,' I said.

'Crafty little swine, hedging your bets,' remarked Clifford companionably, champing almonds and crunching handfuls of raisins with his excellent teeth. Attention to the riches of the English language would not deflect him for a moment from the more serious business of hunting and gathering. His was not a home where almonds and raisins would be there for the taking. A brain must be fed. Clifford was no longer the dedicated young socialist ready to fight the good fight on a diet of tea and buns. But he was still a strong believer in unbelief.

'It beats me,' he said, 'how anyone can swallow all that churchy cant.'

'Those picture books of Bible stories that we all got given as small children, in a way they spoil religion, I think.'

'I didn't get given them,' he said.

'No, you wouldn't. You'd be given Fabian Society tracts —free ones. What I mean about religious picture books,

181

they give us the idea from quite young that God is a very bad-tempered old grandfather type and Jesus is plain soppy, with long hair and in a nightie like a sort of rather tall woman. Meek and mild too, which doesn't help. I like the Holy Ghost best.'

A white dove coming down out of the blue with a blessing and going back into the blue was a better thing to dwell on than all that blood and pain.

'I don't believe in any of it. Religion is the opium of . . .'

'Oh, I know. Shut up and crack some Brazils to put inside dates. I'll stone the dates.'

Abstractions forgotten, Clifford returned to the serious business of getting fed.

Towards the end of January my brother came back from school one evening with his starched white collar filthy and his face far from clean. This was most unlike him.

'Those silly sods in the front compartment were fooling about and I got pushed under the seat,' he explained as I watched him wash his face and hands, 'and I practically ate, it felt like a spoonful, of that filthy dust under there—never been swept since the carriage was built, I'd say. I can still taste the muck.' He gargled and spat. 'It's up my nose too,' he complained. If he had bitten the dust as often as I had, I thought, he would not make such a fuss about a small scuffle. But he had always been a neat and tidy boy, not given to brawling.

My mother for once paid scant attention to his snuffles. She had just come back from Richmond where she had been having her hair done.

'Did you see Aunt Luke and Uncle Jack?' I asked.

'I did look in there for a few minutes.'

'How's Uncle Jack?'

'Quite unwell. Not at all himself.'

My brother sneezed vigorously.

'For heaven's sake sneeze into your handkerchief!' she snapped, quite crossly. It was evidently time to shut up. That night I woke up to hear my parents coming upstairs to bed. As they passed my door I heard them talking quietly together and afterwards, for a while, the murmur of their talk in their bedroom. They sounded serious.

My brother had a cold and a sore throat. He decided to

182

take a day or two in bed. This was nothing new. He would take a few days off on any pretext. A grown man now, he was sick of school. Dr Biggs was called in as a matter of routine. After inquiring about my brother's bow-els, he prescribed bed rest and a light diet. A bottle of medicine (guaranteed brown) would be sent along that evening. My brother had tonsilitis. It would take a few days to get better. Be sure to keep the bow-els open.

The tonsilitis took its time. For once I had not had weeks off, wheezing and coughing, this winter and I envied my brother. After school or at the weekend I would sit on his bed for a game of chess or draughts, or just to talk.

'Mother wasn't in when I got back from school.'

'No. She's gone to Richmond.'

'She's there half the time, these days.'

'Don't you know why?'

'No. Why?'

'It's Uncle Jack. He's going off his head.'

I might have known it. My mother had said he was 'not himself'. People 'not themselves' were either drunk or mad; and Uncle Jack was not a drinker.

'And he's going to die before long,' added my brother.

I was dismayed. 'Why is this happening to him? Why haven't they talked about it?'

'Not everybody knows about it. The parents do, but the grandparents and aunts haven't been told. You're not supposed to know, at least not yet. They say they'll tell you when you're older but you know what parents are, when you're older they'll still put it off or forget or something..I'm telling you because I think you ought to know and basically you're quite sensible though you're a little fool in many ways. You mustn't say I told you.'

'No, of course not. But what is all this about?'

'Uncle Jack has got GPI—general paralysis of the insane. It's a disease that is the consequence of another disease. Have you heard of venereal disease?'

'I've often seen the word. I don't know what it means.'

'It means a disease that can be passed on by a man and woman going to bed together—that is, if one of them already has it, of course. You know about prostitutes —soliciting?'

'I've often read about soliciting in the police court reports in the *Borough News*. I'm not quite clear about what it is.'

'Prostitutes are women who go to bed with men for money. Picking them up in the street and taking them home to bed is called soliciting.'

'Why do the men want to go to bed with them if they don't know them?'

'Well . . . some men get sick of their wives. Some just feel they want to go to bed with a woman . . . almost any woman. That's what happened to Uncle Jack. Years and years ago when he was about twenty-three, working in Nottingham, he got picked up by a prostitute who infected him with a venereal disease: syphilis, it's called. It starts with a kind of sore, something like a cold sore, but not on the mouth.'

'Where, then?'

'Don't be a fool. The other end, obviously . . . After a bit this first sore clears up, but the next thing, and this is the second stage, someone with the disease may get all sorts of upsets—rashes, sore throats, swollen glands—and during this stage it's still infectious, I mean it can be passed on to anyone the infected person goes to bed with. And to any children born from that time on.'

'Uncle Jack and Aunt Luke haven't got any children of their own.'

'Exactly. That's why.'

'I don't see how they could stop having . . .'

'Well, they did. How they did's another story. You can ask someone else about that. But I was going to tell you about the third stage of this disease. The last stage . . . After all the other symptoms have stopped, the sores and rashes and throat infections and whatever, if you've got this disease you won't pass it on any more to anyone you sleep with. But if you have children they will inherit it and will be born all wrong, deformed or with funny teeth or blind or a mess generally, so you mustn't have any children, though you can marry; for a short time, until you die.'

'Why do you have to die?'

'Because in its last stage syphilis can attack the nerves and the brain. Nothing works. Everything collapses. Without working nerves, you have to die.'

'Is that what is happening to Uncle Jack?'

'Yes.'

'And he knew about it all this time, he knew what was going to happen to him? Isn't there a cure?'

'There's no cure. Sometimes it's treated by giving the patient malaria—a high fever may retard it for a time. But there's no cure . . . Yes, of course he knew.'

Towards me down the corridor he came, the slim soldier with the sad eyes, down the corridor he came towards me where I stood beside the white marble bust of the lady. He ruffled my hair.

'Hello, Poodle.'

Goodbye, Uncle Jack.

'Go away now. Talking makes my sore throat worse.'

'Let me look at it. Say *Ah*.'

'Ah.'

'Move your head more into the light. Say *Ah* again.'

'Ah . . . Ah . . .'

'Pooh . . . your breath stinks. It looks awful down there . . . white patches like ice floes breaking up. You're so disgusting . . . see you later, I'll bring you up the evening paper when it comes.'

My mother returned from Richmond much later. She asked me, rather absently, whether I had seen my brother that evening.

'Yes. We played draughts. Talking made his throat worse. I looked down it. It's quite horrible, covered with white fungus like rotting wood.'

My father looked up sharply from the French novel he had been reading. My mother said:

'Perhaps we'd better have Dr Biggs have another look at him.'

She went out of the room and I heard her going rather quickly upstairs.

The next day, as soon as I got back from school, my mother said to me:

'Get undressed and have a bath and go to bed at once. And don't argue. I'll explain later. You can have supper in bed. Don't waste time, go now.'

Astonished, I did as I was told. It was plain that my mother meant business. As I was getting into bed she came into my room. She sat on the bed. She did not look cross.

185

She looked worried. She explained that Dr Biggs had been in that morning to have another look at my brother. For ten days Dr Biggs had thought that my brother had tonsilitis.

But now, it seemed, Dr Biggs was more inclined to think it might be diphtheria.

Diphtheria! I had been there before . . . the choking swab, the dreaded carpet-needle thrust deep into the muscles of my bottom . . .

'And he is coming back at about six to take swabs from all of us and give us all a shot of antitoxin. That's why I thought you'd be more comfortable getting to bed first, with no need to undress and wash after you are sore from that needle.'

That needle. This time it was thrust into the muscle of my upper arm. This time I was too old to yell. The choking swab was pushed down my throat and dollied about. Dr Biggs stood there, as so often in the past, bending over me in bed, every open pore of his nose familiar to me, every yellow fold of his face, those eyes of an old bird of prey too tired to swoop. For once he did not ask how the bow-els were. He asked me if my throat was sore. He looked into my mouth with no change of focus in those dimming eyes. Somewhere over the sea-coast of Bohemia an ancient bird of prey drifted, off course.

They left my room. I heard them go along the landing to my brother's room. They went in and shut the door. My arm, marked purple where the great needle had gone in, ached with a strong, dull pain that would last a long time.

I was kept from school. I was told not to enter my brother's room.

'But that's absurd,' I objected. 'I've been in and out of his room for the last ten days, I've spent hours there. Why stop just because old Whhhher-and-Whhhatski thinks it's diphtheria? Yesterday he thought it was tonsilitis and he probably will again tomorrow.'

'You'll do as you're told,' said my mother.

When Dr Biggs came back on Sunday we learned that my parents and I were, so far, clear. My brother had diphtheria. Dr Biggs took another swab from my throat. The result of this swab would not be known while I was still at

186

home. I was to be sent away. Where to? My arm was swollen up and itching ferociously.

My grandparents had a telephone but at that time we had not. My mother telephoned from the undertaker's across the road. As the day wore on my father's face darkened, my mother's became lined. Telegrams were sent and received. When asked if I could stay at Sherbrooke Lodge while my brother was ill, so that, if my swab was again negative, I could return to school, my grandfather refused. He was afraid of infection. My father raged at this, in view of the many unused rooms in that big house where I could have lived isolated for a week. It was then that he telegraphed his own parents, who lived in a box of a cottage on the outskirts of a village in Kent. It was arranged that I should go there immediately. My mother crossed the road again to the undertaker's, telephoned her father again.

Could he lend us his car and chauffeur to drive my father and me down to Kent and bring my father back? The answer was *No* again. My grandfather would on no account ask his chauffeur to work on a Sunday. It was his chauffeur's day of rest.

It was not my parents' day of rest. By this time we were all blown up and itching like stray dogs. My father cursed my grandfather and his chauffeur in a rich litany of obscenities. My mother looked unhappy, in between hanging up at my brother's door sheets reeking of disinfectant, and packing things in a suitcase for me.

A taxi came to the door. I kissed Umski and the silly Fluffkins goodbye. I would have said goodbye to Bethany, gaunt and straw-coloured, our current maid, but she had run away temporarily to the Salvation Army as she did from time to time, to be saved. When she was saved enough she would run back. When she returned next time, to find a family stricken with pestilence, I guessed she might stay a little longer than usual. Serving in a lazar-house should offer many fruitful opportunities for salvation, without having to travel to the penitents' bench.

'Goodbye, darling.' My mother hugged me briefly. 'I'd better not kiss you . . . Tell Grandma I'll be writing to her about your washing.'

I said goodbye.

187

My father picked up my suitcase and we went down the path to where the taxi waited. Darkness had already fallen on that winter day. The street was wet, shining blackly under the headlights of the taxi as it moved off. The aching thrill of leaving the known for the unknown tingled in my veins and touched up my punctured arm.

'Does your arm itch badly too?' I asked my father.

'Like buggery,' he replied.

The Sunday train service into the country was slow and infrequent. We had to wait a long time at Swanley Junction. There were few people about. Here too the lights shone liquidly along the damp platform and the receding rails. My father broke open a packet of plain chocolate which we munched as we waited for our train to steam in. My arm still hurt and itched but the nature of the discomfort was changing in a way that I recognised: it would be better soon.

The train, when we boarded it, stopped at every station. It was almost empty. The names of the stations could only just be read under their dim lighting. The train puffed on, then stopped again.

'Here we are,' said my father. He hauled my suitcase down from the rack. We were the only passengers alighting. We gave up our tickets to the one porter on duty and stepped through the little booking-office into the lane beyond. There were no lights ahead but the faintly foggy darkness, smelling of fields, was not completely black. We walked between hedges for about ten minutes, then turned into a wider road. This was the main London to Folkestone road but as we walked along it, on that Sunday winter night in 1922, there was no traffic to be seen. A bank of land rose ahead of us. There were steps cut into it, leading to a garden gate. We went through and up a long front garden, round the side of the house to the back door. This was my grandparents' cottage.

There was a white cloth laid on the table with an oil lamp in the middle. The lamp had a white porcelain diffusing globe. The body was made of a metal like pewter—as I learned later, antimony—with figures of people and animals in high relief all round it. My grandparents kissed and hugged me. After the strangeness and the black sheen of the journey, the little room seemed homely and not subject to change.

For supper we had two pies. These must have been the pies my grandmother was baking when the telegram arrived and she had kept them both intact for us to eat cold at supper. The first was a beefsteak pie, full of tender gobbets of meat in a rich juice tinctured with herbs. The second was an apple pie, a perfect apple pie, succulent, sweetly sharp, touched with cloves. Both pies were covered with thick pie-crust that was exactly right, just solid enough to melt in the mouth, just tender enough to satisfy, tasting of the essence of perfect pastry. The finishing touch was the patterns of flowers and leaves with which the pie-crust had been decorated with its own substance, a graceful still life made to be eaten.

After partaking deeply of the two perfect pies I went up to bed by candlelight. The little staircase was steep and narrow. Upstairs I slept in a big bed with an engulfing feather mattress, the sleep of my life.

After breakfast—the bacon was just right, on the verge of crisping but not yet crisp—I walked with my father to the station. While we waited for the train he said he hoped to come down soon to see me. The result of my swab would be through by then. I was not worried about my swab. My father looked at me rather lingeringly when we kissed goodbye before he entered the train.

I walked away, back to the small brick cottage on the bank.

It was one of a row of six or eight semi-detached cottages, small houses with big gardens front and back. The land rose again behind them. At the top end of my grandparents' back garden was a huge cherry tree, big enough to climb and be lost in. It was a country of cherry trees, cob nuts and hops, a rich country in summer. But this was winter still.

The cottage had a kitchen, a scullery and a sitting room downstairs and three rooms upstairs. There was no bathroom. Water was laid on to the scullery and to the lavatory, a brick sentry box just by the back door. There was a range in the kitchen and an oil stove in the scullery. By these simple arrangements some of the best food I have ever tasted was brought to table.

189

The excellence of the food as I remember it is not a wistful trick of memory. It was a fact. In his day my grandfather had been head chef in noble houses, including that of the Duke of Westminster, then the richest man in Europe. Grandpa had cooked for kings. He cooked no longer, except to act as kitchen boy and prepare the vegetables and, of course, to decorate the pies. But he had taught his wife his tricks and the simple dishes, which were all they could afford, tasted like the bread of heaven.

He was a shortish, spare, broad-shouldered old man with blue twinkling eyes behind round gold spectacles, in the days when spectacles were usually oval. His white beard and moustache were neatly trimmed. Though his clothes were shabby, there was nothing messy or unkempt about him. He had definite ideas about hygiene—it is certain there would have been no peeing in the soup in any ducal kitchens under his supervision. When he went off to the lavatory after breakfast he always took with him a basin of water to wash himself. Toilet paper, he said, was a disgusting compromise which failed to do properly the job for which it had been made. A good wash was necessary. That was the one good idea the Hindus had had. No doubt after all that curry their fundaments would feel like balls of fire and crave total immersion, preferably in the Ganges. In the absence of the Ganges, my grandfather would make do with a small basin of water. Had he been better placed financially, no doubt he would have been a bidet man.

A top chef had always been a relatively well-paid job with many perks such as a good house and a servant, not to mention lucrative backhanders from suppliers. My grandfather had never saved a penny. He had squandered his money on horses, even rising to the peak of silliness by launching a racing paper called *Electric Flashes*, confident that it would pay its way. He had filled some of the best chef jobs in the country, with the Earl of Derby and the Marquis of Salisbury, as well as the Duke of Westminster, but he never stayed more than a few years. He would have been the ideal cook but not perhaps the ideal employee, being of independent views with a keen eye for the comical. A brilliant shot, he was sometimes privately invited to take a gun and join this or that lordly boss when there were no guests around; he was admired for his sporting talents and no doubt his easy and amusing manner made him an acceptable companion personally if not socially.

I had never visited my grandparents in this little cottage before, though I had seen them occasionally when they came to London.

'Do you remember coming to stay with us when we lived at Great Barton?' my grandfather asked me as we set out, on my first morning, to visit the butcher.

'Oh yes, I remember a great deal about it.'

'You were very young. We left there in 1913.'

'What happened to Jack?'

'I had to shoot him. He got old and sick. He was a wonderful gun dog, Jack, I've never seen better. You can't beat a curly-coated retriever, though they seem to be going out of fashion now.'

I could still feel my three-year-old fingers burrowing their length into the dense, curly black pelt of the old dog as he lay flopped at my grandfather's feet in the heat of that pre-war summer. He stank strongly. I had loved old Jack. He was always, always there, placid under his rug-like coat, giving off the very odour of faithfulness.

'You're very fond of animals, aren't you?'

'Yes. Except for a few people, I like animals better than people.'

'Do you know why?'

'They never complain or criticise, and if they love you they love you all their life.'

'I remember how you cried when I said I was going off to shoot sparrows. Do you remember that?'

'Oh yes.'

One morning, very early indeed, I had woken up in my mother's bed. Grandpa's head looked round the crack of the door.

'We're just off to shoot . . . sparrows,' he said, twinkling. I burst into tears. Almost the only birds I knew were the sparrows of London.

'He doesn't mean sparrows,' my mother had comforted me, 'he means pheasants and partridges.' That was a little better, but not much. Grandpa was off with my father to

191

bag some illicit game. Jack was an essential part of the household economy.

At Great Barton they had lived at the Mill House, isolated in fields but for the windmill across the yard. The windmill laboured under the wind with huge creaking flails. Mr Manning the miller was blind in one eye: chaff had blown into it. That eye was white. We clambered up wooden stairs going round and round the mill, seeing through small openings the flails sweeping past with a daring closeness. The smell of the corn being ground was unforgettable, so fresh, nutty, heady, satisfying. For the rest of my life after that, not an opened bag of animal feed but it gave off by comparison a whiff of mouldiness. The corn ground in that mill was the stuff of the bread of heaven and all the food eaten in my grandfather's house tasted of it.

'I remember the windmill,' I said, 'and I remember the smell of the garden.'

My father had spread his jacket and laid me on top of a thick clipped hedge. Up through the maze of twigs came the fumes of summer and the garden, warm earth and wholesome rot. A path between shrubs led to the earth closet, a scrubbed white seat with two holes cut in it, a big hole and a little hole. I would sit on the little hole and enjoy the comfortable pigsty reek of the all-welcoming cesspit beneath me. Then there was the scent of flowers, the sweet essence of that garden never again to be captured or forgotten. There was the scent of the magnolia trained round my open bedroom window. There were lilies, roses, pinks and sweet peas, catmint, old man and something unnamed that was ferny or mossy. There was cherry pie, mignonette and the powdery scent of pansies. In that garden there was an air so sweet it could be gulped like a birthday treat by a three-year-old.

'The garden there had a special smell,' I said to my grandfather.

'When I make up a posy from the garden for your grandmother,' he said, 'I always take care to see it smells as good as it looks. That is most important. So I always slip in a sprig of mignonette if possible, or a moss rose or honey-suckle. It's nice to include a glow-worm or two, if there are any about, so that it glows in the dark—your grandmother is always pleased to get a posy with a glow-worm inside it.'

This delightful old man was devoted to his wife, never mind that he had rarely provided for her with any reliability and had often left her racked with worry over tradesmen's debts while he was away catering for shooting parties in Scottish sporting lodges. In his estimation there was no one like his Lu (her name was Lucy). My grandfather lacked a talent for calculation. In many ways he was an artist. He had wanted to be an artist but his father (perhaps wisely) had torn up his drawings.

The family had always lived in Banbury. By tradition, they were the keepers of the original recipe for Banbury cakes, first marketed commercially in the eighteenth century by an enterprising forebear called Betty White. There had always been Banbury cakes. Shakespeare had mentioned them. But it was Betty White, hindered more than helped by an idle and profligate husband called Jarvis, who had put them on the map. The bakery business had prospered but my grandfather, born in 1843, had not wanted to go into it. He had received a sound education at the grammar school, where there was a drawing master exceptionally gifted at developing talent in his pupils. My grandfather drew beautifully. He would spend hours putting the bloom on a still life of grapes, then his father would rage along and tear it up. They both had fiery tempers and my grandfather left home.

There was another brother who left home too, making for Portugal, where he went into the wine business. My grandfather scarcely ever spoke of his early life, all that was known of it was picked up in snatches by my father. Evidently my grandfather was sensitive about the circumstances of that parting from his family. He never went back. It seems that men often grieve over mothers they have left, yet they do not return to them.

'I thought we were going to the butcher's?' I said as we turned away from the village, climbed a stile and continued along a track through an orchard.

'So we are. The meat is better here than in the village butcher's.' Through the trees a wooden shed with an open side came into view. One or two carcases were hanging

193

inside. There was nobody about. My grandfather hollered and after a minute or two a man with a cleaver and a saw appeared through the trees beyond.

The two of them entered into earnest talk. It appeared that this man was a grazier. My grandfather liked to choose his meat, small though that portion every week might be, on the hoof. That way he had the best quality available and could be sure it had been properly hung and was neatly butchered. Hopelessly incompetent though he had shown himself to be in managing money, when it came to matters of taste, smell and texture, my grandfather was meticulous. There could be no compromise with things of the senses.

Somewhere along the line he must have gone to France and trained there as a chef, building on the groundwork familiar to him from the Banbury cake bakery. Most of his friends were French chefs. A close friend of the family was Monsieur Menager, the royal chef, famous for his extravagant use and waste of costly viands at Buckingham Palace. His daughters had been friends of my mother's when they were girls and it was through the Menagers that my mother and father had met.

We walked back together over the fields. It was one of those soft February days with streaks of lemon light through clouds. Nearby, the leafless trees were brown, but massed trees in the distance had the beginnings of a purplish look. Up the steps cut into the bank we climbed, through the garden gate and round to the back door of the cottage.

Everything in that little sitting room was worn with use. It reminded me of the leathery skin of some old draught animal where the hair had rubbed thin under harness. A sagging armchair beside a small bookcase was set at right angles to the fire on one side, a basket chair on the side opposite. My grandfather would sit in the sagging chair, turning quite red about anything in the paper that annoyed him. What made him turn reddest was someone called Lovat Fraser who wrote in one of the Sunday papers in a manner that caused him the most extreme annoyance. What this journalist wrote about I do not remember, though my grandfather was always carrying on about it in furious terms. A number of things annoyed him. He greatly

194

disliked clergymen and what he thought of as their humbug. Once, when the vicar called and my grandmother, seeing him come up the path, bundled darning and cardigans under cushions hastily fluffed up, my grandfather snorted, 'Cloth worship!' and beat it outside to The Lodge. This was a roomy shed in the garden, its shelves stacked with little labelled containers of seed. My grandfather was a skilful gardener and spent much of his time, in good weather, working in the garden or pottering in The Lodge.

I went for long walks alone. A small dog attached himself and followed me everywhere. He was a shaggy terrier of anonymous breed, the sort often seen with poachers and ratcatchers. He was a wanderer but no stray. Somebody fed him. Once he had returned me to my grandparents' cottage he wasted no time hanging about scrounging: he was off. The next day he would be back again, following me. I never knew where he came from. I called him Wozzy.

More than once, walking with Wozzy along a lane that petered out in a woodland track, I had passed three people who must have come out of the only house on that lane, a comfortable-looking red brick house with a white gate opening on to a short drive. It stood in a big garden with trees and shrubs. Under a tree was a drift of snowdrops and the spears of daffodils. Behind the house, part of a tennis court with a summerhouse at the corner could just be glimpsed. More than once on my way to the wood I met these three walking. They were a big rosy man, quite elderly, a much younger plump rosy woman and a fair rosy girl of nineteen or twenty. They smiled as they passed me. The second time they bade me good morning.

'Oh, that was Mr and Mrs Williamson and their daughter,' my grandmother told me when I asked her about them. They had taken the house a year or so ago and had done wonders with the garden which was badly run down. Mr Williamson had retired from a solicitor's practice in Chatham. An only son in the Navy had gone down with his ship on Atlantic convoy in 1918. That may have had something to do with the family wanting to get away from Chatham, though this must be a bit quiet for a girl of Miss Williamson's age, my grandmother decided.

I thought Miss Williamson was very lucky to be living

here. That summerhouse at the far end of the tennis court was a desirable thing to have in one's garden. Not much of it could be seen from the road. I imagined sitting in it. Perhaps there was a little pool there, just out of sight, with leaves reflected in it in summertime.

In the evening, after tea, when the antimony lamp was lit, my grandmother and I would play cribbage or draughts. I had not played cribbage before. I liked the little board with the peg-holes in it. I could see now what my mother was talking about when she told me that as a very small child she would be given a blob of raw pastry to roll out on a cribbage board. It would be baked with the pies in the oven and would come out with an interesting pattern of raised dots. My grandmother was no good at draughts. I always beat her. She had no grasp of the tactics of defence. It was nice of her to play with me.

For supper there was always some delicious light savoury dish. My favourite was flakes of fish cooked in sauce with just a hint of anchovy and cayenne pepper. It was served in a white fluted soufflé dish and eaten with bread and butter. At nine o'clock I went to bed, carrying a candle which cast wheeling banister shadows. On a cold night it was bliss to sink into the feather bed. Everything sad was far away.

One morning when the postman came there was a letter from my father. I was not going to get diphtheria, my swab had proved negative. My brother was no worse, it appeared he only had a mild attack of the disease, but he and my mother were suffering more from the treatment than the illness. Both were swollen and itching from the antitoxin which Dr Biggs was now administering with the same blind faith with which he had previously prescribed his two medicines. Nobody could foretell how long the infection might last. A succession of swabs would be taken and tested until proved negative.

'That is very good news,' said my grandmother with satisfaction. 'I'll write a postcard at once and you shall take it to the letter-box. Your Aunt Hilda will get it by teatime and I expect we shall see Dudley arriving on his bicycle this weekend. His father gave him a new bike for Christmas and he goes all over the place on it.'

196

My cousin Dudley Arnaud lived in Maidstone. He was almost exactly my own age. He had no brothers or sisters. We met seldom but always got on well together. Brattle Place had been the common ground where usually we had met. He was a sturdy boy a little shorter than I with blue eyes and light brown hair cut short to conceal as far as possible its tendency to curl. There was something pleasing that I could not define about the relation between his forehead, his cheekbones and his nose. In appearance a typical English boy, Dudley was by descent half French —his grandfather had been one of the French chefs our grandfather had known. He was not a studious boy but was very knowledgeable about everything that grew or moved out of doors.

'Mother says you're to come and stay with us for a weekend soon, now you're not catching. If you come on a Friday I can meet you off the bus after school.'

Of course it was term-time for him. In the autumn he was going to board at Dover College, at that time not considered a centre of academic excellence though well-placed as a launching pad for a boy like my cousin with an interest in sea birds and in swimming the Channel.

'Do you know about positive and negative swabs?'

'I didn't, but Father explained.'

Dudley's father, Uncle Francis, had a job of deeply morbid interest. He was the public analyst for Kent and from time to time had to examine a bit of body for traces of poison. He could declare the water of certain wells unfit for drinking. He would know all about swabs.

'He said you were lucky to get away with it. If you'd developed diphtheria here you'd have had to go to the fever hospital. They're quite strict about diphtheria. There was an outbreak in Father's area last year and quite a lot of children were packed off to hospital. One or two died —their throats swell up, you know, they can't breathe and they die. Sometimes they cut their throats and stick a tube in to breathe through but they often die all the same.'

'I know. I've often read about it in those old story books where people are always saying, "It doesn't signify," and children die like flies of scarlet fever and diphtheria . . . Where is this fever hospital?'

197

'Somewhere near Rochester, I think. An isolated place.'

After Dudley had gone, promising to come back the next day, I thought about Rochester and that fever hospital, that isolated place where I might have been sent, that place of exile.

Rochester. What did I know about Rochester? Virtually nothing, except that there was a cathedral there. Who would have visited me (goggling at me through glass) in Rochester? Not my mother: she would be at home nursing my brother behind a door draped in antiseptic sheets. My father? Only seldom. He would be too busy and worried; Rochester was too far away. What about Lord Rochester? Scarcely likely; people with titles never lived near the places belonging to their names. The Duke of Norfolk lived in Sussex, the Duke of Devonshire in Derbyshire. If ever I became Lady Clapham Junction I should probably be living on the Isle of Skye. As for Lord Rochester, it was most unlikely that he would be bothered to visit me, even if he lived next door to the isolation hospital. His memory of me would not have been one he would wish to retain. 'I am Lord Rochester,' he had said, only to have the front door shut in his face. I was old enough now to see that a very new lord might take to such treatment even less kindly than a lord who had been a lord for a long time. As a sick visitor Lord Rochester could be written off.

But I did remember something about Rochester, or somewhere near it. Years before, when I had been staying with my other grandparents at Brattle Place, we had all gone one day to a place near Rochester where Dickens had once lived. There was a chair he had sat in, a heavy thing of dark wood. They had made me sit in it. I had no interest in Dickens or his chair. What engrossed me was a nearby park, Cobham Park I think it was called, where we had eaten picnic sandwiches. We had walked through the park towards a lake. There were trees, oak trees probably, but one could not be sure because there were no leaves on the trees, though it was early summer, rhododendron time. Every leaf had been eaten from the trees by caterpillars, myriads of small greenish caterpillars swinging from the branches on filaments of silk, veils and veils of spun silk with caterpillars swinging in the light. Beyond the frail

198

curtain of swinging silk was the lake bordered by rhododendrons, their great bunched flowers reflected in pinks and lilacs from the greenish water, their colours softened by the hanging veils. Over the lake hovered and swooped a rainbow of dragonflies. The sheen of the reflected colours, the pinks and the lilacs drenched in green made misty by the caterpillar veils swaying in pale gold and silver light, held me like an enchantment. Caterpillars and dragonflies, rhododendrons and green water . . . I could have stayed there all day long, staring.

'You must come and sit in Dickens' chair,' they said. I was dragged away into a house to sit in a chair where a man had sat writing books I didn't enjoy.

Young though I was, I had lived long enough to know that a phenomenon like the caterpillars swinging on their silken threads did not happen every year. That miracle of light, colour, movement and stillness might not be seen by anyone for years; by me never again. I knew that then. I sat in Dickens' chair resentfully. The heavy thing would be there for years for fools to sit in when the caterpillars and dragonflies were gone.

That was what I remembered about Rochester, or somewhere near it.

But the isolation hospital would be a hard, lonely place of right angles, cut off by walls or high railings with a padlocked iron gate that creaked when opened by a surly porter who uttered only monosyllables. It would be staffed by brutalised nurses unfit for employment in gentler hospitals where they could be seen by visitors. At a fever or isolation hospital there would be scarcely any visitors, except the occasional undertaker come to collect an infective corpse sealed in its lead coffin. Plain vans would pass occasionally in and out, bearing who knew what. Food would be stale bread and the offscourings of slaughter-houses. Pigs' eyes would float in the skilly. In autumn, the place would be a dumping-ground for the blighted potatoes of greedy farmers. Corrupt doctors would swill rum with the sinister bearded matron after signing certificates stating cause of death as diphtheria when it should have been malnutrition. It would not have been for nothing that Dickens had lived within spitting distance of this place. It would have been affected by his nearness and been anxious to please. Such must have been the place to which I would have been consigned if that swab had proved positive.

My mother had thrown me to the wolves. Even before I left London, in those few hours of telegrams and flurry on that Sunday afternoon, I had been vaguely aware that some conspiracy had been hatched between my mother and Dr Biggs, that the old fool had been got round by her and persuaded to loosen up the regulations governing notifiable diseases so that my brother could be nursed at home behind a decontamination screen of lysolised sheets instead of being sent to a fever hospital—a *London* fever hospital. At the time, I had not thought it through. Now I knew. I had been sent away with the question mark of infection hanging over my head, so that my brother, a grown man, could be nursed, somewhat illicitly, at home. If I had developed diphtheria in Kent . . . too bad, away to the fever hospital in Rochester with me. There was no doubt about it. My mother had had to choose and it was me she had thrown to the wolves.

But the wolves had not devoured me. I had survived. Tempered and hardened, I was free and strong, glad to be away from home, except for Fluffkins and Umski. Here I had Wozzy, my father would come down now and then, and now that I was no longer a health hazard Dudley would often be cycling over to be with me. Only my mother and her family had thrown me to the wolves.

10

One day, walking with Wozzy along the lane where the Williamsons lived, I saw an old man leading a small rough pony between the shafts of a ramshackle two-wheeled cart. His face was covered in grizzled reddish whiskers under a stained felt hat with the brim coming away. He wore mud-coloured work clothes and heavy hob-nailed boots. As he passed me he gave me a wide smile of a few blackened teeth, touched his cap and let out an explosion of unintelligible speech. His whiff and a black lurcher bitch followed behind him.

'That would be old Charlie Platt,' my grandmother told me later. 'Yes, he is difficult to understand, he was born with a cleft palate and losing most of his teeth hasn't helped. I expect he had been taking firewood to the Williamsons. He sells rabbits, pea-sticks, hatching eggs—anything he can get hold of. You must have noticed that tumbledown cottage with all the mess round it on the edge of the wood going down to the brook? That's where he lives. I must make him another pie. He loves a pie.'

'Does he live alone there?'

'Now, yes. Until a couple of years ago he had an old sister living with him but she got pneumonia and died. She kept house for him and used to go out charring at the vicarage and one or two other houses. The place was tidier then. Now he manages on his own but I think he misses his sister's cooking.'

'He lives on rabbit stew, or bacon and fried potatoes, or bread and cheese and onions. I asked him,' my grandfather joined in. 'I could scarcely understand him, but that's what I gathered. Also he misses the puddings his sister used to make. From the smell of him, it must have been his sister who did the washing . . . but he manages well enough on his own. With that speech impediment it's hard to tell whether he's all there or not.'

'His sister was quite normal. She told me once that at one time he had a sort of reputation as a fortune-teller, but that's died down now. She said that as a small boy he was taken to a fair and went with his mother into the palmist's booth. He saw the palmist looking at his mother's hand and when he got home he started picking up his mother's or sister's hand and jabbering, imitating the palmist, you see, but somehow he got it all wrong and looked at the *backs* of their hands. As time went on he told his sister—she could understand him—that when he looked at fingernails they gradually turned into faces and started speaking to him; he read their lips, he said, foretelling the future. I don't suppose he was any worse at it than most fortune-tellers. But he took money off visitors and Constable Mereworth gave him a warning, and anyway, I doubt if anybody would want to go there now, cottage is too dirty. There's no harm in old Charlie . . . must make a pie for him when I'm baking. He does enjoy that. A plum pie. There were more last year than I knew what to do with, I bottled pounds and pounds of them as well as making jam.'

'I could take him a pie.'

'So you could, and save your grandfather's legs. But we'll leave it till one day when Dudley's here, better than your going alone.'

I had noticed Charlie's cottage. Hemmed in with overgrown bushes, bicycle wheels and cart wheels, hutches, water butts and cold frames, it stood in a hollow going down to the brook beyond the wood. It was part brick, part daub, patched with cement and shingles. The tiled roof had a slithery look, like cards being dealt. At the back there was a well-tended kitchen garden.

Next time Dudley came over we had plum tart for dinner. Two more were cooling on wire trays. One was a smaller, covered pie.

'That's pie's for Charlie,' our grandmother said. 'You two can take it along to him this afternoon. It'll be cool enough by the time you're ready. You won't understand him but he'll know who it's from. Bring me the baking tin back. He knows how to turn it out between two plates to keep it

202

intact. You'd better carry it,' she said, addressing me, 'I wouldn't trust Duds not to eat it or drop it.' She ruffled his hair. 'Off you both go. Mind you keep it level.'

We walked slowly. Wozzy fell in at my heels. I carried the little pie in my two hands, carefully. We passed the Williamsons' house, the only one in the lane, and entered the wood. At the end of the wood there was a stile, leading to a footpath through a rabbity field clumped with thickets of bramble. Just out of sight round a curve of the footpath was Charlie's cottage.

'You go over first,' I said, 'and hold the pie while I climb over.' I handed the pie, still faintly warm, over the stile for my cousin to take.

What happened then I do not know. Somehow, between our twenty fingers and the stile, the pie slipped and fell face downward on the short February grass, its tin bottom gleaming.

'Now what!' I sprang over the stile and together we knelt to inspect the damage. Gingerly, I lifted the baking tin by its edges and the underside of the pie was revealed, biscuity brown, miraculously unbroken. But how to get it off the ground and back again in its tin? There was no way. We stood up in some dismay. We heard heavy footsteps approaching from the direction of Charlie's cottage, and the sound of gulping at our feet. Wozzy was gobbling the pie. A black streak shot along the footpath towards us, Charlie's lurcher bitch. There was a scuffle and a yelp, the black bitch was slurping up the remains of the pie as Wozzy made for the brambles, carrying the baking tin. Charlie approached. He was dressed as before. He grinned at us, touching his hat. His few black teeth could just be seen through his whiskers. He made his explosive noises, scrambled speech full of undeciphered meaning, emphasised by expansive gestures of goodwill. He passed on. As he made to step on to the stile, his dirty hobnailed boot with its stiff bent-up toecap came down plump onto the place were the pie had been. His lurcher leapt over the stile after him and the two disappeared among the trees of the wood.

Wozzy emerged, still carrying the baking tin. I took it from him. We headed for home and confession. But as we approached the back door of the cottage we could see our grandmother down the garden talking over the hedge to her neighbour Mrs Griffiths who was hanging out nappies on the line, so we slipped the baking tin into the sink and went away again out of the front door. Grandpa was dozing in his chair with the newspaper trailing over his knees and did not stir as we went past him through the kitchen.

We crossed the road, ran down the long field to the stream. Here among the willows Dudley pulled a quarter bottle of Johnnie Walker from his pocket. He unscrewed the cap.

'Smell that,' he said.

It was not whisky, it was petrol. Petrol then had a homelier smell than it has now, there was more of benzine about it, or brass polish. We both liked the smell and sniffed it up.

'Where did you get it?'

'I siphoned it out of a lorry.'

'Where was the lorry?'

'Parked just off the road on the way here.'

I did not believe him.

'You had the whisky bottle in your pocket?'

'Yes. A bottle is often useful.'

'What about rubber tubing?' I knew about siphons. Siphons were the sort of things my brother used to talk to me about, showing off his know-all expertise, years before I went to school. 'What about rubber tubing?'

'What about it?'

'Well, where is it?'

'Never mind where it is.'

'Did you chuck it away?'

'Of course I didn't.'

'Then it must be in your pocket.'

'Yes.'

'Show it to me, then.'

'Why should I?'

'To prove you're not a liar. I bet you nicked that petrol from a tin in Uncle Francis' garage. Didn't you?'

I sprang at him and we rolled over and over while I frisked his pockets for rubber tubing. There was none. But he was carrying a box of matches.

'What are these for?'

204

'To light the petrol. Look!' And from the high bank of the stream he leaned over and dribbled petrol from the bottle on to the water, then struck a match and tossed it after. The little stream was running strongly and the petrol, as it ignited, flared out in broken ripples of white and yellow, a river of light, miraculous, making and taking reflections, as it plaited itself away between the willows.

We crossed the stream further down where there were stepping-stones, then made across a small heath of birches and dead bracken to a church that stood in its quiet church-yard at a little distance from the village that it served. We went through the lychgate and walked about among the gravestones, reading the inscriptions. Some were too weatherworn and lichened to be deciphered. One gravestone had scratched on it through the moss by a recent hand two words I had often seen before, from the time when I could first read. Chalked on walls, cut into wooden donated seating, scrawled on railway underpasses, their letters distorted by running paint, haste and tremulous illiteracy, these two words, first read by me as *Prick* and *Puck*, here appeared again, popping up in this ageing churchyard with the gibbering persistence of idiots.

'Do you know what those words mean?' my cousin asked me.

'No.'

'Well, if you don't know I shan't tell you.'

Whether he expected me to urge him with strong en-treaties to reveal the meaning of these many-rendered vocatives will never be known. *Prick* and *Puck* had always sounded to me like the names of two silly fairies in a kindergarten play of no possible interest except to school-teachers like the mysteriously disappeared Miss Snead. I drifted away from the desecrated gravestone towards the gate, with Dudley dawdling after.

Beside the lychgate there was a thick old tree, the gnarled ivy-clad bole going up some ten feet, then abruptly trun-cated with only a few thin branches sprouting under the rim. It was obviously hollow. We climbed up and looked down into the hollow but it was too dark in there for anything to be seen from above. We wondered whether there might be an ancient toad down there or something

205

unexpected. Dudley said he would go down inside and see.

'Can you get back?'

'Of course I can.'

I could see that my cousin, after being caught out about not having siphoned the petrol from a parked lorry and not having been pressed to tell all about the fairies Puck and Prick, might be in need of the mini ego-boost the descent into the hollow tree would offer. He dropped down on to the soft mould inside. From above I looked down into the dimness.

'What is there down there?'

'Nothing much. Just earth and stuff. Can't see, really.'

I remembered the box of matches in his pocket.

'Strike a match and have a look.'

There was a pause, then the flare of a match.

'Nothing here but old leaves and a few toffee papers. And some orange peel . . . I'm coming up . . . Give me a hand.'

I hauled him up over the rim of the hollow tree, then we climbed down and made off the long way round that took us across a plank bridge over the stream higher up, thence into another part of the wood leading to the Williamsons' lane. He walked ahead of me along the track, between trees with the buds of leaves unopened but grown bigger since I first walked the wood.

'Did you know you'd got a tear in the seat of your trousers?'

'Not again! Mother will kill me. This has only just stopped being my best suit.'

He was wearing a suit of Donegal tweed with short trousers. There was an inch-long three-cornered tear, probably made when he had slithered down inside the tree.

We passed the Williamsons' house. Daffodils were coming out but there was no sign of human life. They would be at the back, having tea, looking out through French windows on to the tennis court and the summer-house.

'Do you know the Williamsons?' I asked.

'I've seen them. Gran mentions them sometimes. What about them?'

'They have this tennis court. It looks lovely, what you can see of it beyond the daffodils. Look.'

'Seems a decent place. No garage, though, unless its round the back. Have they got a car?'

'I've no idea . . . I see them walking about. I should love to play tennis on that court.'

'Why?'

'I don't know, really. I just want to. It seems somehow special.'

'What's special about it? It looks like an ordinary grass court to me, what you can see of it.'

'Yes, but the summerhouse—you can see the corner of it—I think the summerhouse looks out on a pool, with reflections in it.'

'You've been there, then?'

'No. Not yet, I haven't.'

'Then why on earth are you talking about a pool you don't even know is there?'

'Oh, I don't know . . . I'm hungry. Let's run. Tea will be ready and you know you'll be walloped if you're not home before lighting-up time . . . Come on!'

Tea was on the table.

'Gran,' said Dudley.

'Yes, what is it?'

'I've . . . I've slightly torn my trousers again. I wondered if you, if you could do something about it . . . ?'

'Off with them. Sit down and have your tea while I have a look. Though I don't know why you should expect me to do anything about it with only half an eye.'

Dudley sat down to tea in his underpants. Grandma hitched her spectacles up on to her forehead and squinted at the torn tweed held within an inch of her one short-sighted working eye. Some years before, when they were still living in Suffolk, Grandma had slipped and fallen coming out of church one Sunday. When she stood up she was blind in one eye. Her retina had become detached. In those days a detached retina stayed detached and Grandma had stayed blind in that eye. This had seemed a truly remarkable coincidence to me when I was three, because

207

Mr Manning the miller in his windmill across the yard was blind in one eye too. One-eyed blindness evidently went with the place.

While we ate boiled eggs and bread and butter with strawberry jam and slices of the inimitable succulent raisin cake that only my grandmother has ever been able to make, she sat there peering one-eyed at the tear and mending it with perfect invisible stitching, for she was a fine needle-woman, though the work strained her sight. Dudley was packed off just in time and told to ride straight home and not to dawdle.

'See you tomorrow,' he said, and rode away. It was a Saturday. We had forgotten all about Charlie and the ruined pie. At supper I told my grandparents what had happened.

They took it lightly.

'I'm not surprised,' my grandfather remarked. 'Seeing you two set off I laid a bet with your grandmother that pie would never get to Charlie in one piece—that's a tanner you owe me, Lu.'

'That can wait till pension day,' she replied placidly. The lamplight spread a pool of tranquillity over the supper table, over the white cloth, the yellow butter, the food illumined as if by some unsought blessing. I saw the two worn old faces in that blessed light and wanted never to leave them, never to have to say goodbye. My grandmother looked up.

'I'll play you at cribbage when we've cleared away supper. I'm better at crib than draughts,' she said, smiling at me.

That night I dreamed I was back at Sherbrooke Lodge, in the house of my other grandfather whom I hated. I did not want to stay but could not leave because I was being summoned by the dinner-gong, the tap-tap faint at first but rapid as Alice the parlourmaid, with the skill of a practised drummer, brought the beat up to a strange ringing roll and then let it taper away, *diminuendo*, rapid still but ever more faint until no longer heard. I awoke briefly, then turned over and dropped asleep again.

'Didn't you hear the fire-engine?' said my grandfather at breakfast. 'That bell was enough to waken the dead.'

'Children can sleep through anything,' my grandmother remarked, setting before me scrambled eggs on toast.

I waylaid Dudley as he dismounted from his bicycle. I spoke rapidly.

'Listen. The fire-engine was out in the middle of the night—that hollow tree in the churchyard, it was on fire. I'm telling you so that you don't look guilty when they start talking about it. It's awful, isn't it?'

'Do you think anybody knows it was us?'

'I shouldn't think so; but take that look off your face or they'll start asking you what's up.'

My cousin had the disadvantage of the sort of angel face that is noticeably marked by a sense of sudden guilt. We entered the house.

'Heard about the excitement last night, Duds?' My grandmother greeted him with a kiss.

'Er . . . yes, we were just talking about it.'

'The paper boy told me. They say the lychgate's badly singed, too.' My grandfather chuckled. 'You know what that means, don't you? A jumble sale in aid of the Lychgate Restoration Fund, tea and buns provided, bring your own buns and threepence for the tea. Won't be long before the vicar's round here again, piping his eye about the wickedness of the times and the decay of Holy Church. Cloth-worship!' My grandfather had gone quite red with indignation. He opened the Sunday paper. 'Let's see what Lovat Fraser has to say this week.' Lovat Fraser was guaranteed to make him go redder than ever.

Later my cousin and I talked it over. We both felt guilty and sorry, yet somehow blameless. He had struck the match but it was I who had suggested striking it. Confession would be considered the correct thing but not only would it not restore the tree, it would cause Dudley and myself to be marked people on any future wanderings. We would be bawled out wherever seen. There was nothing for it but to chew on our guilt.

So we chewed on our guilt and swallowed it. We never returned to the churchyard. The grave of Prick and Puck would not again be visited by us and that quiet place would know us no more.

Grandma baked another pie for Charlie, but this time my grandfather took it to him.

'Not one of Charlie's better days,' he remarked on his return. 'Poor chap stank to heaven and gobbled like a turkey, kept making a move to grab my hand and do his act of divination by fingernails, but I sidestepped that by offering him a pinch of tobacco. Rum chap. Must be lonely, though, since his sister died and nobody else understands him.'

'How does he manage shopping?'

'He points at things and knows all the prices. He's understood to that extent. But he can't converse.'

'I expect his lurcher and his pony understand him.'

'No doubt they do. Though their lack of fingernails must be frustrating to the seer in him . . . I saw the Williamsons on the way back. They spoke about you. Mrs Williamson asked how long you were staying and I said that depended on how soon a negative swab came up . . . Their garden seems to be coming along nicely. Tom Jenkins from the village has been working on the tennis court; it was all moss and weeds when they took the place over but they say he's done wonders, it'll be ready to play on by May. Miss Williamson asked if you would be coming back in the summer holidays and I said now you'd rediscovered us I expected you'd be coming back and she said she hoped you and Dudley would go along and play tennis there then, and maybe your brother too if he came down for a holiday when he was better. A nice-looking girl, that. Pity there's such a shortage of young men of the right age because of the war, but I expect she'll find one, the pretty ones usually do. But it's hard on the half-and-halfs, let alone the uglies unless they've got money.'

'Next time you visit us remember to bring your tennis racquet,' my grandmother said.

'Oh yes, I'll remember.'

The week that followed was a happy one for me. I wandered about with Wozzy at my heels, thinking about summer days to come, the drone of bees, the plop of ripe plums dropping from their trees, the plonk of tennis balls on the court beside the summerhouse, the pool reflecting . . . reflecting what? Lilac? Laburnum? Hardly, with ripe plums falling from the trees. Better have the pool reflecting sky and an edge of cloud, a reflection for all seasons. It was a happy week, but it ended.

The next Saturday my father arrived for a flying visit. The news he brought was that my brother, after six weeks of infection, had now been declared free of diphtheria. I could return home. Any day next week would do, he said, as it was now the school holidays again.

It was late afternoon, two days later. I was in the field opposite the cottage, flinging sticks for Wozzy to retrieve. Wozzy did not know that I was leaving him tomorrow. It was a dull day, not cold but heavy.

On the other side of the hedge there were people approaching along the road, talking. Now I could see their heads. It was the three Williamsons. As they drew near the gate I climbed over into the road.

'Hello,' Mr Williamson said, 'we haven't seen you lately. What have you been up to?'

'My father was here over the weekend. We went up on to the downs.'

'Your grandfather was saying he expects you'll be back in the summer holidays. You must come and play tennis with us and bring your cousin. Our court is just about ready and Margaret can't wait to play on it,' her mother said. 'But I don't think you've seen it, have you? . . . the view from the summerhouse . . .' She broke off as her husband stepped out into the road, holding up his hand to stop Charlie, who was pedalling towards us with his black lurcher following.

'I'll pay him that money we owe him, I don't like to keep him waiting . . . Ah, Charlie, I'm glad we've run into you. We were out when you called the other day and Cook hadn't the ready cash.'

Charlie dismounted, all whiskers and teeth. Over his shoulder he was carrying a sack, which he dumped by the hedge. His bitch sprawled down beside it and began to scratch under her elbow, making a little whimpering sound now and then. From beside me, Wozzy kept watch. Mr Williamson took out his notecase.

'Two pounds three and six, wasn't it? Firewood and the rabbit? Have you change for a pound note?'

Charlie shook his head as he was given the notes, and

made negative noises. Mr Williamson turned to his wife, but she said she had no money on her.

'I think I may have three and six,' his daughter said, pulling a purse out of the pocket of her tweed coat. 'Hold out your hand, Charlie, I'm afraid it's all in small change.' She took off her glove. She began counting out the coins—a few sixpences, a threepenny bit, a lot of coppers—her smooth fingers with the buffed, satiny nails contrasting disconcertingly with Charlie's broad and dirt-lined palm. She dropped the coins clinking into his hand one by one.

The black lurcher, pointed head raised, whined as she scratched half-heartedly at her lean rib-cage. Wozzy watched.

As Margaret Williamson dropped the last coin into Charlie's palm he grabbed her hand with a jerky snatch as a dog might lunge at a bone. He bent low over her fingers in pantomime parody of a diplomat kissing hands, but not merely allowing her fingers to rest in his, he was gripping the thick of her hand between his fingers and his dirty thumb; and all the time talking, gabbling his unintelligible language, spluttering droplets of saliva from the glottal no-man's-land behind his few blackened teeth.

There flashed into my mind a memory of the night of the end of the world, the breathless wait for what might come after that first awesome roll of thunder. It had been a moment ominous and static in its expectation of ill, a glimpse of limbo. Here was another moment heavy with a stillness that dismayed.

Mr Williamson's cheeks, which had seemed so rosy, could now been seen not to be rosy at all but only old flesh, faintly bluish, veiled by a minute network of red capillaries. His wife's round blue eyes gazed fixed, mere porcelain marbles. As for their daughter, pretty and pink, passively just not yielding to the drag of Charlie's hand, she stood there like a captured doll. It was a tableau of dismay that could go on for ever, a Worcester china group.

A piercing howl issued from the mouth of the black lurcher, to be joined at once by a higher wail from Wozzy, the waves of canine lament interweaving in a twist of sound now hideous, now almost musical, as the two dogs lifted up their heads, exposed their throats and made their mouths into two round holes. The warbling duet, chilling yet absurd, jerked the stalled moment back on to the tracks of time again.

The tableau shattered like a painted vase.

Charlie dropped the girl's hand, straightened up, pocketed the money, bared his discoloured teeth in an explosive grin of thanks, lifted the sack to his shoulder, wheeled his bicycle out from the hedge, mounted it and rode away along the road. The lurcher bitch loped easily after him. Wozzy watched him go.

There was a pause.

'Well,' said Mrs Williamson. 'We'd better be getting along . . . I expect we shall soon be seeing you again, dear,' she said, addressing me.

'Must be nearly teatime.' Her husband spoke like a wound-up toy.

Their daughter said nothing. She gave me a brief smile as they all moved off. I turned away towards my grandparents' cottage. Wozzy sloped off to wherever it was he went. I felt uneasy, as if something had gone wrong that was not my fault and that I could not put right.

The next day my grandfather walked with me to the station. Wozzy followed us.

As the train puffed away from the platform, I watched the old man and the mongrel terrier getting smaller, as if travelling backwards, away from me.

* * *

My brother had heard the taxi and was at the front door.

'Hello, Ugly!' he greeted me. 'You've grown an inch. What's more, you're beginning to look almost human.'

'Wish I could say the same of you. You look about thirty-five.' I pushed past him. 'Where are the cats?'

'In the drawing room, catching up on their sleep.'

There they were, Umski and Fluffkins, just as I had left them. When I spoke to them they stretched and purred faintly before going back to sleep. Mother came in.

'First priority the cats, I see . . . What about a kiss for your mother?'

She kissed me. Then she held me at arm's length and looked at me with her searching barrister look.

213

'You've changed a bit. You've grown, of course, but it's not just that. You're not quite the same as when you went away.'

Of course not. People who said goodbye and went away did not as a rule come back. The soldiers who had gone away to the war were not the same as those who came back.

'We're having roast chicken tonight and I've made you an apple cake because that's what you like best.'

As if by magic, Clifford appeared. He carried my suitcase upstairs. The stairs seemed wide and shallow. I had often noticed that when we came back from a holiday in an hotel or after I had been staying with my Sherbrooke Lodge grandparents, our staircase at home seemed steep and narrow. Now it seemed wide, with shallow steps. The stair-carpet felt thick. The little staircase in my grandparents' cottage was steep and narrow, thinly carpeted, yet going up it carrying a candle had been an ascent into a state of blessedness.

I looked out of my bedroom window on to the field, the place of my childhood. Now its eleven acres, with red roofs glimpsed beyond trees, seemed hemmed in. Clifford was looking at me.

'Glad to be back?'

'Not really.'

'I can see that.'

'There's no room here.'

'Have these other grandparents you've been staying with got a big house too, then?'

'No. It's tiny, a little cottage. And its shabby, everything's worn out. They're poor. They only spend money on food, they can't afford new clothes and things like gramophone records. But it was lovely there. There was a little dog. I called him Wozzy. He followed me about. He will miss me. I shall go back every holidays. I'm not going to work at school any more, either.'

'Why's that?'

'There's no point. I don't want to do well and go up to Oxford or Cambridge and get a good job and be stuck in an office or the law courts or dish out dinner parties to business friends of some bald husband with a paunch.'

'Husbands don't have to be bald with a paunch.'

'If they don't have to be, why are they?'

We laughed and ran downstairs to a splendid supper. It was lucky for Clifford that my brother's quarantine had not extended over the Easter holidays, or he might have starved. My mother looked older but I had to admire her, with her direct blue gaze, clear features and fair hair now thickly brushed with silvery white. My brother was very brusque with her. They had been shut up together in pesthouse seclusion for nearly two months and I could see he was sick of her. She would never be sick of him.

He left the table as soon as he had finished eating. As he was making for the door, my mother called to him.

'Don't forget to take your tonic, dear.' A bottle of Dr Biggs's red physic stood on the sideboard.

'I'm not taking any more of that lobster's piss,' he answered rudely and went out banging the door. Clifford made a face at me as he helped himself to another slice of apple cake.

'Where's Bethany?' I inquired.

'Bethany's in Wales, beating a tambourine in the train of some travelling revivalist. She'd been away about three weeks last time, so when she came back I took the opportunity of parting with her on the grounds of infection in the house. We parted on the best of terms. She said she would come back to see me, in the intervals, of course, of being saved. But I've engaged another girl, she's starting next week. Lily recommended her—you remember Lily?'

A previous maid of ours, Lily had had the misfortune, by no means uncommon at that period, to lose all her teeth at an early age. Since that time she had never been able to get a set of false teeth that stayed in and were comfortable: if they stayed in they were so uncomfortable she could not eat, if they were comfortable they kept falling out. Lily had given up on teeth altogether and ate only slops. She was married now but still came to see my mother occasionally, when she would sup a basin of bread and milk like a cat.

'Lily says she's an excellent worker with good references.'

'What's wrong with her?' Clifford asked.

'Why should there be anything wrong with her? . . . If you want more, Clifford, there's always bread and cheese.'

215

Or fruit . . . Well, as a matter of fact, it seems she does have a slight problem.'

Clifford kicked me under the table.

'What's her problem?' I asked.

'A pathological fear of spiders. If she sees one, she goes practically cataplectic.'

'What's cataplectic?'

'Temporarily paralysed with shock,' explained Clifford, who knew everything.

'Very awkward for the poor girl,' my father put in. 'She'll never be able to go into the garden to hang out washing on September mornings. There are webs of them everywhere then. I can't see her lasting long. What's her name?'

'You're not going to believe this. Her name's Miss Moffat . . . Phoebe Moffat.'

'Phobic Phoebe,' muttered Clifford.

'Very funny, but pretty awful for the poor girl. Where on earth can she go? There are spiders everywhere.'

'She could take up fishing. There won't be many spiders on a fishing smack.'

'Or she could work in a fever hospital,' I suggested.

'Why a fever hospital?'

'They are very bare and clean and disinfected . . . they are hosed down all the time, so there are no flies for spiders to eat. There are no visitors to bring in insects on their clothes. They are very lonely, isolated places. Phoebe could get a job in a fever hospital. There's one near Rochester.'

'How do you know that?' My mother spoke quite sharply.

'I asked.'

'Surely there's one nearer than that?' said Clifford, munching.

'There must be. But Rochester is the only one I know about, because I asked.'

There was a long pause.

'May I be excused?' I pushed back my chair. 'Come on Clifford, let's go.'

* * *

It was a Saturday morning in May. All the windows were open, the curtains shifting and lifting with the breath of lilac, their fabric speckled with sunlight and swaying leaves. In the hall stood ready two baskets packed with picnic food—cold ham, pork pies, salad, cake, tins of fruit. We had a boat of our own on the river now, or rather, a skiff on hire for the season, moored at a boatyard at Thames Ditton, its locker stocked with primus stove and Woolworth crockery and knives and forks, some doomed to be lost in the river during washing-up.

My brother and I were off for a day on the river. We were meeting a schoolfriend of mine and her sixteen-year-old brother. They were bringing a gramophone and some records. My brother was in blazer and white flannels. I was wearing for the first time a gingham dress with stripes of green and white.

We were finishing breakfast. My father, who had come down later than us, was drinking coffee and opening his letters. There was one from his mother.

'She sounds upsets,' he said. 'A neighbour of theirs went down suddenly with diabetes and died within the week. A girl only twenty. A Miss Williamson . . . Did you know her?' he asked me.

I swallowed on some toast that would not go down easily.

'Yes . . . by sight,' I mumbled.

'How very sad . . . Diabetes often races in young people, you know, if they are unlucky enough to develop it. In older people it can often be controlled by diet but in young people it simply races through them, draining them dry. They have to drink and drink but it runs straight through them: their tissues can't take it up so that they dry up as if they had died of thirst. There is no cure.'

My brother spoke.

'Didn't some Canadian doctor recently isolate some substance called insulin that will improve the prospect for diabetics? But I suppose it's too early yet for clinical trials.'

My own mouth felt dry. I drank from my cup but still felt dry. I remembered Clara, dying in St Mary's Hospital, with her lips not able to slide over her teeth because they were too dry . . . her everlasting goodbye smile as I left her.

217

. . . Miss Williamson, fair and rosy, smiling everlastingly, smashed a volley down the length of the court. The ball skidded off the back line into the bushes . . . the bushes grew and darkened, encroaching on the unmown grass where the white lines had faded and the net had sagged, where docks and thistles had taken over that enchanted tennis court beside the pool where Margaret Williamson would not be seen to play again and I would never go . . .

Insulin was to come too late to save Margaret Williamson, as the Armistice came too late for those wounded soldiers who were to die of their wounds after the guns were silenced. Could it be that for many of us, what might have saved us would come too late, with any luck too late for us to know it came too late?

'You're very quiet,' remarked my mother.

'I was wondering if they would ever discover a cure for diabetes.'

'I expect they will. But by then there'll be some new disease to take its place. However much we twist and dodge, something will get us in the end. We've all got to go. And a good job too,' she added, rattling the breakfast things together as she began to clear them away, 'or we'd all get awfully sick of one another.'

'Even of me?'

'Specially of you,' replied my brutal parent, flashing at me her radiant smile as she rattled away the cups and saucers, plates, spoons and forks and the little killer knives she kept so sharp.

218